THE HAWAI'I
BATHROOM
BOOK

Other Books by John Richard Stephens

Commanding the Storm
Weird History 101
The Wild, Wild West
Wyatt Earp Speaks!
Captured by Pirates
Adventure!
Voodoo
A Skeleton at the Helm
The Book of the Living Dead
Vampires, Wine and Roses
Into the Mummy's Tomb
The King of the Cats and Other Feline Fairy Tales
Mysterious Cat Stories (co-edited with Kim Smith)
The Enchanted Cat
The Dog Lover's Literary Companion

THE HAWAI'I BATHROOM BOOK

Light Reading for the Lua, Airport, Bus, Waiting Room...

JOHN RICHARD STEPHENS

Mutual Publishing

Permissions

Wendell A. Duffield: *Chasing Lava: A Geologist's Adventures at the Hawaiian Volcano Observatory*, Mountain Press Publishing Company, 2003 (pp 102-103).

Elaine Molina: Photographs pp 94, 197, 301

Toni Polancy: *The Hawaiian Pet Book,* Barefoot Publishing, 2003 (p. 6)

____*Hawaii in Love*, Barefoot Publishing, 2001 (p. 35)

Norman Banks: Quote from April 15, 2012 email to John Stephens

Small Trim size
ISBN: 978-1939487-15-5

Design by Jane Gillespie
Second Printing (small trim size), August 2015
Third Printing, (small trim size), February 2016

Mutual Publishing, LLC
1215 Center Street, Suite 210
Honolulu, Hawaii 96816
Ph: (808) 732-1709
Fax: (808) 734-4094
e-mail: info@mutualpublishing.com
www.mutualpublishing.com

Printed in South Korea

to Barbara Main

Contents

Acknowledgments

The author wishes to express his appreciation to Elaine Molina; Martha and Jim Goodwin; Scott Stephens; Marty Goeller and Dorian Rivas; Terity, Natasha, and Debbie Burbach; Brandon, Alisha, and Kathy Hill; Jeff and Carol Whiteaker; Christopher and Doug Whiteaker; Gabriel, Aurelia, Elijah, Nina, and Justin Weinberger; Rachel and Roxanne Nunez; Jayla, Anthony, Sin, and Bobby Gamboa; Pat Egner; Baba and Mimi Marlene Bruner; Anne and Jerry Buzzard; Krystyne Göhnert; Eric, Tim, and Debbie Cissna; Norene Hilden; Doug and Shirley Strong; Barbara Main; Joanne and Monte Goeller; Irma and Joe Rodriguez; Danny and Mary Schutt; Les Benedict; Dr. Rich Sutton; SK Lindsey; Jeanne Sisson; Michael and Roz McKevitt; and to my agent, Charlotte Cecil Raymond.

We are indebted to a number of Mutual authors and writers from whose works material was obtained or cited: Gail Bartholomew, Phoebe Beach, Arnold Bitner, Sam Choy, Carrie Ching, Chris Cook, Lynn Cook, A. Grove Day, William Dorrance, Glen Grant, Van James, Karen Lofstrom, Ian MacMillan, Julie Mehta, Dan Nakaso, Douglas Peebles, LaRue W. Piercy, Ronn Ronck, Sophia V. Schweitzer, MacKinnon Simpson, and Milly Singletary.

At Mutual Publishing, Jane Gillespie, Kate Kincaid, and Courtney Young helped nourish this project along in the editing, layout, and design phases while Mary Beth Mueller helped with copy editing and proofing.

Quick Reading for Rapid or Waiting Room Readers

The Art of Short Writing

In this digital age, our lives now move very quickly. We have to think and act fast. There are tweets, fast food, fast forward, instant replay, instant coffee, instant messaging, express trains, express mail, speed dial, speed dating, sound bites, and a general acceleration of most everything. So it shouldn't be surprising that fast reading has also become popular, as evidenced by the growth of flash fiction. In flash fiction, as Pamela Heffernan noted in *Fiction Factor* magazine, "You're taking a snapshot of a longer story, using a moment in time. Often, it's the story that would have never been told, or included, in a longer piece of work."

Snapshots of longer stories. Moments in time. Never been told. Perhaps not included in longer works. That is exactly what this book is about. The difference is that this book is nonfiction instead of fiction. It's not flash fiction, it's flash fact, with a few fiction vignettes thrown in for good measure.

Reading is Good

Reading sharpens the mind and increases intelligence. Studies show it also improves one's vocabulary and memory. It is much more stimulating and attractive than bouncing around the Internet, staring at a video, pounding on a joystick, or flipping through channels in a vain search for something interesting. Reading is intellectually active and engaging. It's brain candy without the sugar.

And this volume is like a box of chocolates. One can quickly read a selection, then move on to the next, where one finds a different flavor. In this reader, it's okay to start anywhere—at the back or the middle, or just skip around. Bookmarks don't belong here. Open to any page at random and begin reading.

This is great for those with short attention spans. For those with longer attention spans, this is also a book of light reading to lazily help pass time in waiting areas, at the beach, on an airplane, at bedtime, in the can, or any place where there is idle time or a diversion is needed. And there is a chance of not just being entertained but learning something.

Diversity of Topics

This reader contains true stories, eyewitness accounts, snapshots of articles, short quotations, glimpses of history, significant facts, bits of science, and snippets of trivia. The range of topics is broad. What unifies the selections is that they are all about Hawai'i. The more than 250 short pieces and numerous one-liners assembled here cover a multitude of subjects of ancient and modern Hawaiian life. The primary selection criteria used were that the subject be interesting and entertaining, unusual or fun, offer insight into significant events, provide little-known facts, and be humorous or amusing. Brevity, of course, was also a requirement.

Although this book is quick, easy reading, much research went into it. Hundreds of sources ranging from books to magazines, letters, diaries, blogs, newspapers, and emails were scoured for material for these flash-fact pieces.

What You Can Do

Of course, the Hawaiian experience is too broad to cover in one book. We have just scratched the surface. There is so much more fascinating material still to come, which is why another volume is already in the works.

You can participate in the next volume by sending us your ideas and suggestions for topics to include. Something you're curious about, questions you'd like answered, a funny story you have to tell or an unusual or touching experience you wish to share, send it along and we'll take it from there. If you've seen something worth clipping from a magazine or newspaper, we want that too. As long as it's related to our wonderful islands, chances are it'll be included in the next one. See the last page for more information.

Literary Masters

The Most Seductive Siren of the Sea

Hawaii is the home of shanghaied men and women, and of the descendants of shanghaied men and women. They never intended to be here at all. Very rarely, since the first whites came, has one, with the deliberate plan of coming to remain, remained. Somehow, the love of the Islands, like the love of a woman, just happens. One cannot determine in advance to love a particular woman, nor can one so determine to love Hawaii. One sees, and one loves or does not love. With Hawaii it seems always to be love at first sight. Those for whom the Islands were made, or who were made for the Islands, are swept off their feet in the first moments of meeting, embrace, and are embraced.... Truly, Hawaii is a woman beautiful and vastly more persuasive and seductive than her sister sirens of the sea.

—JACK LONDON, AUTHOR OF *THE CALL OF THE WILD* AND *WHITE FANG*

Literary Masters

A Varied Land

...to the proposition that never was so much climate gathered together in one place, can be added that never was so much landscape gathered together in one place. The diversification is endless, from the lava shores of South Puna to the barking sands of Kauai. On every island break-neck mountain climbing abounds. One can shiver above timber-line on the snow-caps of Mauna Kea or Mauna Loa, swelter under the banyan at sleepy old Lahaina, swim in clear ocean water that effervesces like champagne on ten thousand beaches, or sleep under blankets every night in the upland pastures of the great cattle ranges and awaken each morning to the song of sky-larks and the crisp, snappy air of spring.

—JACK LONDON

The Hawai'i Bathroom Book

Famous Surfer Agatha Christie

The Thrill

Okay, Agatha Christie is not famous for being a surfer, but she is very famous and she was a surfer, at least for a short while. In fact, she was one of the very first Brits to surf standing up.

It was in 1922 that she discovered the thrill of surfing. This was before she became the best-selling novelist of all time, with more than four *billion* copies of her books in print. Her first novel, which featured Belgian detective Hercule Poirot, was published in 1920 and her second, featuring Tommy and Tuppence, had just been released. She wouldn't create Miss Jane Marple for another four years.

Discovering Surfing

In 1922 she was touring the world with her first husband Archie Christie, who had been a fighter pilot in World War I, when they were introduced to surfing in South Africa. There, surfing was actually much closer to boogie boarding, but it gave her a feel for the waves, though she said it was painful if you nosedived into the sand. It seems that two U.S. marines brought Hawaiian-style surfing there in 1919.

A World Tour

After touring Australia, New Zealand, Fiji, and other islands, they arrived in Honolulu on August 5th and stayed until October of 1922. On arriving early in the morning at Waikīkī, they looked out their hotel window and saw people surfing. They immediately rushed out to join them, figuring they'd already learned what they needed to know in South Africa. It turned out to be one of those rough days when only experts go out and Agatha quickly wiped out. She decided she should wait for better conditions.

The second time she went out, the waves ripped up her shoulder-to-ankle silk bathing suit. "Almost nude, I made for my beach wrap," she wrote in her autobiography. "I had im-

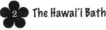

mediately to visit the hotel shop and provide myself with a wonderful, skimpy, emerald green wool bathing dress, which was the joy of my life, and in which I thought I looked remarkably well."

Pain, Suffering, and Bliss

They spent all of their days surfing, but the first few days were hard as they ended up battered and bruised, with their feet torn up from the coral, and sunburnt. Surfing, she said, "was far too painful," but they refused to give it up. Buying some soft leather boots that tied around their ankles, they continued. All of this surfing was done lying on the board. She found it was easier to hire a Hawaiian beach boy to assist her. She would lay on her board while the beach boy swam out to the reef, pulling her along by gripping her board with his big toe. He would then tell her which wave to catch and when to go.

She wrote, "At the word 'now' off you went, and oh, it was heaven! Nothing like it. Nothing like that rushing through the water at what seems to you a speed of about two hundred miles an hour; all the way in from the far distant raft, until you arrived, gently slowing down, on the beach, and foundered among the soft flowing waves. It is one of the most perfect physical pleasures that I have known."

A True Surfer Gal

After ten days, she began rising to her knees and eventually tried to stand up. The first few times her board flew out from under her. As the

A modern surfer gal getting ready to take on the waves at Hanalei Beach on Kaua'i. John Richard Stephens

boards didn't have leashes, her Hawaiian beach boy usually tried to retrieve it for her and then towed (or toed?) her back out. She soon mastered the art of stand-up surfing like a true surfing wahine.

According the Pete Robinson, the founder of the Museum of British Surfing, there is only one other Brit who is known to have surfed standing up before her—that was Prince Edward. Robinson is still trying to find out whether Agatha Christie continued surfing after returning to England.

Did you know...

It's thought that standing up while riding a surfboard was first developed by the Polynesians in about 1000 AD—around the time of the first crusades and well before Marco Polo.

Did you know...

The Hawaiian Islands are the peaks of the world's largest mountain range, most of which is underwater.

Did you know...

Hawai'i is the only place in the fifty states where you can see the stars of the entire northern and southern hemispheres. Here, stars that can't be seen from the mainland are visible, along with the stars that aren't visible from Australia.

Hawaiian Kangaroos

Escape of the Wallabies

Kangaroos are usually found in Australia or in zoos, but there is at least one band of wild pint-sized kangaroos near Honolulu. They are Brush-Tailed Rock Wallabies, which stand about two-feet high. Wallaby is a generic name for all small and medium-sized kangaroos. In Australia, there are some 'roos that are as small as rabbits.

Back in 1916, a developer purchased a family of three Rock Wallabies from animal collector Ellis Joseph. He wanted them for his private zoo at his residence in ʻĀlewa Heights. The 'roos were being temporarily kept in a tent when neighborhood dogs tore into the enclosure and killed the joey. The two parents escaped into the wild.

They Look Cute and Harmless (because they are)

Biologists describe them as being gentle, shy and harmless. They're vegetarian, eating mainly Christmas berries, grasses, roots, and bark—mainly non-native plants. One 1984 study noted that there were seemingly old and blind 'roos that were otherwise healthy, so it sounds like they must hang together and watch out for one another. At any rate, they seem to have settled in nicely, without causing any damage, which goes to show that some introduced species are not harmful to the environment.

An Endangered Species?

'Roos on the Loose

At their peak, the Hawaiian kangaroos ranged from Nu'uanu to Halawa Valley with an estimated population of up to 250, but wild dogs and new housing developments cut their habitat to Kalihi Valley along Likelike Highway and by the 1990s their estimated population had dropped to about a hundred. After funding cuts in the early 1990s, wildlife biologists were no longer able to continue monitoring them, so no one knows how many there are now. The wallabies live in caves and crevices of the almost inaccessible cliffs and are rarely seen. Even the biologists sometimes only saw them when they were trapped in cages to be tagged and tested.

Exploring the Neighborhood

In 2002 a couple of residents in Foster Village found one in their backyard grazing on their lawn. Wildlife officers were called in and the knee-high hopping marsupial was captured in their backyard shed. After a quick checkup, the wallaby-on-walkabout was released back into Kalihi Valley. Three years later another one somehow made its way onto the second floor of the Tripler Army Medical Center. It, too, was released back into the wild.

Not Your Aussie 'Roo

Since their relatives in Australia are considered threatened, wildlife experts are glad to have another wild population. The Hawaiian kangaroos now look different than their Aussie cousins and even the size and shape of their skulls are different, leading some to suspect they might have evolved into a separate species. Probably not, since it usually takes a long time for a line of animals to separate into two species, but they might be considered a subspecies. If they do become a separate species, then they'll be the only species of kangaroo that is not Australian. Since the Australian Rock Wallaby populations are dropping, Hawaiian kangaroos might qualify as an endangered species.

An Island Treasure

Israel Kamakawiwoʻole

Bruddah Iz

Even in death, Israel "Bruddah Iz" Kamakawiwoʻole continues to attract new fans with a sweet, falsetto voice that belied the troubled, morbidly obese giant who remains an icon in the islands.

"Iz," as he's commonly known in Hawaiʻi, grew up in Mākaha where he got into drugs and struggled with his enormous weight. He also became the focal point of the original music group Makaha Sons of Niʻihau, and later the Makaha Sons. But artistic and philosophical differences with the band led Kamakawiwoʻole to turn solo in 1993.

A Turn Around

Generations of fans, especially Native Hawaiians, were touched by Kamakawiwoʻole songs steeped in Hawaiian tradition, cultural hardship, and revival. He won over even more fans by later urging children to stay away from gangs and drugs.

Early one morning, unable to sleep, Kamakawiwoʻole went into a studio and improvised the lyrics and chord changes to record his iconic version of "Over the Rainbow/What a Wonderful World," accompanied only by the simple sounds of his ʻukulele.

Favorite Entertainer

Just weeks before his death, Kamakawiwoʻole watched the televised Nā Hōkū Hanohano awards from a hospital bed when his *N Dis Life* CD won Kamakawiwoʻole four Nā Hōkū Hanohano awards—for album of the year, male vocalist of the year, island contemporary album and graphics. He was also named favorite entertainer of the year.

Over the Rainbow

Kamakawiwoʻole weighed more than seven hundred pounds when he died in June 1997 at the age of thirty-eight due to respiratory problems related to obesity. He became one of only five people to lie in state in the rotunda of Hawai'i's state capitol and more than five thousand people streamed through to pay their respects. An estimated ten thousand mourners later gathered for his funeral at Kamakawiwo'ole's beloved Mākua Beach on the leeward coast of O'ahu.

—Dan Nakaso (*Things Hawai'i, New Edition*)

It Is What It Is
Learn Your AEHs

The Hawaiian alphabet has only 13 letters—seven consonants and six vowels, including the 'okina ('), which is actually a glottal stop, although it's considered a vowel; therefore the alphabet is A, E, H, I, K, L, M, N, O, P, U, W, and the 'okina. Hawaiians get by just fine without B, C, D, F, G, J, Q, R, S, T, V, X, Y, and Z. Imagine, never using an R, T, or S, which are three of the four most popular consonants in the English language. Since vowels make up about forty-six percent of the Hawaiian alphabet and are used in a much wider variety of ways than consonants, vowels definitely dominate the Hawaiian language. In fact, every word ends with a vowel. As guitar virtuoso Leo Kottke observantly pointed out, when introducing his song "Gewerbegebiet," "The Germans have done for consonants what the Hawaiians have done for vowels."

Did you know...

'Ukuleles evolved from the Portuguese braguinha, which was brought to Hawai'i in 1878, although the first person who could play it didn't arrive until the following year.

When Lava Flies at You, Run Away

A Dangerous Job

A helicopter is silhouetted against a 1,500-foot fountain shooting out of the Pu'u 'Ō'ō vent in 1984. MARDIE LANE, NATIONAL PARK SERVICE

Working around lava is a dangerous profession. Dr. Wendell Duffield is a geologist who, for several years, worked at the Hawaiian Volcano Observatory on the Big Island. One day he was observing a lava geyser when it suddenly started to shoot lava straight at him. He and a German geologist were watching the Mauna Ulu lava fountain from Pu'u Huluhulu—a nearly 300-foot-tall, forest-covered cinder cone that is roughly 2,000 feet away. Mauna Ulu is in Kīlauea's East Rift Zone which, with a brief pause, shot fountains of lava up to 1,770 feet high—higher than the Empire State Building—from 1969 to 1974. As the lava flowed into a nearby crater, it created lava falls that were higher and wider than Niagara Falls.

While Wendell and his companion were watching, some hardened lava must have blocked part of the fountain's base, because the fountain began to shoot horizontally, instead of straight up, so that the fountain was firing blobs of molten lava right at the two geologists.

Wendell wrote:

On the Firing Line

Suddenly and with no recognizable warning, Hans and I found ourselves squarely in the fallout zone. Inch-wide pieces of hot rock and still-molten clots were targeting Pu'u Huluhulu, and Hans and I stood perilously close to the bull's-eye. Without hesitation or discussion—for even the most loquacious and impractical of academicians will waste no time trying to explain what is happening while "fire" is falling all around him—we ran directly away from the offending fountain.

Since the established foot trail on Puʻu Huluhulu included a series of switchbacks across the slope facing Mauna Ulu, we crashed through the tangle of rain forest in the opposite direction. We were wearing metal hardhats like those used at construction sites, and the clots of hot, pasty cinder ricocheted off our helmets with unmistakable pings, clunks, splats, and thwacks. Both Hans and I garnered a few burn holes in clothing and minor skin burns where clots penetrated cloth. I was wearing an Oʻahu State Prison shirt, and it was never the same after this shower of fire. After just a few minutes and couple hundred yards of crashing cross-country through the forest, we were out of the danger zone.

—Dr. Wendell A. Duffield (*Chasing Lava*)

A Hawaiian Volcano Observatory geologist collects samples of spatter erupting from another fissure on Kīlauea's East Rift Zone in 2011. Matthew R. Patrick, USGS.

Butchered Pronunciations

The Unforgivable

Although we mean well, most of us mispronounce many Hawaiian words and names. A lot of it is because common usage is wrong, so that is just way we learned it. That's forgivable. What is bad is when someone who doesn't know how to pronounce something is so confident they're right that they insist on teaching others to mispronounce it.

Make a simple Internet search for "Kaua'i pronounced." This generates some interesting results. Some people take the easy way out, saying it's "Hawaii with a 'K'," which is fine as long as they know how to properly pronounce "Hawai'i." Others give these variations: ka-why, Ka-wi, kaua-ee, Ko-Ah-Ee, kawa-ee, kuh-WAH-ee, kah-oo-ah-ee, and koo-EYE.

Perhaps It's the Accent

Sometimes people's accents get in the way. The UK's *Sunday Tribune* says it's "Koowy-ee," while Ireland's *Independent* insists it's "ka-wa-i" and Canada's *Welland Tribune* pronounces it "k-WHAA-ee." And then there's *The Rotarian* magazine which simply says it's "Cow-eye."

Say That Again

One can't help but wonder at the travel website that has "Kauai (pronounced Kauai)" or where someone less-than-helpfully wrote it's "Kauai (pronounced Hawaii)." So how *do* you pronounce Hawai'i? Well if you're referring to the *island* of Hawai'i, it's pronounced "the Big Island." And, according to Henry Frederic Reddall's book, *From the Golden Gate to the Golden Horn*, O'ahu is pronounced "war˘ hoo."

Hawai'i Jones and the Lost City

The Creation of Indiana Jones

Indiana Jones was created by director-producer George Lucas, who is best known for the *Star Wars* movies, but the character he originally envisioned was considerably different from the one who ended up on screen. Lucas's idea was for Jones to be "an international playboy like James Bond." It was Steven Spielberg and Harrison Ford who turned Jones into the fallible, uncertain, reluctant, yet highly resourceful, adventurer-professor that became so popular. His exploits were primarily modeled after matinee serials and pulp magazines of the 1940s and 1950s, but a number of the movies' story and character elements were inspired by real people.

Some of the most commonly cited people who helped influence the character of Indiana Jones are explorer-naturalist-adventurer Roy Chapman Andrews, archeologist-explorer Giovanni Battista Belzoni, archeologist-explorer Colonel Percy Harrison Fawcett, archeologist-professor Sir William Matthew Flinders Petrie, and historian-explorer-treasure hunter Hiram Bingham III.

Hawai'i Jones

It is Hiram Bingham III who is of interest to us. He was born and raised in Honolulu, the son and grandson of two notable missionaries, the elder of which played a significant role in Hawai'i's history. Hiram Bingham I was the leader of the first group of Protestant missionaries who introduced Christianity to the islands. He helped create the spelling system for the Hawaiian Language, he had a hand in designing Honolulu's Kawaiaha'o Church, and he was one of the founders of the Punahou School to educate the missionaries' children so they wouldn't have to be shipped off to schools on the mainland.

Hiram Bingham III attended Punahou School from 1882 to 1892 before he went off to earn a B.A. at Yale University, a degree from the University of California, Berkeley, and his Ph. D. at Harvard University. He then taught history and politics at Harvard and Yale, in addition to serving as preceptor at Princeton under Woodrow Wilson. Eventually he became a U.S. Senator.

The Lost City of the Inca

He is usually credited with the 1911 rediscovery of Machu Picchu—"the Lost City of the Inca"—high in the mountains of Peru, though he actually just brought the site to the world's attention. Much like Columbus's "discovery" of the Americas, there were already people living at Machu Picchu when he arrived. He wrote about his adventures in his book *Across South America: an Account of a Journey from Buenos Aires to Lima by Way of Potosí, with Notes on Brazil, Argentina, Bolivia, Chile, and Peru.*

It was his many experiences as an explorer, adventurer, and perhaps even as a professor that likely contributed to the character of Indiana Jones.

Did you know...

Hawai'i is the most isolated population center on Earth, with the nearest points being between Hilo on the Big Island and San Francisco in California 2,315 miles away.

Did you know...

In Hawai'i, the name "Hawai'i" has no meaning, beyond that it's the name of the state and the Big Island, but in other parts of Polynesia, versions of the word mean "ancestral homeland" or it is the name of the underworld where everyone goes when they die.

Raiders of the Lost Ark

George Lucas and Steven Spielberg were vacationing in Hawai'i when Lucas first told Spielberg about his idea which would evolve into *Raiders of the Lost Ark*, inspired by the action serials of the 1930s and '40s. The first Indiana Jones movie starring Harrison Ford contained opening scenes set in the jungles of South America, but these were mainly filmed on Kauai with local actors playing the South American natives. They spray-painted two gray donkeys brown and then for the mountain shots they used helicopters to fly these donkeys to a remote location along the Nā Pali Coast.

Robert W. Watts, the film's production manager, wrote in *Honolulu* magazine, "We shot the trek to the exterior of the South American temple and Indy's flight from the Hovito Indians a few miles up the Hulai'a River from Nawiliwili. The Hovito Indians were played by local Kauaians who were persuaded to have their hair cut in an Indian pudding-basin style. The Waco biplane came from the U.S. mainland. The mountain in the opening shot was Anahola. The exterior of the temple was in a pit-like location about ten miles from Lihu'e, off the road in the direction of Po'ipu. This pit with a pool and waterfall was filled with mosquitos, and despite spraying they made our lives a misery. Thank goodness for insect repellant! The final scene of the airplane flying away was done at sunset over the Menehune fishponds in Nawiliwili."

The entire movie was shot in just seventy-three days and with a budget of about $18 million. It became the highest grossing film of 1981, taking in more than $384 million world-wide. The following year it won four Academy Awards, including Best Picture.

Hāʻupu, in the background, looks down on the Menehune Fishpond after the pigs have flown away. JOHN RICHARD STEPHENS

Uncommon Knowledge

Bad Weather Pigs

On Kauaʻi there's a saying that when the pigs—or piglets—follow one another around Hāʻupu's summit, then bad weather is coming. The pigs or piglets are puffy clouds and Hāʻupu is a mountain range between Poʻipū and Līhuʻe on the southeast corner of Kauaʻi. So when the weather is calm and you see the puffy pig clouds around the summit of Hāʻupu, know that bad weather is on its way.

Fried Poke

Diving for Octopus

Sometimes we take it for granted that here in Hawai'i we're surrounded by the ocean, allowing us access to the freshest seafood in the world. When I was a boy, my family would put on tabis and goggles, wade out to waist-deep water around the reefs of Lā'ie Bay, and pick limu. At other times, we would catch lobster for dinner, or would go diving for octopus with my friends.

Traditional Foods

Those kinds of fresh ingredients were part of the traditional Hawaiian diet. Although today's food is high in fat and sodium, I believe that the work being done by people like Dr. Terry Shintani with the Waianae Diet is an important force in educating people to eat healthier. At least we can still learn to appreciate some of the traditional Hawaiian foods like steamed fish, limu, or fresh poke.

I sponsor an annual poke contest that has become very popular. One of the main reasons I do it is to educate people. I've always said, "Look, raw dishes like sushi and sashimi have made it big-time, with international followings. Other popular dishes are actually half-cooked sashimi, so why shouldn't poke become accepted on an equal scale?"

Experimenting with Poke

One day, when we were all just sitting around sharing new ideas, I said, "Let's make some poke and sear it real quick on the teppanyaki grill." We tried many different kinds of poke before we found the best-tasting one.

It's funny now to look back at when we first introduced the fried poke at our restaurant. The first thing people said was, "Eh, don't buy the fried poke—that's Sam Choy trying to sell his old poke." When you think about it, it's almost natural that local people might think that.

I said, "Aw, come on you guys. Give me a break. What more do I have to do to prove myself to you?" Then we decided to offer samples of the fried poke in little cups. The next day, the fried poke was the hottest thing on our menu. It just took off. Today, we serve an average of about a thousand pounds of fried poke a week. It's just phenomenal.

(WITH SAM CHOY: COOKING FROM THE HEART)

Literary Masters

These Beautiful Islands

No alien land in all the world has any deep strong charm for me but one, no other land could so longingly and so beseechingly haunt me, sleeping and waking, through half a lifetime, as that one has done. Other things leave me, but it abides; other things change, but it remains the same. For me its balmy airs are always blowing, its summer seas flashing in the sun; the pulsing of its surfbeat is in my ear; I can see its garland crags, its leaping cascades, its plumy palms drowsing by the shore, its remote summits floating like islands above the cloud wrack; I can feel the spirit of its woodland solitudes, I can hear the plash of its brooks; in my nostrils still lives the breath of flowers that perished twenty years ago.

—MARK TWAIN IN AN 1889 DINNER SPEECH AT DELMONICO'S
IN NEW YORK TO HONOR TWO BASEBALL TEAMS THAT HAD
JUST RETURNED FROM TOURING THE PACIFIC, INCLUDING HONOLULU.

Did you know...

The depth of the Pacific Ocean around the Hawaiian Islands is 3.4 miles, while the deepest part is the Mariana Trench near Guam, which is 6.8 miles deep.

Mark Twain

Samuel Langhorne Clemens (1835-1910), who had only recently begun to use the world-famed pseudonym of "Mark Twain," arrived in Honolulu in March of 1866 to spend four months as a roving reporter for the *Sacramento Union* for his first excursion outside of the then-United States. His Hawai'i travels gave him material for a series of twenty-five sketches written in his inimitable style, with one of these being a notable journalistic scoop on a celebrated sea disaster, the burning of the clipper ship *Hornet,* a piece of writing that made him a "literary personage." His Hawai'i adventures enabled him to embark on a new and lucrative profession, that of a popular lecturer. Perhaps the most often quoted remark in Hawaiian literature is Mark Twain's characterization of the future fiftieth state as "the loveliest fleet of islands that lies anchored in any ocean." As late as 1884, he began to write a novel with a Hawaiian setting.

A tireless sightseer, Twain began riding around O'ahu in 1866 and reporting his adventures in the capital of the kingdom of Kamehameha V. After a tour of the neighboring island of Maui, where he climbed to the summit of the giant crater of Haleakalā and viewed the green 'Īao Valley, he took a schooner to the Kona Coast of Hawai'i, rode around the southern end of that island, and scrambled about the Kīlauea district, marveling at the titanic energies of the active volcano. After visiting the sugar plantations of the Hāmākua region, he rode along the deep gash of Waipi'o Valley, crossed the Waimea tableland, and caught the little steamer *Kilauea* at Kawaihae on his return to Honolulu.

His letters cover not only the sugar and whaling industries, which were of interest to American businessmen of the time, but also the Hawaiian trade, whose exports brought high fees to the United States customs service. Much of the material deals with scenery and climate, politics, social conditions, history and legends, Polynesian lore, the monarchy, religious affairs, horse-traders, and even the "millions of cats" of Honolulu. No mention is made of leprosy, brought into the kingdom before 1854, probably because Twain did not wish to frighten off the businessmen who would be his most important readers.

—A. Grove Day (*Books About Hawaii, Fifty Basic Authors*)

Isle Lore
A Human Menagerie

The Hawaiians have a wonderful sense of metaphor. Here is how they refer to certain types of people:

- **Someone who is too wily to get caught:** A parrotfish that's slippery with slime.
- **A man who constantly thinks of sex:** A boar.
- **Someone who jumps from lover to lover:** A flying fish.
- **A strong warrior:** A fierce rooting hog.
- **A loud person:** A mud crab on a rocky point.
- **Someone who is observant:** The ka'upu, the bird that observes the ocean.
- **A person who is well-off or rich:** A feathered bird.
- **A thief:** A gripping cuttlefish.
- **Someone who is unruly:** A wild goat of the wilderness.
- **Those who spread malicious gossip:** They are said to have a jutting beak.
- **A person who talks too much:** A Mynah bird.
- **Someone who talks constantly:** Lightning snout.

Did you know...

Queen Lili'uokalani had a pet Galapagos tortoise, which weighed 560 pounds and lived to be between 150 and 200 years old.

Presenting the Scholars

In 1831 native scholars—which is what the missionaries called their students—of the Christian schools were presented to a group of chiefs. It was quite a display. Missionary Hiram Bingham described it this way:

> During this visitation of the chiefs at Kaʻawaloa, numerous schools were called before them to show themselves for examination. Their coming together presented a novel scene, exhibiting something of the taste and habits of Hawaiians. Long processions of scholars and teachers, coming in from different quarters, after dark, moved in single file with flaming torches of the candle-nut, and loud-sounding conchs. Some of the schools, with their torches and conchs, came winding along around the head of Kealakekua Bay, high on the steep and craggy precipices, which once echoed back the thunder of the guns of Capt. Cook's ships in hostile strife with the natives. Then near where that navigator fell in the preceding generation, the schools, embracing thousands of men, women, and children, just coming to the light, formed an immense column, still flourishing their fiery banners, and blowing their many shells of various keys, with as much spirit as if they expected the fortifications of darkness were about to fall before them.
>
> —HIRAM BINGHAM (*A RESIDENCE OF TWENTY-ONE YEARS IN THE SANDWICH ISLANDS*)

"...by the second half of the 19th century, the literacy rate in Hawaii was as high as in most parts of American and in a good many less advanced European countries. Between 1850 and 1900, Hawaiians wrote and mailed about a million letters to each other, according to statistics on the sale of postal stamps."
—Gavan Daws
("FUTURE COURSES OF HISTORICAL EXPLORATION" *HAWAII OBSERVER*, APRIL 29, 1975)

Early Hawaiian Scholars

Our knowledge of the ancient Hawaiian culture depends heavily upon the classic work of early Hawaiian scholars. David Malo, born in 1795 near Kealakekua, during his youth was a retainer of the high chief Kuakini, brother of Queen Ka'ahumanu. He became a Christian soon after the arrival of the New England missionaries. In 1831, he entered the mission high school at Lahainaluna. Endowed with an alert and inquiring mind, he devoted himself to the study and writing (in the Hawaiian language) of the history and customs of his people. He died in 1853 at Kalepolepo, Maui, where he had been pastor of the Congregational Church. Malo's volume, *Hawaiian Antiquities*, written around 1840, was not translated until 1903.

"We have the testimony," by the author of the introduction to his work, "of one who was born and grew up to manhood under the tabu system, who had himself been a devout worshipper of the old gods, who had been brought up at the royal court, and who was considered by his countrymen as an authority on the subjects on which he afterwards wrote." Some of these subjects include pre-European daily life, geographical terms, land and water divisions, plants and animals, food and drink, household objects, classes of people, religion, healing, magic, canoes, festivals, agriculture, fishing, sports, and ancient heroes.

A fellow student of Malo at Lahainaluna was Samuel Manaiakalani Kamakau, who was born in 1815 in Waialua, Oahu. Kamakau entered the school in 1833, where he remained for seven years, both as pupil and as teacher's assistant. He began publishing in 1865, the first of more than two hundred newspaper articles which were translated by Mary K. Pukui and appear in two books: *The Ruling Chiefs of Hawaii* and *Ka Po'e Kahiko: The People of Old*.

Another member of the Lahaina group was S. N. Haleole, author of *The Hawaiian Romance of Lā'ieikawai*, translated by Martha Beckwith. He was born about 1819 and entered Lahainaluna in 1834.

A valuable book of early memoirs in the native language is *Fragments of Hawaiian History*, by John Papa ʻĪʻī, who joined the court of Kamehameha I at the age of ten and became the companion of the future Kamehameha II. The selections were made from articles appearing in the newspaper *Kūʻokoʻa* from 1866 through 1870.

—A. GROVE DAY (*BOOKS ABOUT HAWAII, FIFTY BASIC AUTHORS*)

A Matter of Faith

Tiki

Tiki the God

Said to be the deified ancestor of the Polynesian people, first man and first god, the procreative power from whom all life flows, Tiki, under various names and in different languages, formed the root of Polynesian religion for many hundreds of years. Tiki appeared in creation chants and old mythologies. He was a human, yet divine; a god, with human traits. The image of all men, he became a demigod. Maori legends linked him to Tane, the life-giving god. Marquesans paired Tiki with Tangaroa, the god of the sea.

Tiki ruled the supernatural forces that governed daily life, and manifested himself in the natural world. He gave protection or brought disaster at will. His worship was essential.

Tiki's Tikis

Tiki's image, carved in stone or wood, summoned the god's presence and guided ritual. Hundreds of different tiki statues evolved to hold the spirit of his myriad expressions—nature gods and ancestral forces alike. Maori women used to wear small charms around their necks, tiki, to protect them against barrenness. In Hawaii, master artists created sculptures, kiʻi, to capture the divine powers. Across Polynesia, on archipelagoes thousands of miles apart, each design was a prayer, each showed reverence for Tiki's vast, unseen spiritual world.

But no one knows how old Tiki is, or where exactly he is from.

—SOPHIA V. SCHWEITZER (*TIKI OF HAWAIʻI*)

 The Hawaiʻi Bathroom Book

An All-Around Dog

Poi Dogs

Mutts vs. Purebreds

In Hawai'i, we call our mutts "poi dogs." Where does the poi come in?

In very early Hawai'i, dog meat was a delicacy for humans. Dogs were fed poi, the beaten root of the taro plant, to fatten them up for feasts at which they were part of the main course.

Some kama'āina (longtime Hawai'i residents) say a true poi dog must not carry the characteristics of any one breed, but be very mixed. Others insist a poi should have some of the characteristics of his Polynesian ancestors. Early Hawaiian dogs were descended from canines who came with the first Polynesian settlers. They were small, short-haired and short-legged, with distinctive pointy ears and slightly up-curled tails. Not aggressive barkers, they fit in well with Hawai'i's laid-back lifestyle.

Well Mixed

"Perhaps poi dogs are beloved here because we islanders are so ethnically diverse," muses Pamela Burns, Hawaiian Humane Society executive director in a newsletter. "Or maybe it's their convenient and cuddly size, just big enough to scare a burglar but still small enough to fit on your lap or lie next to you on the pune'e for a nap.

"Since they are a blend, poi dogs tend to have personalities that blur the distinction commonly attributed to particular breeds and no one characteristic stands out—neither too mellow nor too active, not too independent nor too territorial, not too loud nor totally silent.

Poi Dogs No Ka Oi

"Whatever the reason, poi dogs make great pets and recent research shows that the people of Hawai'i continue to choose them as companions far more than any other breed," Burns concludes.

—TONI POLANCY (*THE HAWAI'I PET BOOK*)

O'ahu's VIPs

Surfing Commander-in-Chief

President Barack Obama is our most famous living Hawaiian. Born in Honolulu, he went to school in the lower Makiki district, next to the Punchbowl. He worked at the Baskin-Robbins Ice Cream Shop on South King Street and bodysurfed at Sandy Beach. After he went off to college at Columbia University and Harvard Law School, he would return home to visit his grandmother and his mother, who earned her doctorate in anthropology at the University of Hawai'i. He's lived other places, but he still considers O'ahu his home. Now when he comes for vacations, he usually stays at beach houses in Kailua.

More O'ahuians

Jim Nabors lives near Diamond Head and for a while Tom Selleck was his neighbor. Some people say Selleck once owned a ranch upcountry on Maui, but apparently he just stayed there on a vacation or while filming.

Other past and present Honolulu celebrities include Daniel Dae Kim, Jack Lord, Don Ho, Carrie Ann Inaba, Tia Carrere, and Buster Crabbe, who starred in many serials during the 1930s and 1940s as Buck Rogers, Flash Gordon, and Tarzan the Fearless, among others. Jack Johnson lives on O'ahu's North Shore, as does Paul Theroux, who also tends bees and produces Oceania Ranch Pure Hawaiian Honey. Famous Amos chocolate-chip cookie creator, Wally Amos has lived in Lanikai on O'ahu since 1977. He also founded Uncle Wally's Muffin Company, which sells home-style and gourmet muffins throughout the country.

Sometimes Visitors Want to Change Things

One of the first things Captain James Cook did after arriving in the Hawaiian Islands was change the kingdom's name. In order to curry favor with the guy who paid for his voyage, the Earl of Sandwich, he rather arrogantly dubbed Hawai'i the Sandwich Islands. Then he left. But the Hawaiians were stuck with this name for more than half a century.

Then when Captain William Brown arrived in Honolulu Harbor in 1795, he renamed it Fair Haven, in spite of the fact the Hawaiians called it Kou. Apparently the normally very hospitable Hawaiians didn't care for Captain Brown, because they quickly killed him.

Luxuriant Hawai'i

Hothouse Kona

Hothouse flowers grow in rank profusion round every house, and tea-roses, fuchsias, geraniums fifteen feet high, Nile lilies, Chinese lantern plants, begonias, lantanas, hibiscus, passion-flowers, Cape jasmine, the hoya, the tuberose, the beautiful but overpoweringly sweet ginger plant, and a hundred others...Pineapples and melons grow like weeds among the grass, and everything that is good for food flourishes. Nothing can keep under the redundancy of nature in Kona; everything is profuse, fervid, passionate, vivified and pervaded by sunshine. The earth is restless in her productiveness, and forces up her hothouse growth perpetually....

—ISABELLA BIRD (*THE HAWAIIAN ARCHIPELAGO*, 1875)

 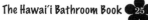

It Is What It Is
Kona Confusion

Kailua on the Big Island is in the Kona district, but the U.S. Postal Service calls it Kailua-Kona so they don't accidentally send its mail to the Kailua on O'ahu. People often refer to the town as Kona, but technically there is no town by that name.

Kailua-Kona's Main Street in 1908 near where the Kona Inn is now. BAKER-VAN DYKE COLLECTION.

Did you know...

Huli-Huli chicken was invented in 1955 by Ernie Morgado, the co-founder of Pacific Poultry.

Sports-Crazy

Sports for Everyone

Maui was sports-crazy! Everyone participated by playing, coaching or as a spectator. Many managed to do all three, finding fun and excitement in an otherwise quiet community. While individual ethnic groups retained their traditional sports, such as Japanese sumo wrestling and a Filipino ball game called *sipa*, immigrant groups immediately adopted American sports as well.

Island-Style Baseball

In 1908, only 13 years after the arrival of the first immigrants from Japan, organized Japanese baseball teams filled diamonds in Lahaina and Wailuku. Ethnicity, as well as locale, played a part in the formation of teams and leagues, with names such as the Pāʻia Portuguese, the Puʻunēnē Nippons, and the Filipino Plantation League. Athletic associations abounded in each community, however small.

Hawaiian Football

Athletes on Oʻahu, not limiting themselves to established rules, invented island-style barefoot football, a highly popular sport on Maui from the 1920s through the 1940s. Playing the game with no shoes, a natural outgrowth of the local habit of going shoeless, reduced the cost of participating. Enthusiastic fans watched talented toes punt the ball up to 80 yards.

Golf

Golf mania hit Maui early. The first links in Kahului opened in 1912, followed shortly by the construction of small courses throughout the island. Even Makawao School had its own course in the 1920s. The territory boasted its first municipal golf course when Waiehu opened in 1930.

— GAIL BARTHOLOMEW (*MAUI REMEMBERS*)

 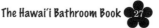

A Lunch, Fit for a King

A few months after King David Kalākaua began his reign in 1874, he went on a tour around the world. One of those who accompanied him was one of his old schoolmates, William N. Armstrong, who held the titles Attorney General, Minister of State, and Royal Commissioner of Immigration. Armstrong later wrote of the trip, relating one amusing incident that occurred in Egypt.

> While en route to Egypt it was assumed that the Khedive of that country had never heard of Hawaii, and that the party would, therefore, modestly visit the Pyramids and quietly proceed to Italy. On arriving, however, at Suez, the party was received by a deputation of high officials of the Khedive's government, who conveyed it in the state railway carriage to Cairo, as the guests of the ruler.
>
> I will here make an exception to my resolve not to enter into any details, by giving a curious incident of this trip to Cairo. On leaving Suez, the chief official of the Egyptian party asked if it was his Majesty's pleasure to lunch on the way. The King cordially replied that it was. Thereupon a telegram was sent to the proper station, "Prepare lunch for the King of the Sandwich Islands." On arriving at the station, the King, his suit, and the officials, were formally taken into a room, the doors of which were guarded by soldiers, and several large piles of sandwiches were presented to the King. The chief official at once stormed about it, and inquired what was meant by offering such a lunch. The keeper of the station was brought in, and meekly explained that the telegram given to him verbally was, "Prepare a lunch of sandwiches for the King."
>
> —WILLIAM N. ARMSTRONG (*AROUND THE WORLD WITH A KING*)

The Long and the Short of It

The longest Hawaiian first name recorded on a birth certificate so far is Keliihokulanileikulamakakeanuenueohaleakala. This name has 43 letters in it. The shortest name is I.

Gecko Encounters

Where I live on Maui, the pretty green geckos with the red spots—the Gold-Dust Day Geckos—stay outside and are generally out and about during the day. Every night we have Stump-Toed Geckos on the outside of our windows catching insects attracted by the lights. Occasionally they're seen during the day, but they're mainly nocturnal. At night, the Common House Geckos come out. Almost all of the geckos inside our house seem to be Common House Geckos, but it's hard to tell for sure since Common House Geckos, Stump-Toed Geckos, and Indo-Pacific Geckos sometimes look very similar.

My girlfriend, Elaine, found one of these guys on our kitchen counter one day and we could tell something was wrong. It ran when we touched it, but it wouldn't go very far. We finally realized that it had gone blind. I made it comfortable outside in an orchid pot and tried to feed it, but it wasn't interested. I kept an eye on it for about twenty-four hours and watched the Gold-Dust Day Geckos gather around to inspect it. It was as big as they were, if not bigger, so I knew they couldn't eat it. They just seemed curious. Eventually it vanished while I was sitting about ten feet away. That was about the time the sun reached the flowerpot, so perhaps it went in search of shelter—they are nocturnal—or maybe a bird ate it. The life of a gecko can be tough.

War Clouds from Half a World Away

Germans in Hawai'i

Honolulu had an influential German population when World War I broke out in Europe in 1914. Henry Berger conducted the Royal Hawaiian Band and composed many of Hawai'i's favorite songs. Commercially, H. Hackfeld & Co.—one of the "Big Five" and its subsidiary B.F. Ehlers department store—were still wholly owned in Germany. Other still-familiar German names include Isenberg, Pfleuger, Schuman, Spreckels, Stangenwald, Straub, Von Hamm Young and Von Holt.

A Fierce Debate

For several years the United States waged a fierce internal debate on whether to join the hostilities or not. Isolationists argued that it was not "our" war, an argument that was quite popular as the horrific weapons of modern warfare—machine guns, poison gas and unrestricted submarine warfare—slaughtered people in unprecedented numbers. Still, before hostilities were officially joined, young Americans aching for adventure volunteered for such outfits as the Lafayette Escadrille.

Liberty Dogs

Germany's use of submarines—including the sinking of the British passenger liner RMS *Lusitania*, in which 1,201 lives were lost (128 of them American)—eventually turned public opinion to enthusiasm for entering the conflict. Coupled with "Beat the Hun" propaganda demonizing the enemy, the cause to send Johnny "Over There" created anti-German loathing in the U.S. in which dachshunds were renamed "liberty dogs" and companies such as H. Hackfeld were divided up and given names like American Factors.

—MacKinnon Simpson (*A Century of Aloha*)

Parrotfish Poop

Look at All that Sand

Have you ever looked around while sitting on one of Hawai'i's many beaches and wondered where all that sand came from? Probably not. But it *is* an interesting question; or rather, a question with an interesting answer.

In most places, sand consists of granular particles of minerals and rock—usually quartz, which makes up most of the world's sand—but not in Hawai'i. There is no quartz here. Some of our sand is fragments of volcanic materials, but much of it is parrotfish poop.

Big Eaters

Parrotfish are so named because their teeth are fused together, giving them the appearance of a parrot-like beak. They use their tough teeth to eat coral. They want the living material attached, but to get it they chomp off clumps. You can actually hear their loud crunching when you're snorkeling. They even nibble away dead coral to get the algae off of it. The chewed up coral passes through their digestive tract and the hard bits of coral come out the back. In a year, an 18-inch Parrotfish can poop an amazing 700 pounds of sand, and they've been doing this for millennia. These guys are champion sand-makers.

Grinders

Parrotfish have bones in their throats that further grind up the coral. Sometimes they even eat rock. And they're not the only ones. Sea urchins also grind up rock and coral into sand. An urchin chews off coral with the mouth on the bottom of its shell using its five beak-like teeth and the sand is ejected from a hole in the top of its shell.

Beautiful, But Watch Out

Male Parrotfish are some of the most beautiful fish in the ocean, with their florescent blues, greens, oranges, and pinks. But when startled, they will suddenly eject a cloud of sand, so you don't really want to swim right behind them. This propensity is probably why the Hawaiian name for the female redlip parrotfish is uhu pālukaluka, which means "diarrhea parrotfish." If they knew this, no doubt they'd be mortified and highly offended.

Way Back in the Day
The Changing Face of Honolulu

In 1886, the Prime Minister of the Hawaiian Kingdom, Walter Murray Gibson, gave a speech on the "Progress of Hawaii Since 1836" to commemorate the jubilee birthday of King Kalākaua. In this excerpt he talks about how Honolulu had changed in those fifty years.

> Fifty years ago the tide flowed where now are some of our busiest streets; a small coasting schooner anchored where now may be seen steam vessels carrying the Hawaiian flag across the ocean...Kalo patches and grass huts, unshaded by any tree, except where the cocoanut fringed the shore, have been replaced by substantial buildings and busy streets, and the whole shaded by such a wealth of lovely foliage...busy haunts of a commerce...brought with rapid strides to its present high condition by the wise and patriotic effort of the King whose jubilee we now celebrate [in 1886].
>
> —WALTER MURRAY GIBSON (*THE DIARIES OF WALTER MURRAY GIBSON*)

"Honolulu streets are amusing. The blocks of houses are tropical, with most reasonable lowness, and are of cement in facings; and the great number of Chinese shops and of Chinese, with some pretty Chinese girl faces and children's faces, enliven the streets.

—John La Farge

Honolulu 1825

The town of Honoruru, the Capital of the Sandwich Islands, is rather a considerable place; it is situated upon a plain, immediately at the foot of a high range of hills, and extends itself along the shore to the distance of about 3 miles....

The town itself occupies about a quarter of this space. The habitations, with the exception of a few houses...are all built with straw...some of the best of them are very large, and capable of lodging fifty or sixty persons...Very little attention has been paid in the forming of this cluster of huts into anything like a town or Village: here and there however, sufficient regularity has been observed to form a street or two. As a small piece of ground is generally attached to each house, encircled by a mud wall, or fence of long sticks, the Village has a strangling and irregular appearance. There are four or five decent houses erected by Americans, one or two of stone, the others of wood;...Karaimoku possessed a very large well-built stone house; which he was just finishing as we arrived....

The Springs from the Mountains are...turned into various channels, by which large patches of stagnate water are formed around the town: here the taro plant flourishes in great luxuriance....

There are also large salt water ponds formed immediately along the shore, and the vicinity of the Village. These are constantly well supplied with fish, on which, together with the taro, the Natives almost entirely subsist.

— ROBERT DAMPIER AND DAVID W. FORBES
(ENCOUNTERS WITH PARADISE: VIEWS OF HAWAI'I AND ITS PEOPLE 1778-1941)

Waikīkī Then and Now

Waikīkī and Diamond Head, with the Royal Hawaiian and Moana Hotels in the 1930s.

Waikīkī Beach as it looks today. Carol M. Highsmith's America, Library of Congress, Prints and Photographs Division

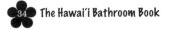

Downtown Honolulu looking toward Nu'uanu Valley in the early 1860s.
HAWAI'I STATE ARCHIVES

The Streets of Honolulu in 1870

The street was filled with a motley throng of Yankees and Hawaiian men and women, the latter being very fat and big, all barefooted, with wide, loose dresses. Some of them were very stylish but all were barefooted save me. The shops were mostly kept by Europeans but a great number by Chinese and a few Hawaiians. The lower part of the town is no way different from that of a third-rate Australian town. The streets are unpaved but there are footpaths formed. The wholesale places are nearly all kept by whites but most of the retail by Chinese who are drapers, bakers, boarding house keepers, etc. The laborers are kanaka. We walked up the street about a mile, seeing throngs, and across the street the funeral of one of the sailors of the man-of-war. We spoke to several natives, asked questions, but found no-one understood us. I asked one woman if the king lived at a respectable looking house we came to; she answered something in kanaka.

—PATRICK O'LEARY

Fixing Honolulu's Problems

Honolulu grows today with the same problems that burden most American cities—freeways, excessive traffic, parking deficiencies, air and water pollution, diminishing open spaces, the destruction of natural amenities, the loss of historically significant buildings, over crowding, social inadequacies, insufficient recreational facilities, and so on. But Honolulu itself is not the same as any other city, and therefore these problems, though similar, must have dissimilar solution—solutions planned by sensitive, imaginative and understanding persons—solutions that are particularly sympathetic to the regional requirements and conditions. And in the planning process, the safeguarding of Honolulu's individuality should certainly be the primary objective.

—GEOFFREY W. FAIRFAX (*THE ARCHITECTURE OF HONOLULU*)

Prison Life in 1855

In 1855, while the whaling ship *Arab* was docked in Lahaina on Maui taking on supplies, a sixteen-year-old sailor named William Stetson and a few others went ashore and ended up in Lahaina's prison. The prison, which doubled as a jail, consists of a two-story gatehouse, where the prison master and his family lived. Running off on each side of the gatehouse is a high coral-block wall that encloses the large prison yard, roughly 150 feet square. Towards the back of the yard is a building that resembles a small church or an old schoolhouse. This is the cell block and contains eight prison cells.

Stetson described what it was like being a prisoner in his journal. You can't say the Kingdom of Hawai'i was tough on crime. It almost sounds like a free vacation.

The view from inside the Lahaina prison yard, showing the gatehouse. JOHN RICHARD STEPHENS

Joining Friends

But within the white washed walls of the Lahaina calaboose, we were not destined to undergo much hardship. The first person who greeted us upon our entrance was Kirby, the man who in the morning had warned us not to go too far from town and now he had the laugh on us for our disregarding his advice. Moody was also in there for a fellow prisoner to us and with these we had a very sociable time.

The cell block of the Lahaina prison.
JOHN RICHARD STEPHENS

Good Food

A dinner of excellent poe [sweet potato] and fish were furnished us by some of the kanaka prisoners and we made a hearty meal of what we had been looking for all day where we least expected to eat it. We then had a comfortable smoke and layed ourselves out on the greensward in prison yard to await the issue and see a little prison life.

Companionship

There were no white men in with us excepting Moody and Kirby and the rest of the prisoners were about ten dozen kanakas [sic, perhaps two dozen?], male and female all had the freedom of the prison yard and mingled promiscuously with each other. And if there were about a dozen or twenty good fellows in there, together they might lead a very pleasant life for some time.

Prison Cells

The only time the prisoners, in common cases, are shut up is at night and then they are put in large wooden cells which are capable of accommodating four persons each and this number is usually placed together when they behave themselves.

The cells are entirely unfurnished but the prisoner is at liberty to furnish it in any order that his funds will allow him to. And he is also free to have any groceries for his palate that he can procure, but each prisoner is allowed but one loaf of bread per day as prison fare. No restrictions are placed on the use of cards or tobacco and any sedate individual could therefore lay back all day with a pipe in his mouth and enjoy himself at a game of euchre as well as though he was comfortably stowed away in a beer house.

—WILLIAM STETSON

Crime and Punishment

Catching Murderers

Honolulu has been changed and civilization has advanced since I joined the police force, but the chief elements of crime and detection don't change. Crimes are committed by human beings. They may use different instruments and different techniques from year to year, but their motives are the same as those of people who committed crimes forty-five years ago.

The qualities most important for a detective trying to catch a burglar, a robber, or a killer are unlimited patience and attention to detail. In a real tough murder case, the man who pays attention to every small detail and finds out the meaning behind each one of them – there's the man who will catch the murderer.

— DETECTIVE JOHN JARDINE (*CRIMES IN HONOLULU*)

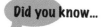

Did you know...

The Honolulu Fort was built to deal with rowdy sailors and foreign residents. It operated from 1816 to 1857 as a prison and insane asylum.

The Hawai'i Bathroom Book 39

Hilo Hattie

The Rise of Hilo Hattie

Hilo Hattie was a much-loved comic singer, dancer, and actress, who is one of Hawai'i's Golden People—one who effectively blended together different cultures.

Her real name was Clarissa "Clara" Haili (later Clara Inter and then Clara Nelson). She was born in Honolulu in 1901 with 100% Hawaiian ancestry. She began performing informally in 1920s, while working as a teacher at Waipahu Elementary. In 1936, she took a ship to a teachers' convention in Portland, Oregon. On the return journey, Don McDiarmid and the Royal Hawaiian Hotel orchestra were performing his song, "When Hilo Hattie Does the Hilo Hop." McDiarmid normally had a sultry hula dancer perform it seductively, but one night the dancer fell ill so Clara took over, doing it in her comic style. It became such a huge hit that Hilo Hattie became Clara's stage name. Her other mildly risqué hits were "The Cockeyed Mayor of Kaunakakai" and "Princess Pupule has Plenty Papayas."

Hilo Hattie, Betty Grable, and Elvis

In California during World War II, she was a regular performer for the Red Cross, cheering up the returning wounded servicemen, but it was her many appearances on the *Hawaii Calls* radio show (1935-1975), which was broadcast on more than 750 radio stations, that made her famous around the world.

Hilo Hattie recorded several live albums and appeared in

the movies *Song of the Islands* (1942) with Betty Grable, *Tahiti Nights* (1944), *Miss Tatlock's Millions* (1948), *City Beneath the Sea* (1953), *Ma and Pa Kettle at Waikiki* (1955), *Kismet* (1955), *Suicide Battalion* (1958), and *Blue Hawaii* (1961) with Elvis Presley. She also made occasional guest appearances on the TV show *Hawaii Five-O* (1968–1970).

Hilo Hattie Stores

She succumbed to cancer in 1979. That same year a souvenir manufacturer, wholesaler, and chain of retail stores took on her name. Now many people know the Hilo Hattie stores as places that feature locally made gifts and products. But in spite of the passage of time, Hilo Hattie (the entertainer) remains one of the world's favorite Hawaiians.

From Personal Experience

How Hilo Hattie was Born

Don McDiarmid was leading the band and Clara wanted him to let her do the Hilo Hattie number, but he was reluctant. In an article written by Don in the April 1947 issue of "Paradise of the Pacific," here's the way he tells it:

> Although I enjoy writing any type of song, my biggest thrills have come from creating mental personalities. It's fun to form a picture of a new song character and wait and see what finally happens. Sometimes the result is just what I'd expected.
>
> Aggie Auld, former Hula darling of the Royal Hawaiian Hotel, was first to introduce "Little Brown Gal." She was all I had dreamed of, with her charm and grace, and beautiful long black hair. Ku'u Lei also ran true to form as "South Sea Sadie," a character she has portrayed with much success in Hollywood. Napua Woodd was pleasantly surprising with her streamlined interpretation of the "Old Kama'āina

from Lahaina," which she featured in the Hawaiian Room of New York's Lexington Hotel.

But the greatest shock of all was the fate which befell my most popular brainchild, "Hilo Hattie," at the hands of Clara Inter. I had conjured up an exotic eyeful, tall and slender, voluptuous and glamorous. Well, if you've seen Clara in the role, I need say no more. She is neither tall nor slender, neither streamlined nor glamorous. But I hasten to add that Clara is doing alright for herself and for the song.

—Don McDiarmid (*Paradise of the Pacific*, April 1947)

Doing all right indeed she was. Members of the band recall the first time she did the number at the Royal Hawaiian Hotel. They agree with a version of a story in an unidentifiable publication that reported the incident thusly:

When Clara asked the conductor if she could do Hilo Hattie, he stared at her in disbelief. He grudgingly consented to play accompaniment for her, making no secret that he thought she wasn't the type for this song. Hattie, a charming person, is a bit buxom and not a glamour girl.

Hilo Hattie's version of "Hilo Hattie" brought a tremendous ovation in the same place where the number had failed, and she had to make encore after encore. The amazed composer jumped from the bandstand, tears streaming down his face, as he confessed to Hattie he obviously had erred in visualizing a streamlined glamour girl for the song. "I never dreamed a character looking like you would put the number over," he admitted.

—Milly Singletary (*Hilo Hattie: A Legend in Our Time*)

Did you know...

The Kingdom of Hawai'i had one of the world's most literate populations.

Ain't Comin' Back to New York

Here is an example of Hilo Hattie's humor, in Harry S. Decker's "Becky (I Ain't Comin' Back No More)," she sings about Izzy Cohen who came to Honolulu in 1861 and refused to return to New York, so he had to write a letter to his wife, Becky, breaking the news, saying (in a New York Jewish accent), "Tell my relations I'm here at Waikīkī. Hanalula is the only place to be. You should see those hula dollies. They're better than the Minsky follies....Those hula dollies, how they can shake. They wiggle and they tremble like an earthquake. And then they show how and you yell '*wow!*' Shoot me while I'm happy now. The rumba, boogie-woogie, jitterbug, oi! It's too darn slow for this Yiddish-a boy. Now give me a girl with a skirt of shredded wheat, with a rope around her neck and bagels on her feet. Oh, Becky, Becky, I ain't comin' back no more."

> *"Hilo is a beautiful city, and indeed I would have been proud to have been born there, but the great Kahuna decided I should be born in Honolulu."*
>
> —Hilo Hattie

> *"I've seen it in newspapers. I've even been asked if Haili Street was named for me. (That's my maiden name.) I've even had the same question about the Haili Church and that was built in 1859 by Protestant Missionaries."*
>
> —Hilo Hattie

Academia Nut

Dr. Rodney Chang, a Honolulu dentist who also lives in Volcano on the Big Island, earned *ten* college degrees from a variety of universities, including the University of Southern California, Loyola University in Chicago, and the Union Graduate Institute in Ohio. Besides his D.D.S., he also has an associate degree, two bachelors, five masters, and a Ph.D. in Art Psychology.

What's in a Name?
(Hawai'i, a.k.a. the Big Island)

- **Hawai'i (island):** this is an ancient name that doesn't appear to have a translation.
- **Kona (district):** leeward.
- **Kailua (town):** two seas, or two ocean currents.
- **Kalaoa (town):** the choker (referring to a stick used for catching eels).
- **Kohala (district and mountains):** this is an ancient name that doesn't appear to have a translation.
- **Waikoloa (town):** duck water.
- **Waimea (town):** reddish water.
- **Honoka'a (town):** rolling bay.
- **Hāmākua (district and coast):** this is an ancient name that doesn't appear to have a translation.
- **Mauna Loa (volcano):** long mountain.
- **Hilo (district and town):** first night of the Hawaiian moon calendar, new moon.
- **Puna (district):** spring of water.
- **Mauna Kea (volcano):** white mountain
- **Kīlauea (crater):** spewing eruption.
- **Ka'ū (district):** this is an ancient name that doesn't appear to have a translation.

Pele

Goddess of Volcanoes

In the pantheon of ancient Hawaiian worship—or, rather, of the worship of the group from the twelfth century to the nineteenth—the deity most feared and respected, especially on the island of Hawai'i, was the goddess Pele. She was the queen of fire and goddess of volcanoes, and her favorite residence was the vast and ever-seething crater of Kīlauea, beneath whose molten flood, in halls of burning adamant and grottoes of fire, she consumed the offerings of her worshippers and devised destruction to those who long neglected her or failed to respect her prerogatives.

Pele's Family

Her assistants and companions, as related by tradition, were her five brothers and eight sisters, all of them clothed with especial functions, and all but little less merciless and exacting than Pele herself. The first in authority under Pele was Moho, king of steam. The others were charged, respectively, with the duties of creating explosions, thunders and rains of fire, moving and keeping the clouds in place, breaking canoes, fighting with spears of flame, hurling red-hot masses of lava, and doing whatever else the goddess commanded.

Pele's Heiaus

As the family claimed tribute of the entire island of Hawai'i, to receive it they frequently visited the active and extinct craters of other districts, and earthquakes heralded their departure from Kīlauea. The temples of Pele were numerous, particularly in the neighborhood of old lava-flows, and their priests were always well sustained. The crater of Kīlauea was especially sacred to the goddess, and the earth around it could not be safely disturbed.

Attractive and Courageous

Pele was as courageous as she was personally attractive. She had taken an active part in the wars of her father, and with her own hand had slain a chief who attempted to abduct her. Her brothers were devoted to her, and her bright eyes and queenly presence commanded the respect and homage of all who approached her.

—KING DAVID KALĀKAUA (*THE LEGENDS AND MYTHS OF HAWAII*)

"*[Pele] could at times...assume the appearance of a handsome young woman.... At other times the innate...character of the fury showed itself, and she appeared in her usual form as an ugly and hateful old hag, with tattered and fire-burnt garment, scarcely concealing the filth of her person. Her bloodshot eyes and fiendish countenance paralyzed the beholder, and her touch turned him to stone.*"

—Joseph Emerson

(*THE BURNING ISLAND:*
A JOURNEY THROUGH MYTH AND HISTORY IN VOLCANO COUNTRY, HAWAI'I)

Did you know...

Hawai'i County is one of seven counties in the United States that has the same name as its state; the others being New York, Iowa, Arkansas, Oklahoma, Utah, and Idaho counties.

Kona Nightingales

Singing of the Nightingales

Most of Hawai'i's famous coffee is grown in the Kona district, on the western side of the Big Island, after former plantation workers—mainly of Japanese descent—took leases on coffee farms high on the volcanic slopes overlooking the Kona coast and created a booming coffee industry during the 1920s and 1930s. The new coffee farmers struggled and lacked the income to buy luxuries such as trucks, forcing them to turn to donkeys to carry loads of coffee beans down the steep volcanic slopes, and haul loads of groceries and supplies back up again. The donkeys became known as Kona nightingales, a backhanded tribute to their loud braying.

Becoming a Tourist Attraction

After World War II, coffee farmers started using surplus Jeeps instead of donkeys. Some of the donkeys went wild and migrated down toward the ocean to live on dry, flat lands by the sea, turning the Kona nightingales into a tourist attraction. The donkeys have since been moved to fenced preserves, where they will no longer be endangered by the increased traffic on Queen Ka'ahumanu Highway.

—DAN NAKASO (*THINGS HAWAI'I, NEW EDITION*)

Did you know...

Hawai'i is the only state that grows coffee. While Kona coffee is the most famous, coffee is also grown on O'ahu, Maui, Moloka'i, and Kaua'i.

Don't Call It Shaved Ice!

John Richard Stephens

Don't Do It

Some people get very up-set whenever anyone calls it "shaved ice." It's like finger-nails on a chalkboard to them. It's "shave ice," which makes sense when you think about it. They make it by shaving off a thin layer of ice from a big block. Shaved ice would refer to the big block that just got the shave, since it has been shaved, while shave ice would refer to the soft mound of ice that was shaved off.

176 Flavors (more or less)

Like snow cones, flavored syrups are poured onto the ice, but unlike snow cones, some shops make their own syrups. Snow cones usually come in cherry, grape, apple, bubble gum, and root beer. At most stands, you can get shave ice in those flavors too, and about thirty more. A few might offer more than a hundred flavors. Chances are you'll never see a shark's blood snow cone. Actually that's what they call strawberry coconut here. But how about apricot, tamarindo, cherimoya, pickled mango, lychee, or melona cheesecake? And we actually do have a dill pickle flavor shave ice, and a buttered popcorn flavor, and tiramisu flavor.

The Extras

Then there are all the extras. On the bottom you can get ice cream, azuki beans, bits of mochi, and/or gummy bears. Poured on top you can condensed milk, sweetened coconut cream, chocolate caramel cream, or li hing powder, which is salty, sour, and sweet. These are known as snowcaps.

Getting Creative

Then they start to get creative. New Orleans may have the Frog in a Blender (green apple and cherry swirled with a gummy frog on top), but we have the Shark Attack!, which has a Blue Hawaii as a base to represent the ocean, then they splash Tiger's Blood (cherry coconut) on top around a Sour Patch Kid gummy and then stick a gummy shark or two on the side.

A Bit More About Dessert

First Shave Ice

The first commercial sales of "shave ice" began in the 1920s when heaps of flakes were produced with a hand-held planning device. A decade later, hand-cranked Japanese machines were imported and businesses such as the Hale'iwa Vegetable Market found an additional source of revenue, especially in beach communities like the North Shore. The original shave ice, served in a cup with flavored syrup, sold for five cents. In the 1970s, the price rose to an exorbitant 15 cents! Now, the shave ice of Hale'iwa stores such as Matsumoto's and Aoki's is internationally famous, and these stores are popular destinations for tourists and locals alike.

—GLEN GRANT AND BENNETT HYMER (*HAWAI'I LOOKING BACK*)

Did you know...

Moloka'i once produced more honey than anywhere else in the world, up until an epidemic wiped out the hives in the 1930s.

Samurai Shave Ice

Actually, shave ice wasn't invented in Hawai'i. It's one of those great cultural ideas that was brought here and enthusiastically adopted. As far as anyone can tell, shave ice originated in Japan during the Heian Period (794 to 1185), where they shaved blocks of ice with swords. One can easily imagine a great Shogun warrior taking a strong stance with his feet wide apart and knees slightly bent as he brings down his razor-sharp samurai sword to shave off some ice for his kids.

They don't do it quite like that anymore. The Japanese plantation workers brought it here and now we're beginning to export it to the world. If you can't come to Hawai'i to get a shave ice, you can now get one in places like New Jersey. They even have a flavor we don't have—the toxic waste-flavor shave ice.

More Frozen Treats

Gourmet Treats

Hawai'i is great! Where else can you get gourmet popsicles with flavors like Lavender Chocolate Flake, Passion Fruit Orange Guava (Pog), Kona Koffee, Mango Cream, Coconut Lime, Pineapple Ginger, Starfruit Lemongrass, Watermelon Cucumber Cayenne, and Kula Strawberry Maui Goat Cheese (probably made with cheese from the Surfing Goat Dairy in Kula). You can even get popsicles made with tequila or champagne, such as Li Hing Mui Margarita pops or Guava Strawberry Mimosa pops. Slices of kiwi or chunks of Grand Marnier-infused strawberries are distinctly visible in some of them.

The Forbidden Isle

Ni'ihau is a privately owned island that sits about eighteen miles west of Kaua'i and is home to between 100 and 200 people who speak Hawaiian as their primary language. There are no cars, telephones, radios or televisions. They do have solar electricity, but no running water. Newspapers and most books are also not allowed, although the school does have a computer. Since it's privately owned, generally only invited guests are allowed, though occasionally there are some tours and hunting safaris. There is also a small U.S. Navy outpost there. These restrictions are what give the island its nickname, the Forbidden Isle. It's also known as the Hawaiian Island.

The majority of Ni'ihau's population lives here at Pu'uwai. DOUGLAS PEEBLES.

The Revolt of Mamie Stover

*Jane Russell as Hawai'i's most suc-
cessful "dance hostess."* TWENTIETH
CENTURY-FOX

The Military Floods In

After the Japanese attack on Pearl Harbor, thousands of military personnel flooded the islands, some to stay, some in transit to conflicts elsewhere in the Pacific. The military had money to spend and island businesses were eager to take it. Movie theaters and restaurants made money hand over fist—as did bars and brothels.

Honolulu's Brothels

Most of Honolulu's houses of ill fame were to be found in Chinatown, on River Street. They did a roaring business, particularly when a big ship came into port. Old folks remember going shopping in Chinatown and having to push through lines of sailors, standing in the street and waiting their turn.

Rising to the Top

Several years after the end of the war, mainland novelist William Bradford Huie called on his experience of wartime Honolulu to write *The Revolt of Mamie Stover.* This 1953 novel details the adventures of a mainland prostitute who sails to Honolulu, graduates from working girl to madam, defies restrictive laws, and eventually becomes a married woman and wealthy property-owner. Huie picked a risqué subject, but avoided coarse language and graphic detail. The novel successfully skirted the edge of the permissible and became a best-seller.

Huie published a sequel, *Hotel Mamie Stover,* in 1963,

which attracted none of the attention given to the first Mamie Stover novel. Both novels are now out-of-print and hard to find. The few copies in island libraries are non-circulating.

Mamie at the Movies

The novel is perhaps better known for the 1956 movie version, which starred Jane Russell as the curvaceous temptress. The movie turns the novel's narrative of vice triumphant into a morality tale: Mamie is punished for her evil ways by losing the man she loves.

The novelist, James Huie, died in 1986. During his lifetime he published twenty-one books, fiction and non-fiction. Several other Huie books were made into movies: *Wild River* (1960), *The Outsider* (1961), and *The Americanization of Emily* (1964).

—KAREN LOFTSTROM

Blast from the Past

The Red-Light District

Iwilei is an industrial section of Honolulu that lies adjacent to the dock area and seems very ordinary. But its past is a story to tell.

Hospitality with Benefits

With the discovery of Hawai'i by Captain James Cook in 1778, Hawai'i's reputation for aloha and hospitality began to spread around the world aided by the behavior of some of the local women who swam out to greet visiting ships. Many would spend the evenings and nights aboard in the company of sailors starved for female companionship. Initially no payment was asked.

However, the women grew canny as they realized that the sailors had useful items to trade for their favors. Iron nails, sailcloth, knives, and daggers which were then valuable became staples for trade. Soon women no longer swam to the ships and instead the sailors came ashore, thus starting a commercial enterprise which continued as Honolulu became a favorite re-provisioning stop for the increasing number of vessels plying the Pacific. Unfortunately, it was not all a blessing as the visiting seamen brought with them venereal diseases and pestilences previously unknown to the islands with devastating results.

The Government Gets Involved

By 1860 the legislature created an act to mitigate the situation.

> "Whereas, the evils and diseases arising from prostitution are widespread and apparent, carrying death to thousands of the Hawaiian race, and preventing the increase of the population; and it being impossible to suppress and crush out prostitution but that its evils and diseases may be combated, circumscribed and diminished,...
>
> Therefore be it enacted by the King...that a system of regulation of prostitution be established including the registration of prostitutes, regular medical examination of them...and treatment of infected prostitutes by the health department free of charge."

Kamehameha IV (Alexander Liholiho) signed off on the Act which was the thinking regarding prostitution up to and into World War II. Providing a prostitute registered as such and passed regular medical examinations, she was free to ply her trade.

Containment

While prostitution was condoned, it was to be somehow contained. What was needed was a "red-light district."

Iwilei was a natural choice as it was the location of a railroad terminal and near to the interisland steamship docks. And it was out of sight of the central business district, only a few blocks away.

Sometime before 1900, a "stockade" with five entrances was established in Iwilei. Police rules were posted near the entrance and a policeman patrolled therein to control unruly clients.

As time went on, the enterprising madams of Iwilei expanded the reservation several blocks. The district acquired the dubious reputation of a world-class bordello, with Honolulu compared to the wide open and exotic ports like Port Said, Marseilles, Port au Prince, and the Yoshiwara district in Japan.

Writers like Somerset Maugham wrote vaguely titillating stories based on the stockade at Iwilei, a curious development for a city whose legitimate commerce was under the ironclad rule of the descendents of missionaries. Something had to be done. In 1905 the legislature repealed the governing Act. Committees were formed to study the situation. In the meantime nature took its course and the trade continued to flourish under the old rules.

Inserting the Gas Works

While Honolulu, then a growing city of almost 40,000 residents, enjoyed most modern developments, it lacked a gas distribution company. A gas distribution franchise in Hawai'i (Hawai'i was then a U.S. territory) was created in 1904 by an act in Washington to manufacture pipeline gas using a process that liberated the gas contained within crude oil. Because it was a dirty process, the gas works was placed in Iwilei, removed from the central business district and residential areas. No fewer than 180 "ladies of the evening" were displaced but simply moved over and became neighbors of the gas works.

It's a Raid!

One night in November of 1916, the police swooped down on the stockade and closed it off. The girls were rounded up, arrested, given suspended sentences of one year and ordered to desist from their amorous pursuits. But Iwilei continued having its subterranean economy, which grew in leaps and bounds during World War II when thousands of servicemen were located or passed through the Islands.

—WILLIAM DORRANCE (*O'AHU'S HIDDEN HISTORY*)

Hunting Wild Cows

A Kapu on Cows

When cattle were first introduced to Hawai'i, King Kame-hameha I placed a kapu on killing them, except for some of the bulls to keep them from becoming too numerous. After thirty years the cattle were becoming a problem. As rancher William Lee described the situation in 1851, "Instead of keeping our herds reduced to a reasonable number, they are in some instances allowed to increase to an alarming extent, and thousands of half-starved creatures are seen ranging over the country destroying everything within their reach."

Hawaiian Mountainmen

Cowboys from Monterey, California, were brought over to teach the Hawaiians how to lasso cattle, jerk the beef, and cure the hides, but they soon left. In their place, Hawaiian mountainmen, licensed by the king and the government, began hunting wild cattle solely for their hides, receiving $1.25 for every bull hide and $1.00 per cow hide. It was reported that 222,170 pounds of these hides were shipped primarily to the mainland in the first six months of 1859.

Much like the cowboys and sailors of the day, these mountainmen lived a rough life of deprivation with few comforts. On getting paid,they'd go into town and quickly dispose of their income, then return to their Spartan life in the mountains.

Traditional Saying

Only when the water gourd isn't full do you hear it gurgling. (Those who are ignorant have an awful lot to say.)

The Cattle Hunter's Camp

In 1859, the *Pacific Commercial Advertiser* published this description of one of the camps.

A Rustic Life

The cattle hunter's camp was situated on a side hill among Koa trees, sheltered from trade winds which blow cold and fresh there, and trees furnished firewood, no small consideration at that elevation. The hut was built of three walls of stone, open to the south, roof of koa wood logs and plastered over with grass and mud. The floor was the ground covered with hides. There were many flies. A large fire was constantly kept burning in front, and for an acre or so around the ground was covered with drying hides.

The hut fifteen by twenty feet furnished a sleeping place for twenty-five to thirty cowboys. The corral made of sticks and hides had about sixty horses.

Trapping Cattle

The pen into which cattle were to be driven was about a half acre, built of strong posts and rails and had an entrance like the upper part of Y opening toward the side from which cattle were to come.

The cowboys drove about 200 cattle of all sizes which they had assembled on the mountain side in with a great roar. With them were perhaps 1,000 wild hogs which had got into the trap by being in the cow country. The next day and later at their leisure the cattle were lassoed, taken out of the pen and slaughtered.

—ANONYMOUS

Filmed on Kaua'i

Kaua'i has many prime film locations, and because of this, you can see it in many movies, sometimes pretending to be the jungles of Africa or the rice fields of Vietnam. Here are just a few of the movies with scenes filmed on Kaua'i:

- *The Descendants* (starring George Clooney; 2011)
- *Avatar* (Sam Worthington, Sigourney Weaver; 2009)
- *Pirates of the Caribbean: At World's End* (Johnny Depp; 2007)
- *Pirates of the Caribbean: On Stranger Tides* (Johnny Depp, Penélope Cruz; 2011)
- *Tropic Thunder* (Ben Stiller, Jack Black, Robert Downey Jr.; 2008),
- *Jurassic Park* (Sam Neill, Laura Dern, Jeff Goldblum; 1993)
- *The Lost World: Jurassic Park* (Jeff Goldblum, Julianne Moore;1997)
- *Jurassic Park III* (Sam Neill, Tea Leoni; 2000)
- *Godzilla* (Matthew Broderick;1998)
- *George of the Jungle* (Brendan Fraser; 1997)
- *To End All Wars* (Keifer Sutherland; 2000)
- *Outbreak* (Dustin Hoffman; 1995)
- *Journey 2: The Mysterious Island* (Dwayne Johnson, Michael Caine; 2012)
- *Six Days Seven Nights* (Harrison Ford; 1998)
- *Body Heat* (William Hurt, Kathleen Turner; 1981)
- *Dragonfly* (Kevin Costner; 2002)
- *South Pacific* (Mitzi Gaynor; 1958)
- *Throw Mama from the Train* (Danny DeVito; 1987)
- *Fantasy Island* (Ricardo Montalban;1977 TV series)
- *King Kong* (Jeff Bridges, Jessica Lange; 1976)
- *The Thorn Birds* (Richard Chamberlain; 1983 mini-series)
- *Honeymoon in Vegas* (Nicolas Cage, Sarah Jessica Parker; 1992)

- *Uncommon Valor* (Gene Hackman, Patrick Swayze; 1983)
- *Flight of the Intruder* (Danny Glover, Willem Dafoe, 1991)
- *Donovan's Reef* (John Wayne; 1963)
- *Seven Women from Hell* (Denise Darcel; 1961)
- *The Hawaiians* (Charlton Heston; 1970)
- *Blue Hawaii* (Elvis Presley; 1961)
- *Miss Sadie Thompson* (Rita Hayworth, José Ferrer; 1953)
- *The Wackiest Ship in the Army* (Jack Lemmon, 1960)
- *Beachhead* (Tony Curtis; 1954)
- *Diamond Head* (Charlton Heston; 1963)
- *Voodoo Island* (Boris Karloff; 1957)

Meet Your Neighbors

Who's Who on Kaua'i?

Kaua'i is arguably the most beautiful of all the isles, although each of the other islands have spots that rival it. The North Shore is particularly stunning, so it's not surprising many celebrities are drawn there. These include Pierce Brosnan, Ben Stiller, Todd Rundgren, Glenn Frey, and Charo. Sylvester Stallone once owned a large property there, but he divided it up and sold it. Bette Midler's home is there and she also owns more than 1,000 acres in Wailua, mostly forested. Michael Crichton and surf champion Andy Irons lived there until they passed away. Drew Barrymore and Natalie Merchant are rumored to own homes somewhere on the island. Buffy Sainte-Marie owns a goat, flower and Christmas tree farm on a remote mountainside in Kaua'i which she bought in 1969 just four days after arriving in Hawai'i.

Meet the Kamehamehas

This photograph of the royal family was taken around 1853. King Kamehameha the Great's second son, King Kamehameha III is in the center, accompanied by his wife, Queen Kalama, on the left. Behind them are their nephews and his successors—Prince Alexander Liholiho, who became King Kamehameha IV, and Prince Lot Kapuāiwa, who became King Kamehameha V. To the right is his niece, Victoria Kamāmalu, who became kuhina nui as Ka'ahumanu IV. BISHOP MUSEUM

" *We are descendants of the chiefs who took care of the bones of Kamehameha the Great...So many people want to know where he is buried. The only thing we know is that when the two chiefs came back from hiding the bones, Ho'oulu went to his wife and she had just given birth to a son. Hawaiians had an instinct to name a child after an event. So the child was named Haihe'ekai, which meant the receding waters. So figure that one out: did the waters recede? They must have gone into an underwater cave.*"

—Lydia Namahana Mai'oho, Kahu of Royal Mausoleum

(*VOICES OF WISDOM*)

The Monarchy

The two ruling dynasties of the years of the Hawaiian monarchy (European style) could claim unbroken genealogical roots to the original pair Wakea and Papa who appear as the somewhat mythic progenitors of the ranking alii of old Hawaii in all versions of the *Kumulipo: The Hawaiian Creation Chant.* Proof of rank was kept in heroic chants of ancient times: the mele inoa, the kuauhau and the moolelo. Although not subjected to writing until the nineteenth century, there is ample reason to believe the accuracy of the data contained in these chants. Hawaiians had for centuries entrusted the substance of their history to the memorizing faculties of court historians, usually junior members of the chiefly line.

—JOHN DOMINIS HOLT (*MONARCHY IN HAWAI'I*)

The Royals

Capitals of the Kingdom

When King Kamehameha I formally created the Kingdom of Hawai'i in 1810, he held his court in Honolulu, where it had been since the previous year. He moved the kingdom's capital to Kailua-Kona on the Big Island in 1812.

Liholiho—Kamehameha I's first son—became King Kamehameha II in 1819 and the following year he moved the capital to Lahaina on Maui's west coast. Kamehameha I's second son, Kauikeaouli, became King Kamehameha III in 1825 when he was eleven years old. He moved the capital back to Honolulu in 1845, where it remained until the kingdom was overthrown in 1893. The American businessmen who led the illegal coup—which, in a vague way, was similar to the rebellions in Texas and California that eventually led to their statehood—retained Honolulu as the capital.

Bombs Away!

The Other Occupants

As near as I can tell, almost every house in Hawai'i has geckos living inside it—at least, every house I've stayed in had them and it seems like everyone else's has them too. It's considered good luck to have geckos in your house. The good thing is that they eat bugs—particularly cockroaches and spiders. The bad thing is that they leave little presents for you everywhere in the form of gecko feces. At least their scat is relatively dry, compact, and easy to clean up. It's easily recognizable by its tiny cigar shape with a dab of white at one end.

Under Assault

Unfortunately I've had one or more of these little guys poop on me from the ceiling. The first time I was in the bathroom reading a magazine when a little packet landed on the page in front of me. I looked up and there it was on the ceiling looking down at me. They seem to take careful aim. Of course it's impossible to know what's going on in their tiny reptilian brains, but I suspect that—like monkeys in the zoo who throw their poop at people and laugh about it—the geckos might think it's funny. I don't. I haven't done anything I can think of that might have upset them.

Counterattack

They usually do it when I'm sitting on the couch. I chased one of them around a bit with a feather duster as an expression of my displeasure and to teach it a lesson, but it wasn't long before he or she did it again. This time I was chased it down onto the floor, where I gently pinned it down with the feathers. Reaching under, I got a hold of it and it let out a loud shriek or squawk. Perhaps it thought I was going to eat it, but I just banished it outside.

Who's the Boss?

A few days later I was hit by another pellet and looking up

I saw a gecko on the side of a ceiling beam looking down at me with its tail raised in the same way. I chased it again, but it got away. Could the same gecko have found its way back into the house? It sure looked that way to me. Perhaps it felt the need to re-establish itself at the top of the dominance hierarchy and wanted to show me who's boss.

The Assaults Continue

The little buggers have done it about a dozen more times, taking careful aim to always hit my left arm. When they do, I chase them around to show my disapproval, but so far I haven't been able to catch one again. If I do get a hold of one, I'll banish it down the street about half a block away. Hopefully it won't be able figure out how to get back to our house and will be forced to find someone else to disrespect.

Did you know...

In order to deal with sugarcane beetles, giant toads were introduced to O'ahu in 1832 and within two and a half years there were a million of them.

Did you know...

Roman women wore bikinis a couple of centuries ago, but these strategically placed bits of fabric made their first appearance in Hawai'i on Waīkī-kī Beach in 1952.

Did you know...

Hawai'i established its health department in 1850, while Massachusetts—the first state to set one up—didn't have theirs until 1869.

Fictional Description of Real Life

Hotel Street at War

They left Wu Fat's at ten-thirty.... They decided to take a taxi out. They dodged catty corner across Hotel to the GI taxi stand in front of the Japanese woman-barber shop and fell in at the end of the mob that was jamming the cab stand almost as badly as the other mob had jammed the bar. Everything was jammed, even the Japanee woman-barber shop had a waiting line.

The cab was moving slowly in the traffic up Hotel Street that was lit up like a carnival. They passed the arcade two doors down from the Army-Navy Y, where a mob was shooting electric eye machine guns at lighted planes or waiting to get their picture taken with their arm drunkenly around the... Japanee hula girl against a canvas backdrop of Diamond Head and palms. Something to Send Home, the sign on the photograph booth said.

The cab moved at a walking pace past the crowded hotdog stand next door to the Y where a bunch waited to use the dime automatic photograph machine, their mass overflowing onto the already jam-packed sidewalk. Then on past the dark palm studded lawn on the Y itself, with the Black Cat across the street and also overflowing. A number of drunks lay passed out on the Y lawn.

—JAMES JONES (*FROM HERE TO ETERNITY*)

" *Kaimuki was the saddle between the Heights and Diamond Head; it was also a densely settled community of the more well-off Japanese. except for the big square of it between 13th and 18th Avenues against the flank of Diamond Head which was the government's cut of Kaimuki that was called Fort Ruger. It was almost symbolic, the way Maunalani Heights dominated the well-off Japanese of Kaimuki.* "

—James Jones

From Here to Eternity

From Here to Eternity, a book by James Jones, was first published in 1951. The best-selling novel was the basis for a 1953 hit movie, a six-hour 1979 television mini-series, and a thirteen-episode 1980 television series.

Raw and Gritty

The book was based on the author's own service at pre-World-War-II army bases on O'ahu. Jones painted a less-than-rosy picture of army life: the officers are petty tyrants and the enlisted men drink, gamble, and shack up with "wahines." An officer's wife carries on an affair with a sergeant; some of the characters are homosexual.

Censored

The book was even blunter before the publisher demanded cuts. Much of the profanity was removed, as were some explicit references to homosexuality. Even so, the book was controversial; a Catholic group called the National Organization for Decent Literature tried to get it banned.

It's a Hit

The publicity may have backfired, as the book was a bestseller and won a National Book Award. It was racy and transgressive (for the time). It exposed a side of army life that many ex-service-members, recently returned from World War II, could accept as the ugly truth.

From Here to the Movies

The film version may have been watched by more people than ever read the book. It featured popular actors (Montgomery Clift, Burt Lancaster, Frank Sinatra, Deborah Kerr) who turned in powerful performances; it was shot on location on O'ahu; it featured what were (for the time) explicit sex scenes. Most articles about the movie show a still of a swimsuit-clad Burt Lancaster and Deborah Kerr kissing in the surf at Halona Cove. (In the book, the characters do the horizontal hula.)

The movie was turned into a mini-series some twenty-six years later, then a short-lived TV series. The book is still in print. In 2012 the book was republished with all of the deleted material restored.

—KAREN LOFSTROM

We're on a Highway to Mokapu

Interstates that Aren't Interstate

Hawai'i has four interstate highways that are not interstate, since they can't connect to any other states. Actually, it's more accurate to say that O'ahu has four interstates. They are H-1, H-2, H-3, and H-201. The western end of H-1—the Queen Lili'uokalani Freeway—is the farthest west you can go on the interstate highway system. The other islands don't have any because they don't have a large enough military presence.

Freeways for Defense

Inspired by the German Autobahn system, President Eisenhower established the interstate highway system in 1956 on the grounds that it was necessary for the country's defense; the idea being the country needed the freeways for moving troops, supplies, and equipment to and from military bases, rail terminals, major airports, and seaports. It was a great idea where almost everyone benefited.

The Problem's Even Bigger

We're not the only state to have non-interstate interstates. Alaska also has four. Puerto Rico has three interstates and it's not even a state...yet. Setting Puerto Rico aside for a moment, if they can figure out how to extend H-3 to Alaska, then two-thirds of the problem will be solved.

The Weird and the Wild

Silverswords

Silverswords are very unusual Hawaiian plants that can only be found on Maui's Haleakalā volcano. They can live up to fifty years, but usually make it to about twenty. Like banana plants, it blooms late in its life and then the plant dies. The single flower stem shoots up to a height of three to seven feet and sprouts up to 600 maroon flowers.

They look similar to an agave, but you'll never get tequila from a silversword. Oddly, they are a member of the sunflower and daisy family, even though the plant looks nothing like sunflowers or daisies. But if you get up close, then you can see the flowers do look a bit like daisies, but with a large center and very small leaves. They are very tough plants and are able to withstand Haleakalā's harsh environment of freezing temperatures, high winds, strong sunlight, and dehydration.

The lifecycle of the silversword is shown here with the young plant on the right at the edge of the photograph, then for much of its life it looks like the one in the back on the right, finally it blooms and dies like those in the foreground, and eventually it disintegrates like the remains in the middle. JOHN RICHARD STEPHENS

Kapu

Do This, Don't Do That

Kapu is often translated as "taboo," but "restrictions" is more accurate. Taboos are things society determines are improper or unacceptable. In modern Western society, incest and polygamy are taboos. The ancient Hawaiian system of kapus were restrictions that applied to certain people or certain time periods. Sometimes they applied to everyone, including the king, but more often they applied to everyone except the king and the kāhuna. Sometimes they only applied to females. Then there were kapus that would come and go depending on the time of year. For example, ʻopelu (mackerel scads) were only kapu from roughly January through July, while ula (lobster) and moi (threadfish) were kapu from sometime in May through sometime in August, and aku (skipjack tuna) were kapu from roughly June through January. Violators were often executed as human sacrifices, even if they violated the kapu on accident.

What's It Good For?

Some think that the kapu system may have begun as a way to define gender roles, but it gradually evolved to delineate the classes, giving privileges to those with rank and status and keeping the rest of the people in their place. Ancient Hawaiian society was divided into four classes—the aliʻi (royalty or chiefs), kāhuna (holy men and master craftsman), makaʻainana (your average Joe, just about everyone), and the kauwā (the outcasts, sometimes used as slaves and human sacrifices).

A Word to Remember

Now here is a beautiful-looking word: ‘ili‘ili. It looks even better without the ‘okinas as iliili. The word means "pebbles." In the hula ‘ili‘ili or pebble dance, four smooth, flattened lava rocks are used—two of which are held in each hand by the dancers—and clacked together similar to castanets.

What Does It Mean?

The Name, Honolulu

Honolulu is a name made by the union of the two words— "Hono" and "lulu." Some say it means "Sheltered Hollow." The old Hawaiians say that "Hono" means "abundance" and "lulu" means "calm," or "peace," or "abundance of peace." The navigator who gave the definition "Fair Haven" was out of the way, inasmuch as the name does not belong to a harbor, but to a district having "abundant calm," or "a pleasant slope of restful land."

"Honolulu" was probably a name given to a very rich district of farm land near what is now known as the junction of Liliha and School Streets, because its chief was Honolulu, one of the high chiefs of the time of Kakuhihewa [chief of O‘ahu], according to the legends. Kamakau, the Hawaiian historian, describes this farm district thus:

"Honolulu was a small district, a pleasant land looking toward the west, a fat land, with flowing streams and springs of water, abundant water for taro patches. Mists resting inland breathed softly on the flowers of the halatree."

—W.D. WESTERVELT (*LEGENDS OF OLD HONOLULU*)

Reasons to Visit Hawai'i

- Mild, even, warm temperature.
- Green-covered grandeur of mountain slopes.
- Abounding displays of beautiful flowers.
- Physical wonders: mountains, canyons, cliffs, valleys, volcanoes.
- Ocean shoreline panoramas.
- Comfort of simple, colorful, light clothing.
- Outdoor life: sightseeing, swimming, sunning on the beach, sports.
- Interesting, exotic mixture of people
- Hawaiian entertainment: music and hula.
- Food sensations: fruits, nuts, Asian and other national dishes.
- Island-hopping: each with different attractions.

The Weird and the Wild

Lots of Bugs

It is estimated that the total number of ancestral species which gave rise to the 3,722 known endemic insects was between 233 and 254. There is a reason to believe that the future modification of these last numbers may be downward rather than upward. The significant conclusion reached here is the fact that perhaps only 233 to 254 fertilized female insect immigrants could have given rise to the entire endemic insect fauna! (It will be of interest to note here that only 14 original colonizations have given rise to the entire Hawaiian land-bird fauna.) Of all the data that indicate extreme insularity for the Hawaiian Insecta, these seem to be the most striking. How few have been the successful immigrants over the several millions of years available for dispersal and colonization.

—O.A. BUSHNELL (*THE GIFTS OF CIVILIZATION: GERMS AND GENOCIDE IN HAWAI'I*)

How to Fight Da Bugs

Declutter! The more junk, the more places for da buggers to hide. Crucial in the kitchen, or wherever food is stored, cooked, or eaten. Keep the trash out of the yard, too; don't store firewood and lumber against the wall of the house. Roaches will live there and stroll into your house for a snack.

Clean! Don't leave dirty dishes in the sink, on the table or the stove. Wipe the food crumbs and spills off the counters and the table; sweep the floor. Clean kitchen cupboards regularly. Any edible garbage should be put into a roach-proof covered container, lined with a plastic bag. If you use an outdoor garbage can, regularly clean the can and the area around it.

Keep 'em out! Store food—including pet food—in roach-proof containers. Seal large cracks in your foundation or exterior walls; check the seal or caulk around the windows, doors, pipes, and air-conditioning unit. Inside, plug up openings in walls, baseboards, flues, etc.

If you've done all that, will your house be roach-free? Well... no. This is the tropics, after all. You'll probably need to use some of those cockroach sticky traps.

Boric acid works too; it's a white powder, sold in drugstores. You can squirt the powder into cracks and corners, or mix some of the powder with a dab of peanut butter, put it on a small plate or plastic lid, and leave it out in areas where the roaches like to hang. The powder is toxic to insects, but only mildly irritating to humans and pets. Use it in areas, like cupboards, where pets and children won't try munching it.

You might also befriend your household geckos, rather than going "EEEK!" and throwing them outside. Geckos just love them some tasty roaches. True, the geckos leave little dots of gecko poop, but lots of local folks feel that cleaning up gecko poop is a small price to pay for having fewer roaches.

—KAREN LOFSTROM

Geckos Galore

Common House Gecko
(*Hemidactylus frenatus*)

As its name implies, this is the most common gecko in Hawai'i. They're also called the Leaf-Toed Gecko. It was introduced in the 1940s and they are now found on all the main islands. They change colors depending on their surroundings and the time of day. They can vary from a pale translucent cream to dark brown with a diamond-back design. Their tails are usually thinner right behind their legs and then get larger before they start to taper off. They often have short, stubby spines on their tails. These geckos tend to be more aggressive and territorial, since there are both male and females. Many other gecko species are all females and reproduce parthenogenetically without the need of males. This is one of the few species of lizard that makes vocal noises.

Mourning Gecko
(*Lepidodactylus lugubris*)

The second most common gecko is also found on all the main islands. They're brown or gray with V- or W-shaped designs running down their backs. It has a dark racing stripe that runs from their nose to their eyes and from their eyes to their shoulders. Mourning Geckos are all female and very vocal.

Stump-Toed Gecko
(*Gehyra mutilata*)

These vary in color from light brown to dark brown and from gray to black. Often they have dark or light spots. Some have a white line that runs from their nose to just past their eyes. They have wide toes with claws on only four of their toes or just a tiny claw on their fifth toe, which gives them their other name of Four-Clawed Gecko.

Indo-Pacific Gecko
(*Hemidactylus garnotii*)

This gecko tends to have a narrow snout that sort of resembles that of a fox, so they are sometimes called Fox Geckos. They vary from cream color to brown to black with a variety of patterns and have a row of short, blunt spines down each side of its tail. They are all female. They are on all of the main islands, but are largely being replaced by Common House Geckos. These sometimes live in people's houses.

Tree Gecko
(*Hemiphyllodactylus typus*)

These vary in color with gray, brown, or black patterns and sometimes have small white spots. They can be a translucent pink. These are nocturnal and all female. They're not as vocal as others and aren't often seen around houses.

Orange-Spotted Day Gecko
(*Phelsuma guimbeaui*)

These are found in the Kāne'ohe and Kailua neighborhoods of O'ahu. They are easy to recognize as they are green with orange or reddish spots and lines and a powder blue area on their shoulders and the tip of their tail. But when the weather is cool or they're inactive, they turn gray or black. They prefer living in tall trees, such as palms.

Tokay Gecko
(*Gekko gecko*)

These guys can grow to be about a foot long and are found in Lanikai and above Kāne'ohe in the Ko'olau Mountains, O'ahu. They have orange, red or purple spots on a greenish-gray background in females and a bluish-gray background on males. They live in large trees, but sometimes live in people's houses, usually in attics. Their eggs can take up to six months to hatch in cooler weather. These geckos make loud vocalizations. They have been known to eat mice.

Madagascar Giant Day Gecko
(*Phelsuma madagascariensis grandis*)

These geckos are also green and about a foot long. They have reddish-brown spots and a line that runs from its nose back towards the center of its eyes. They're found in Manoa on Oʻahu.

The Adventure Continues

Here I Am, Sitting in My Tin Can

The International Space Station orbits above Hawaiʻi in 2010. Docked to the space station on the left is a Russian Soyuz manned spacecraft, and next to it is a Russian Progress unmanned cargo vehicle. AN ISS EXPEDITION 25 CREW MEMBER, NASA

Did you know...

Hawaiʻi shares the same latitude on the globe with Guadalajara (Mexico), Cuba, the Sahara Desert, Southern Egypt, Northern Sudan, Mecca (Saudi Arabia), Hanoi (Vietnam), and Hong Kong.

Local Grinds

Hungry?

Understanding Hawai'i's local "grinds" requires learning a bit of Island history. During the nineteenth and early twentieth centuries, immigrants from throughout the Pacific Rim, Polynesia, Europe, and Asia arrived in the Islands to work on Hawai'i's sugar and pineapple plantations. While working side-by-side and living as neighbors, generations of immigrants intermarried and shared one another's rich and colorful secrets of their cultures. Lunchtime in the integrated plantation schools was often a flurry of exchange, as the laborers' children swapped Japanese bentos for Hawaiian laulau and Korean kim chee for Portuguese malasadas. The result of this intermingling was the birth of a distinctly local flavor—a "mixed plate" menu influenced by cooking styles that originated in China, Japan, Korea, Hawai'i, Portugal, Europe, and the U.S. continent.

Mixed Plate

Local-style comfort food today includes Asian-style noodle soup called saimin, Filipino chicken adobo, Korean kalbi short ribs and kimchee, Portuguese bean soup and sweet bread, sushi, teriyaki chicken, and Chinese-style manapua (steamed pork buns). This smorgasbord of flavors also sparked the evolution of unique local dishes that deserve mention: loco-moco is a mouth-watering, savory breakfast dish consisting of two scoops of rice buried under a hamburger patty and a fried egg, covered in a pool of thick, dark gravy. Huli huli chicken, another favorite, is half a chicken broiled over charcoal outdoors on a spit that's constantly huli'd (turned) to roast both sides evenly.

Spam®

No discussion of Hawaiian local grinds can exclude Spam®, that canned, pink, pre-World War II mystery meat that appears in dozens of local dishes, including fried rice, saimin, and Spam musubi (fried Spam on rice, wrapped with seaweed).

Plate Lunch

The everyday plate lunch—the staple food of hard-working, local residents—consists of two scoops of sticky rice, one scoop of macaroni salad, a bed of shredded cabbage, and a heaping pile of protein, ranging from hamburger steak to teriyaki chicken to pork adobo to kal-bi short ribs. Followed up by a shave ice—a heaping "snow-cone" with flavored syrup and li hing mui powder (made from Chinese sweet-sour preserved fruit) sprinkled on top—you have a "Hawai'i State Meal."

—CARRIE CHING (*THINGS HAWAI'I*)

"I look at food as something sacred, almost like religion, because of how important it is in nourishing the body and because, when it's prepared and presented in the right way, it can really bring joy. When I cook, it comes from my heart."

—Sam Choy

Did you know...

In the old days, poi was fermented before it was eaten, giving it a sour taste. Now people prefer it fresher and sweeter, often adding sugar to it.

Ko'olau of Kalalau Valley

Hansen's Disease

Hansen's Disease, formerly known as leprosy, was brought to the islands in the nineteenth century. Native Hawaiians had no natural immunity to the disease and many of them fell victim to it.

Exile

As there was no known cure at the time, all that could be done was to isolate the sufferers, so that they couldn't infect others. The Hawaiian government of the time, the monarchy, set aside the isolated settlement of Kalawao, on Maui, as a place of quarantine.

Thousands of Native Hawaiians submitted quietly to the new regulations that tore them from their homes and families and exiled them to a distant place. A few resisted, hiding from the authorities, evading capture.

Going into Hiding

One such resister was Ko'olau, a Kaua'i cowboy. He was diagnosed with the disease and told that he must go to Kalawao. He and his wife Pi'ilani feared that they would be separated. In the winter of 1892, the young couple, with their son and a few relatives, fled over treacherous mountain trails, over the spine of the mountains, to Kalalau Valley.

This broad green valley could be reached only by boat or by narrow cliffside trails. Once populous, it was now sparsely inhabited. Other Hansen's Disease sufferers had taken refuge there; Ko'olau and his family planned to join them.

Ko'olau Shot the Deputy

But the government would not leave them to their self-imposed exile. In 1893, local officials landed and demanded that the lepers leave for Kalawao. All but Ko'olau and Pi'ilani agreed to go. Ko'olau resisted arrest and ended by shooting (and killing) Deputy Sheriff Louis Stolz.

Calling in the Military

The new government (the Hawaiian monarchy had been overthrown by white businessmen) decided this defiance must not be allowed to stand. Koʻolau must be captured or killed. Soldiers were sent to the valley. The cowboy managed to evade capture and killed two soldiers. After that, he and his family were left alone, to eke out a living in the upper reaches of the valley.

The End Comes at Last

Within a few years, Koʻolau's son Kaleimanu and then Koʻolau succumbed to Hansen's Disease. The indomitable Piʻilani, who had cared for them and buried them, came out of the valley in 1897, fully expecting to be arrested and punished. Fortunately the government absolved her of all blame.

Koʻolau in Fact and Fiction

The writer Jack London, visiting the islands in the early 1900s, heard about Koʻolau and wrote a story about him: "Koʻolau the Leper." Very little of the story is true, but it ensured that Koʻolau would be remembered. A kinder, truer remembrance was dictated by his widow Piʻilani, who told her story to John Sheldon. It was published in 1906, in Hawaiian; more recently, it has been translated into English and re-published in 2001.

In Piʻilani's words:

> "...this entire valley from its high cliffs to the flat terraces of earth became our home, and the dark clouds of Kane were our ridgepole. I have love for Kalalau—who indeed would not! It is the bosom, the grave, the peace, where lie the bones of my man and our child whom we lovingly bore."

—Karen Lofstrom

The Worst Gossips

The U.S. Commissioner to the Hawaiian Kingdom, David Gregg, wrote in his diary in 1858, "Thus it is always with Honolulu society. It is full of jealousies and scandals. No one can live in it without subjecting his character to the severest test. The Missionaries are the worst gossips and the most inveterate scandal-mongers. Their wives and daughters are far beyond anything St. Paul ever condemned in the way of tittle-tattle and mischief making."

Uncommon Knowledge

Hawai'i's Land Use

Hawai'i's Total Land:	4,158,400 acres	
Total Rural Land:	3,527,100 acres	82%
Total Federal Land:	361,200 acres	9%
Total Developed Land:	217,600 acres	5%
Total Water Areas:	52,500 acres	1%

Note: Rounding errors resulted in the missing three percent.

Total Rural Land:	3,527,100 acres	
Forest Land:	1,627,400 acres	46%
Rangeland:	1,082,400 acres	31%
Crop Land	126,900 acres	4%
Pastureland:	60,300 acres	2%
Other Rural Land:	630,100 acres	18%

Note: Rounding errors created the additional one percent.

The difference in the amount of federal land between the charts above and below apparently stems from different definitions of federal land between the U.S. Dept. of Agriculture, which is the source for the preceding data, and the State of Hawai'i, which is the source for the following data. Neither of these should include U.S. National Park land.

Who Owns Hawai'i

Here are the top ten land owners of Hawai'i (in acres), along with the percentage of Hawai'i's total land.

1. State Government
   (including Dept. of Hawaiian
   Home Lands):   1,534,792   37%
2. Federal Government   530,792   13%
3. Kamehameha Schools
   (Princess Bernice Pauahi Bishop estate)   363,476   9%
4. Castle & Cooke (all on Lāna'i,
   except 233 on the Big Island)   118,859   3%
5. Alexander & Baldwin Inc.
   (primarily on Maui and Kaua'i)   113,135   3%
6. Parker Ranch (all on the Big Island)   106,883   3%
7. Moloka'i Ranch (all on Moloka'i)   58,418   1%
8. Robinson Family (all on Kaua'i)   50,671   1%
9. Robinson Aylmer (all on Ni'ihau)   46,044   1%
10. Grove Farm (all on Kaua'i)   36,139   1%

Note: After these statistics were collected, Castle & Cooke sold the Island of Lāna'i to Lawrence Ellison, the CEO of the software company, Oracle Corporation.

A Corporation or a Hui

Advantages of a Hui

In most cases when groups of investors in real estate in postwar Hawaii have publicly registered with the Territory or State, they have done so as a business partnership, as distinct from a corporation. This has mainly been because of certain tax advantages to the partnership arrangement when investing in real property.

In the local idiom of Hawaii such a partnership is often called a hui. This is a word that appears in the Hawaiian language and in major Chinese dialects. In both Hawaiian and Chinese it can mean a "group," which can be of many kinds. The meaning ordinarily understood in business dealings in Hawaii is something like "investment group," and this was probably taken from a South China dialect. As used in the Islands the word can also refer to small corporations. Whether the group registers with the territory or state has had no bearing on whether the word applies.

—George Cooper and Gavan Daws (*Land and Power in Hawai'i*)

Strange Partners

A land hui organized in the early 1960s included: the Democratic governor's chief aide on Maui; a gambler identified in court proceedings as being by 1970 the head of organized crime on Maui; a member of the old haole monied class. At some point a man joined who, in the late 1960s, went to work for Hawaii's largest government employees union and who also became a Democratic legislator.

—George Cooper and Gavan Daws (*Land and Power in Hawai'i*)

What *Was* He Thinking?
Anywhere But New York City

It's reported that initially, President Franklin Roosevelt wanted to establish the United Nations on Ni'ihau. He couldn't remember the island's name and had never been there, but he insisted it was "the most interesting and heavenly spot he knew on earth." He described it as being northwest of O'ahu and owned by an old sugar family. It's possible he was slightly confused and meant Kaua'i. His other two preferences were the islands of Flores in the Azores and the Black Hills in South Dakota.

Lucky Cats

A Lucky Cat Christmas ornament made by a Hawaiian company. JOHN RICHARD STEPHENS

Lucky Cats are a fixture in almost every retail business in Hawai'i. They come in many sizes and are usually seen somewhere near the cash register. Some businesses have five or six. The folklore belief is that they draw in customers, bringing good luck and fortune.

Lucky Cats come from Japan, where they are called *Maneki Neko* (招き猫 or 招猫), which means "Beckoning Cat" or "Inviting Cat." They are always sitting, holding one paw up next to its ear or cheek. Some have the right paw raised, some the left, and a few have both forepaws raised. There are people who believe that cats with the left paw raised bring in customers, while having the right paw raised brings luck and fortune, but there's no consensus. Others believe the same thing, but reverse the paws. Some believe the higher the paw is raised, the more luck it will bring or the wider its range will be for drawing in customers. Then there are those who believe the larger the cat is, the more effective it will be. Some shops have Lucky Cats that are about two-feet tall.

White Christmases

Santa tiki at the Tiki Lounge in Kihei on Maui. It looks like Santa didn't get his milk and cookies. JOHN RICHARD STEPHENS

Hawai'i is north of the equator, so Christmas isn't celebrated in the middle of summer as it is in Australia and New Zealand. Still, the islands are in the tropics. We have two seasons here—the wet season and the dry season. To visitors from colder climes, both can seem to them like summer; particularly if they are staying on the leeward, or dry, side of whatever island they're on. Perhaps it will rain for a few days as a tropical storm passes by, but it could be bright and sunny the rest of the month. There's no "white Christmas" here, unless the beach sand is white, or you drive up to Haleakalā on Maui or Mauna Kea and Mauna Loa on the Big Island for some skiing, sledding, snowboarding, or for making a tiki snowman.

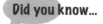

Did you know...

The Big Island is twice as large as all the other islands combined.

The Natural and the Supernatural

Like most indigenous peoples, the ancient Hawaiians felt a deep connection with nature. They experienced the forces that caused thunder and lightning or created sunshine and rainbows to be the same elemental forces that allowed them to stand, to walk, and to chant. These natural forces were so powerful and so alive to the Hawaiians that they were called by name and recognized as beings. Thus, an entire pantheon of gods, goddesses, and demigods was associated with the elements of water, snow, clouds, and fire, and dwelt in fish, animals, plants, and other natural phenomena. The gods Kū, Kāne, Lono, the goddess Pele, and the demigod Māui are just a few of the supernatural beings remembered today in Hawai'i.

The ancient Hawaiian fisherman, kalo (taro) farmer, canoe builder, and kapa or cloth maker, were in constant converse with nature and, thereby, in regular discourse with the gods. The soil, stones, plants, wood, wind, clouds, and light all expressed a meaning-filled content. For this reason, the ancient Hawaiians were sensitive to and revered the world around them. By reading the "Book of Nature," Hawaiians developed effective medical arts based entirely on natural remedies. Their knowledge also enabled them to develop and manage fishponds, some of the most advanced aquaculture in the Pacific. This is not to say that the ancient Hawaiians had a perfect society without injustice, illness, or environmental destruction. In some respects, however, their culture exemplified how a human community could be self-sufficient and enjoy a harmonious and mutually beneficial relationship with nature.

—Van James (*Ancient Sites of Hawai'i*)

Sailing the Open Ocean

An Accidental Discovery?

Up until 1976, anthropologists were convinced the Polynesians discovered the Hawaiian Islands by accident, in spite of accounts of their amazing navigational skills. Scholars just couldn't believe it was possible to navigate thousands of open-ocean miles without an astrolabe, sextant, chronometer or compass. The early Europeans and other seafaring cultures were forced to hug the coastlines until they came up with the grid of longitude and latitude that they superimposed on the world, along with the tools they needed to identify where they were on this imaginary grid. But those scholars were wrong. It's now known the Polynesians did in fact navigate across the Pacific.

Advanced Navigation

When Captain Cook left Tahiti during his first expedition to the South Pacific, he was accompanied by a highly skilled Polynesian navigator, astronomer, and meteorologist named Tupaia. Wherever they went in the Pacific, Tupaia was able to able to act as translator for Captain Cook. He drew a map of the major South Pacific island groups that extended more than 2,500 miles. He was able to predict the weather and always told them when they were about to reach landfall. And Cook was amazed that even when they were in the Indian Ocean, Tupaia could always accurately point in the direction of Tahiti.

In the 1970s, in spite of the anthropologists' theories, some Hawaiians were convinced their ancestors didn't need instruments to navigate and they formed the Polynesian Voyaging Society to prove it. They built a 62-foot-long, double-hulled voyaging canoe named *Hōkūleʻa* and set off from Maui for Tahiti without any navigational instruments. They reached their destination thirty-five days later, proving it was possible.

How They Did It

The Polynesians intensely studied astronomy, using the stars for navigation, but this was just one tool in their kit. They also studied the currents, the directions and types of swells, the shades of the water, and the various sea creatures. They noted the color of the sky and the sun, the direction and strength of the wind, along with the motion of various cloud formations. They followed migrating birds and they knew they were near land when they saw birds heading out to sea to feed. Years spent living close to and on the ocean enabled them to spot subtle clues and recognize their meaning.

DNA studies indicate the ancestors of the Polynesians came from the Asian mainland, passing through New Guinea from 6,000 to 8,000 years ago, before spreading across the South Pacific around 3,000 years ago. Interestingly, there is also evidence that at least some of the Polynesians of Rapa Nui, also known as Easter Island, have a bit of Native American in their DNA. While it is possible—as Thor Heyerdahl demonstrated with his *Kon-Tiki* expedition—that ancient Native Americans from somewhere like Peru sailed to Rapa Nui, it's much more likely that the Polynesians sailed their ships all the way to the Americas, since we now know they had the skills to do it.

Did you know...

The calls from a group of coqui frogs can be as loud as a lawnmower.

Aloha Friday

Until the 1960s, Hawai'i bosses expected their office employees to wear the same suits and ties, dresses and nylons, worn in mainland offices. The employees looked business-like, even though many of them hated the hot, uncomfortable, expensive clothing.

Aloha Shirts and Mu'umu'us

Relief arrived courtesy of the Hawaiian fashion industry, which aimed to sell more aloha shirts and mu'umu'u to local folks. In 1965, Bill Foster, Sr., the president of the Hawaii Fashion Guild, started lobbying for what he called Aloha Friday. He asked the big firms to let their employees wear aloha attire on Fridays, during the summer. The custom, once accepted in downtown Honolulu, spread everywhere. Employees were happy to be cool and comfortable; employers saw that just as much work, or more, got done when clothing was casual.

Aloha Every Day

The experiment was so successful, in fact, that Aloha Friday in summer soon became Aloha-every-Friday and eventually Aloha-every-day-of-the-week. Most local businessmen wear aloha attire all the time, and put on suits only for extremely formal occasions. (The ladies? That's complicated.)

Not a Tourist

Of course, respectable businessmen don't usually wear aloha shirts in brilliant colors, emblazoned with surfboards and hula girls. That is left for the tourists. A lawyer or banker's aloha shirt is usually made from reverse-print cloth (the reverse of the fabric, not the printed side) in a small, subdued pattern. The collar points are buttoned down. The shirt proclaims: I'm reliable! I'm trustworthy! I'm not a tourist!

The Mainland Catches On

Aloha Friday, in the meantime, has spread to the U.S. mainland, as Casual Friday. Casual Friday has already become Casual-every-day in some industries, such as the computer industry.

Live Aloha Bumper Stickers

Driving along, you might see a car with a Live Aloha bumper sticker. What does that mean? Is that for some crazy cult?

No, not a cult. Just the Hawai'i Community Foundation, hoping that people will see the bumper sticker and remember to live with aloha. Or, if you've got the sticker on your car, hoping that you drive with aloha: no honk, no cut off, let people merge, wave thanks.

It was just a bunch of friends at first, talking about how to make Hawai'i better. They decided that it started with individual responsibility: deciding to live aloha and give to others. To spread the word, they started giving out free bumper stickers.

Want one? Send a stamped, self-addressed envelope to Live Aloha, 165 Waokanaka Place, Honolulu 96817, and you'll get a free bumper sticker and a little card that reminds you to:

> Respect all elders and children.
> Leave places better than you find them.
> Hold the door. Hold the elevator.
> Plant something.
> Drive with courtesy. Never drive impaired.
> Attend an event of another culture.
> Return your shopping cart.
> Get out and enjoy nature.
> Pick up litter.
> Share with your neighbors.
> Create smiles.

The group has distributed over 600,000 free bumper stickers since it started in 1993.

—Karen Lofstrom

The Legend of Barking Sands

Back in ancient times an old Hawaiian fisherman lived on the western coast of Kaua'i. He didn't have much in his grass hut on the beach, but it didn't matter because he had his dogs and he loved all nine of them.

During the day he would take his canoe out fishing, and so his dogs didn't run off and get lost while he was gone, he had three stakes in the sand and would tie each of his three dogs to each stake.

When he was out at sea one day he was caught in a tropical storm and had to struggle against wind, rain, tide, and giant waves for many hours. By following the barking of his dogs, he was able to find his way home. When he finally reached the shore that night, he was completely exhausted and barely able to crawl to his hut.

He awoke late the next day and on going outside he discovered the three stakes were there, but his precious dogs were gone. He looked all over for hours, but there was no trace of them—just three mounds of sand near each stake. Oddly, when he stepped on one of the mounds, he thought he heard a low bark. Taking another step, the same thing happened.

Frantically he dug into the mound, thinking the storm had buried his dogs beneath the sand, but as he was digging, the hole would quickly fill back in with sand. He tried to dig into another mound, and another, but the same thing happened. He tried sweeping away the mounds with his arms, but it was no use. He couldn't find any sign of his dogs, other than the bark when he stepped in the sand. Finally he had to give up his search and he returned to his hut alone.

He gave up fishing. Instead, he spent his days walking the beach in search of his lost dogs and with his steps he could hear their barking. His friends thought he'd gone mad, but they could do nothing for him. He had no interest in other dogs; he just wanted his back. Slowly he withered away and eventually died. Some thought it was from a broken heart.

Years, decades, and centuries have passed, but anyone who walks on that beach today hears the old fisherman's dogs barking as they walk, which is why the beach on the western tip of Kaua'i is called Barking Sands.

How Does Sand Bark?

So what makes Barking Sands' sand bark? Scientists say that the grains of sand on that beach are uniform in size, highly polished, and nearly spherical. When you step on them, they rub together, producing a sound that is reminiscent of barking. It is loudest during the hottest part of the day when the sand is very dry. The best results are obtained from sand in the tidal area. For the most part, wet sand doesn't make much noise, although water-saturated sand can be made to squeak when the water is receding. The sand of dunes can also make booming sounds during avalanches.

Feral Chickens

Wild chickens are common on all the islands, but Kaua'i is particularly known for them. They wander alongside the highways, hangout in shopping center parking lots, and sunbathe at the beaches. Many of them were domestic chickens that became feral after Hurricane Iniki slammed into the island in 1992. They add to the Garden Isle's rustic feel.

Launching Rockets from Kaua'i

A medium range ballistic missile is launched in 2007 from the Pacific Missile Range Facility at Barking Sands as part of a Star Wars anti-missile test. U.S. NAVY

Part of Barking Sands is open to the public, but the rest is the U.S. Navy's Pacific Missile Range Facility. This is described by the U.S. Army's Joint Task Force—Homeland Defense as "the world's largest instrumented, multi-dimensional testing and training missile range. Nestled in relative isolation, ideal year-round tropical climate and an encroachment-free environment, it remains the only range in the world where submarines, surface ships, aircraft and space vehicles can operate and be tracked simultaneously."

The facility is used for testing a wide variety of new weaponry, such the Helios Flying Wing and the Advanced Hypersonic Weapon which, when successful, will be able to travel at eight times the speed of sound.

Traditional Saying

Oki pau ka hana i ke one kani o Nohili.

("Strange indeed are the activities at the sounding sands of Nohili." This is said of someone who is acting strangely. Nohili is a part of Barking Sands Beach, which some believe to be haunted.)

A Meeting with Kamehameha I

British naval captain George Vancouver first met Kamehameha when he visited the Big Island as part of Captain Cook's crew on Cook's second and third voyages in the 1770s. He later returned to the Hawaiian Islands several times during his own famous explorations of the Pacific from 1791 to 1795. It was in 1793 that he met Kamehameha once again. At that time Kamehameha was the chief of the Big Island and had not yet invaded Maui or O'ahu. Kamehameha was about thirty-five years old when this meeting took place.

Cheerful and Sensible

About noon I was honored with the presence of Tamaahmaah [Kamehameha I], the king of Owhyhee [the Big Island], whose approach had been announced some time before his arrival.

Not only from Captain King's description, but also from my own memory, as far as it would serve me, I expected to have recognized my former acquaintance by the most savage countenance we had hitherto seen amongst these people; but I was agreeably surprized in finding that his riper years had softened that stern ferocity which his younger days had exhibited, and had changed his general deportment to an address characteristic of an open, cheerful, and sensible mind; combined with great generosity, and goodness of disposition. An alteration not unlike that I have before had occasion to notice in the character of Pomurrey at Otaheite [Pomare of Tahiti].

and am in
Your Majestys
most devoted Friend & Servant
TA MAAHMAAH
King of the Sandwich Islands

King Kamehameha's signature on an 1810 letter to Britain's King George III. Apparently he used both this and the modern spelling of his name.

After the usual ceremonies and assurances of friendship had passed between Tamaahmaah and myself, he said that his queen, with several of his friends and relations were in the canoe alongside, and requested they might be admitted on board. This was instantly granted, and I was introduced to her majesty, who we had previously understood was the daughter of Kahowmotoo, by his favorite wife now on board, Namahanna. [Note: Vancouver seems to have this backwards. Namahana-i-Kaleleokalani was the mother of Kamehameha's favorite wife, Kaʻahumanu.] The meeting of the daughter and her parents sufficiently indicated the relation, and the affection that subsisted between them. She appeared to be about sixteen [she was about twenty-four], and undoubtedly did credit to the choice and taste of Tamaahmaah, being one of the finest women we had yet seen on any of the islands. It was pleasing to observe the kindness and fond attention, with which on all occasions they seemed to regard each other; and though this mode of behaviour in public would be considered as extravagant in the polished circles of society, yet to us, so far removed from the civilized world, the profusion of tenderness was very admissible, and could not be regarded without a warmth of satisfaction at thus witnessing the happiness of our fellow creatures...

The sole object of this visit was to invite and intreat our proceeding to Karakakooa [Kealakekua Bay]: to their solicitations I replied, that our boat was examining Tyahtatooa [Kailua Bay], and that on her return I should determine. With this answer they were perfectly satisfied, but observed, that I should not find it so convenient as Karakakooa.

I was much pleased with the decorum and general conduct of this royal party. Though it consisted of many, yet not one solicited even the most inconsiderable article; nor did they appear to have any expectation of receiving presents. They seemed to be particularly cautious to avoid giving the lead cause for offence; but no one more so than the king himself, who was so scrupulous, as to enquire when and where it was proper for him to be seated. The inhabitants, who had assembled round the ships, were by this time very numerous; on being denied their requests to be admitted on board, which was observed towards all but the principal chiefs, they remained perfectly quiet in their canoes, and in a most orderly manner carried on an honest and friendly intercourse.

(CAPTAIN GEORGE VANCOUVER'S *A VOYAGE OF DISCOVERY TO THE NORTH PACIFIC OCEAN AND ROUND THE WORLD.*)

"How shall we account for this Nation spreading itself so far over this Vast ocean?"

—Captain James Cook, 1778

The Native Journey

Escaping Death

The god images and offering scaffold on the mauka side of the Hale o Keawe at the Pu'uhonua o Hōnaunau. Such images were not thought to be gods, but conduits through which the spirit or power of each god flowed. ELAINE MOLINA

Safe Haven

In ancient times, Pu'uhonua o Hōnaunau was a safe haven to kapu (taboo) breakers, defeated warriors, deserters, and refugees of all kinds. (Punishment for breaking many kapu was death.) If a kapu breaker made his way to the pu'uhonua without being captured, he could be pardoned of his crime after a series of ritual procedures administered by the local kāhuna.

Several places of refuge were located on each of the Hawaiian Islands and they helped to balance the rather severe scale of kapu justice. Pu'uhonua o Hōnaunau was not desecrated in 1819 when the traditional religious practices were abolished and temples were destroyed because the Kamehameha dynasty was connected to this place. Many of their ancestors bones were kept here and, therefore, the site was revered and protected.

Pu'uhonua o Hōnaunau

The pu'uhonua is dated at about 1550 AD by the National Park Service and is partially enclosed by a ten-foot-high, seven-foot-thick, one-thousand-foot-long, uniquely constructed lava rock wall separating the refuge from an ali'i residence. No mortar holds this massive rock wall together. On the royal grounds are Heleipōlala Fishpond and the royal canoe landing at Keone'ele Cove, both once forbidden to commoners. As this area was kapu, refuge seekers had to swim across Honaunau Bay in order to reach the pu'uhonua. Within the enclosure are three heiau platforms of varying dates. The most recent of these, Hale o Keawe, from about 1650 AD, has been restored with a thatched hale (house), ki'i (images) carved from 'ōhi'a logs, a wooden lele (altar) for offerings, and a wooden fence. This building served as the temple mausoleum, housing the bones of some twenty-three chiefs, beginning with Keaweikehahiali'iokamoku. The mana (spiritual power) of these bones gave greater power and protection to the pu'uhonua. Hale o Keawe was first known as Ka Iki 'Āle'ale'a, the "little light of joy."

Redemption

Once within the refuge precinct, a kapu breaker would be absolved by a kahuna pule (priest). Sometimes the offender would be free to return home within only a few hours, other times days were required for purification ceremonies. In 1782, a battle at Moku'ōhai three miles to the north drove many defeated warriors to seek refuge at Pu'uhonua o Hōnaunau. There was one recourse for those who could not reach a refuge: A high chief or chiefess could act as a pu'uhonua and forgive kapu breakers of their crimes. Queen Ka'ahumanu was such a pu'uhonua.

—Van James (*Ancient Sites of Hawai'i*)

Hawai'i Regional Cuisine

A new generation of Hawai'i-born master chefs—including Sam Choy, Alan Wong, and Roy Yamaguchi—spearheaded a revolution in Island cuisine in the 1990s that encompassed all the multicultural flavors of local foods, while adding a contemporary edge with fresh, Hawai'i-grown ingredients and creative, first-class presentation that became known as Hawai'i Regional Cuisine.

Although similar to Pacific Rim Cuisine in its blending of flavors from the East and West, Hawai'i Regional Cuisine is unique to the Islands in its devotion to local produce, meats, and fish in innovative creations with a local twist. Dishes include fresh-caught fish, like opah, ono, or 'ōpakapaka, baked in coconut milk and crusted with macadamia nuts, mixed greens grown in the lush windward region of Waimānalo, kālua pork spring rolls, pūlehu beef from the Big Island served with pineapple from O'ahu's central plain, grilled Kahuku shrimp, fern shoots gathered in Waipi'o Valley, and goat cheese from Puna served in delectable Chinese wontons.

—CARRIE CHING (*THINGS HAWAI'I*)

From Farm to Plate

Hawai'i Regional Cuisine has evolved as Hawai'i's singular cooking style, what some say is this country's current gastronomic, as well as geographic, frontier. It highlights the fresh seafood and produce of Hawai'i's rich waters and volcanic soil, the cultural traditions of Hawai'i's ethnic groups, and the skills of well-trained chefs...who broke ranks with their European predecessors to forge new ground in the 50th state.

—JEANETTE FORSTER AND JOCELYN FUJII

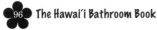

What Does It All Mean?
(Maui)

- **Maui** (island): the name of an ancient Hawaiian trickster demigod.
- **Wailuku** (district, town): water of destruction, because King Kamehameha I's army killed so many Maui warriors there that their bodies dammed the river.
- **ʻĪao** (valley): cloud supreme.
- **Kahului** (bay, town, harbor): probably means "the winning."
- **Pāʻia** (town): noisy.
- **Haʻikū** (town): speak abruptly, or sharp break.
- **Hāna** (coast, bay, town): bay.
- **Haleakalā** (volcano): house of the sun.
- **Makawao** (district, town): edge of the forest.
- **Pukalani** (town): heavenly gate.
- **Kula** (town): open country away from the sea near the base of a mountain, or uncultivated land or fields.
- **Mākena** (town): abundance.
- **Molokini** (island): many ties.
- **Wailea** (town): water of Lea (canoe makers' goddess).
- **Kamaʻole** (three beaches): childless. This might be roughly the equivalent to the Christian concept of virginity, which would have meant little or nothing to the ancient Hawaiians.
- **Kīhei** (town): a cape, or cloak.
- **Māʻalaea** (harbor): red color, or red ocher.
- **Lahaina** (district, town, harbor): cruel sun (said to be named for droughts).
- **Kāʻanapali** (town): the duplicating cliff.
- **Nāpili** (bay, town): the joinings, or pili grass.
- **Kapalua** (town): two borders.

Did you know...

Most of the world's macadamia nuts are grown on the Big Island.

Criminal Masterminds

Just Like in the Movies

In what may be Hawai'i's only train robbery, Kaimiola Hali stopped a train in 1920 near Mānā on Kaua'i and stole $10,000 from the paymaster of the Kekaha Sugar Company. The police found the money in a swamp near his house and his suspicious behavior exposed him as the culprit. He was a big Western movie fan.

Butterfingers

Late one night in 1923, two masked robbers broke into the Territorial Treasurer's Office, which contained $7.5 million in securities and $750,000 in cash. They were confronted by the night watchman who pulled off the mask of one of the robbers. The other fled, dropping his gun.

He Didn't Learn the First Time

Orieman Fujihara was sentenced to die and then to life in prison twice. On the Big Island in 1901 he was sentenced to hang for first degree murder, but this was commuted to life in prison in 1909 and he was pardoned by the governor in 1919. Then in 1931 he was sentenced to life again for setting a man's house on fire.

In Disguise

In 1934, David and George Wong from Lahaina, robbed the Bank of Hawai'i in Pā'ia. This was Hawai'i's first bank robbery. They took off with $979.31, but Maui isn't that big, so they should have known they wouldn't get away for long. Neither wore a mask, but one of the brothers tried to disguise himself by drawing on a mustache with an eyebrow pencil.

Assisting the Police

Gregg Inoshita, then age 48, was arrested at a convenience store in Waikīkī in 2009 and charged with being the primary suspect in two bank robberies—one at the Central Pacific

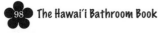

Bank in Mōʻiliʻili and the other at the Hawaii National Bank in Kaimukī. At the Central Pacific Bank, the robber gave a note to the teller saying he was armed and wanted money, which the teller promptly handed over. Perhaps he subconsciously thought the police were overworked and was determined to help them out or maybe the excitement was just too much for him, for police say he left his Hawaiʻi identification card on the counter, making their job a whole lot easier.

The robber must not have gotten away with enough Franklins in the first heist, for the cops say he hit the second bank two days later. This time he used a taxi as a getaway car and paid the driver with stolen loot. Taxis, of course, keep records of where and when their customers are picked up and dropped off, so it would be easy to locate the driver, who in turn would make an excellent witness.

HONOLULU POLICE DEPARTMENT.

CrimeStoppers released a picture which may have come from the ID and the arrest was soon made. His accomplice, Gisele Souza, then age 45, was probably not pleased.

Bank photograph from the third robbery. HONOLULU POLICE DEPARTMENT.

You're Wrong, Officer

In 2008, Ellis Cleveland, then age 38, was arrested in Honolulu, accused of robbing three banks and attempting to rob a fourth. At the time, he was out on bail, scheduled to begin trial the following month on drug charges. The robber did not wear a mask nor try to hide his identity, so he was photographed by the banks' cameras. Notes were handed to tellers in each of the robberies and police said they found Cleveland's fingerprint on one of them. More than $800 was taken in the first robbery and $923 in the second. The third time, the note was illegible—three tellers couldn't read it—so the suspect left empty handed. The fourth time, $1,555 was taken.

Detective Taro Nakamura noted in his statement that when he told Cleveland he was suspected of robbing four banks, Cleveland exclaimed, "Four! I didn't do four. I only robbed three banks. But it doesn't matter because I'm not talking to you guys. I want a lawyer."

Crime and Punishment
Injustice in Paradise

A Sordid Potboiler

It had all the ingredients of a best-selling sordid potboiler: The setting is a lazy Pacific town where Polynesians and Asians live amicably under the patriarchal control of a small, Caucasian sugar oligarchy. A good-looking white woman claims that late one night she is abducted from Waikiki and taken to a lonely tropical road where she is raped and beaten by several Hawaiian "hoodlums." A few hours later five island men of Hawaiian, Japanese, and Chinese ancestry are arrested. Circumstantial evidence strongly points to them as the alleged rapists. Because the victim's husband is an officer in the United States Navy, the Admiral of the Pearl Harbor fleet, who has strong racial prejudices, applies political pressure to make an example of the defendants. This is called "protecting white women."

Conflicts, Incompetence and Vigilantes

As the trial of the alleged rapists bogs down in conflicting evidence, exposing the police force's incompetence, the husband, assisted by two navy buddies and his mother-in-law, takes matters into his own hands. One of the Hawaiian defendants is kidnapped as he stands in front of the courthouse, supposedly makes a "confession" to the husband, and then is murdered in a fit of insane jealousy. The husband and his accomplices attempt to dispose of the corpse, but are arrested following a high-speed automobile chase.

Vigilantes on Trial

The murder trial of the husband, his naval friends, and the grief-stricken mother-in-law attracts national attention as one of the nation's leading criminal lawyers agrees to represent the four defendants. Relying on the "unwritten law" that allows a husband to vindicate his wife's honor; the case for the defense becomes a *cause cèlébre* for politicians who doubt that a non-white community in American territory can govern itself. When a measure of justice prevails and the defendants are found guilty and sentenced to ten years in prison, the pressure from Washington, D.C. is irresistible—the sentence is commuted by the governor to one hour spent in his office, sipping tea. The defendants then depart the islands, leaving behind a racial sore that will take decades to heal.

—GLEN GRANT (INTRODUCTION TO *RAPE IN PARADISE* BY THEON WRIGHT)

<u>Literary Masters</u>
The House Without a Key

Introducing Charlie Chan

Earl Derr Biggers (1884-1933) graduated from Harvard in 1907 and worked in newspaper and advertising offices before *The House Without a Key* was published in 1925. In this novel he introduced readers to the suave Chinese policeman Charlie Chan and it became the best known of Earl Derr Biggers' many detective stories.

The leading character of the book is John Quincy Winterslip, scion of a family of Back Bay, Boston, who comes to Honolulu to persuade his Aunt Minerva to return from her lingering sojourn in the tropics. The murdered man is Minerva's brother, Daniel, who had gained his early wealth by shady means in the blackbirding (slave) trade. A dozen suspects are examined and dismissed on the basis of clues (such as cigarettes, a brooch, and an illuminated wrist watch) collected by the indefatigable Chan, until the one who could not be suspected is trapped. The Waikiki setting of the early 1920s is used as an integral part of the solution.

The "house without a key" is the beach residence of Dan Winterslip, where people could come and go in the days when burglary was uncommon. However, the name was attached to a portion of an inn which became part of the Halekulani Hotel, a charming outdoor cocktail restaurant and lounge that still functions today.

The adaptations of the novel were filmed twice. The first movie was released in 1926 with the same title as the book, while the second came out in 1933 as Charlie Chan's Greatest Case.

Chang Apana

Charlie Chan is supposed to be modeled on Chang Apana, a celebrated and picturesque member of the Honolulu Police Department about whose exploits Biggers had heard. He met Chang when he visited Hawaii in 1919, during which time he gathered material for his novel.

Chan in the Movies

The character of Charlie attracted such popular interest that Biggers later made him the detective hero of a series of stories set in various parts of the world: *The Chinese Parrot* (1926), *Behind That Curtain* (1928), *The Black Camel* (1929), *Charlie Chan Carries On* (1930), and *The Keeper of the Keys* (1932). The Chan character was early portrayed in the films by Warner Oland, and the figure of Charlie Chan, with his fractured English and gnomic quotations, is still appearing on television re-runs.

A product of its time, the character of Charlie Chan is generally derided today for fostering stereotypes.

—A. Grove Day (*Books About Hawaii: Fifty Basic Authors*)

Did you know...

Queen Keōpūolani had a fort built in Lahaina on Maui in 1831 to deal with disorderly sailors and armed it with a cannon raised from a nearby sunken Russian warship.

Con Man or Superspy?

Villain Named After a Restaurant

For thirteen years—1968 to 1980—Steve McGarrett and his squad of crack detectives from *Hawaii Five-O* pursued a diabolical Red Chinese villain, Wo Fat. (If the name of his nemesis sounds familiar, it should. *Five-O* producer Leonard Freeman borrowed the moniker from a downtown Honolulu restaurant which served Chinese cuisine from 1882 until 2005.

Deep Fraud

Despite the TV plots, and some action prior to World War II, Honolulu had never been known for much international intrigue. Then Ron Rewald showed up. A flashy high-roller with an oceanfront estate, a chauffeured Rolls and a string of polo ponies, Rewald combined his and Sunlin L. S. Wong's names with those of three famous kama'āina families, and formed an investment firm: Bishop, Baldwin, Rewald, Dillingham & Wong. Offering unbelievably high interest returns, Rewald was wildly successful for a time, as investors poured millions into his operation. In 1985 he was convicted of operating a classic Ponzi scheme and sentenced to eighty years in a federal lockup for bilking more than $20 million from some 400 investors.

Rewald's defense—that his firm was actually a deep cover front for the Central Intelligence Agency—is still embraced by conspiracy theorists today, with occasional books and TV specials "proving" that he was abandoned (and almost assassinated) by the agency.

His defense failed, and Ronald Ray Rewald was packed off to the Federal Correctional Institution at Terminal Island. He was released in 1995 after serving a decade of his eighty-year sentence.

—MacKinnon Simpson (*A Century of Aloha*)

 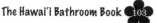

The O'ahu Prison in 1898

"The Oahu prison is on the west side of the town, and right at the mouth of the Nuuanu Valley. It is modeled after the Charlestown prison, and thus far has proved large enough to contain the criminals of the country. All prisoners who are sentenced for over three months are sent there. It accommodates one hundred and seventy, and the usual number of inmates average about one hundred and fifty."

—A. D. HALL, HAWAII (1898)

Extreme Hawai'i

The World's Widest County

Honolulu County includes all parts of the Hawaiian Islands that don't belong to any of the other counties or the U.S. military. That means the Northwestern Hawaiian Islands are part of Honolulu County, making this the widest county in the world. It is 1,381 miles long, which is the same distance as from Los Angeles to Kansas City, or from Dallas to New York City. Honolulu County is even wider than most countries.

Did you know...

In mythology, Maui—the trickster demigod—carved a giant fishhook out of his dead grandma's jawbone and used it to pull the Hawaiian Islands up from beneath the ocean.

Common Misconceptions About Hawai'i

You need a passport to visit Hawai'i

The islands have been a U.S. possession since 1898, and a state since 1959.

We don't use American money

Wrong. Mainland tourist dollars are good here.

We are all Hawaiian

Folks here usually distinguish between Native Hawaiians, who descend from the original Polynesian settlers, and Hawai'i residents, who came to live here later. People usually hear "Hawaiian" as "Native Hawaiian." Don't say Hawaiian when you mean "Hawai'i resident."

Thanks to centuries of intermarriage, most Native Hawaiians are of mixed blood. According to the latest census, some 10% of the state population is Native Hawaiian or other Pacific Islander.

We all speak Hawaiian

Only a few thousand people, most of them elderly, speak it as their mother tongue; thousands more have learned Hawaiian in school. However, most islanders know a few common Hawaiian words—as well as Japanese, Chinese, Korean, and Filipino words. All are part of the vocabulary of Hawaiian pidgin, a local dialect of English that a lot of people *do* speak.

Islanders wear coconut bras and grass skirts

Before the missionaries came, women didn't wear anything except a waist wrap, a pa'ū, and sometimes a kīhei, or cape, when it was cold. Both were made out of bark cloth. Grass skirts? Unknown.

The coconut bras and grass skirts are worn only by women dancing in tourist-oriented stage shows. They ditch the dang things as soon as the performance is over.

No one, in real life, has ever worn a coconut bra. Some South Pacific islanders do wear leaf or grass skirts. In the nineteenth century, Gilbert Islanders were imported to work on the sugar plantations. Hula troupes performing for tourists adopted the Gilbertese grass skirts to emphasize their 'ami, hip movements.

Hawaiians live in grass huts

Islanders lived in grass huts before the European explorers and missionaries arrived. Those days are long gone. Now, the only grass houses you'll find are the ones in tourist theme parks.

Islanders surf

Some of us do. We also bicycle, run marathons, play baseball and football, or just veg out in front of the TV or the computer.

No hot and cold running water in Hawai'i

All towns here have electricity and plumbing. If you build a house out in a rural area, you may have to install rain catchment tanks and a solar water heater. However, off-the-grid housing is the exception rather than the rule.

No fast food places here

Hahahahaha! We got! We got! We don't have all the chains found on the mainland, but we have our own chains, like Zippy's.

It never snows in Hawai'i

Got snow on Mauna Kea, or White Mountain, on the Big Island. That's a dormant volcano, one of the two large volcanoes on the Big Island. The other volcano, Mauna Loa, or Big Mountain, gets a light sprinkling of snow every now and then.

O'ahu is completely urban

Some 26% of the island has been built up; 15% is used for agriculture; the rest is left in its natural state. If you want wilderness on O'ahu, all you have to do is drive a short way, park, and hike.

If you liked your vacation in Hawai'i, you can move here and it will be vacation year round

Inexpensive housing is scarce, jobs are hard to find, everything costs more than it does on the mainland, and lots of local folks work two jobs. They're the ones doing your hotel laundry and busing your restaurant dishes. Year-round vacation? No way!

—KAREN LOFSTROM

Did you know...

In Hawai'i, dog licenses are renewed every two years. For the years 2009 and 2010, the state issued 103,695 dog licenses.

Did you know...

Grass skirts—also known as shredded-wheat skirts—are not a part of traditional hula, which uses skirts made from ti leaves.

Did you know...

The total land area for the Northwestern Hawaiian Islands, not including the Midway Islands, is only 3.1 square miles.

The Decline of Surfing

Surfing dog at Waikīkī in 1932.

Everybody Surfs

On days of good surf, Maui's seaside villages would be vacant, for Hawaiians highly valued sports, and surfing most of all.

Ali'i, or chiefs, excelled at surfing, as did many commoners. Both men and women mastered wave-riding skills, enjoying not only the thrill of the ride, but also prestige. Adults relied upon long, narrow boards, rugged outrigger canoes or their bodies alone to speed them through the surf, while children joined in the fun on banana trunks.

Nineteen ancient Maui surfing spots have been identified at Waihe'e, Waiehu, Wailuku, Hāna Bay, Mokulau, and Lahaina, although undoubtedly more existed. Missionary Charles Steward remarked on what he observed at Lahaina in 1823,

"It is a daily amusement at all times, but the more terrific the surf, the more delightful the pastime to those skillful in the management the boards...hundreds at a time have been occupied in this way for hours together."

It's Those Pesky Missionaries Again

Queen Ka'ahumanu herself loved to surf Lahaina's waters. Ironically, her conversion to Christianity was a force in the suppression of surfing, as the missionaries considered surfing frivolous. Surfing was also suspect because it fostered gambling, promoted the intermingling of scantily dressed men and women, and encouraged sexual freedom. Missionary pressure, along with the deterioration of traditional life that occurred after the arrival of foreigners, ensured surfing's decline.

Die-Hards

By 1854, surfing had almost disappeared. Lahaina was the only place in Hawai'i where enthusiasm for the sport remained, and even there it was on the downturn. Few surfers remained to challenge the waves at the turn of the century.

—GAIL BARTHOLOMEW (*MAUI REMEMBERS*)

Did you know...

The earliest surfboards in Hawai'i were up to 20 feet long and weighed more than 150 pounds.

An Observation

The State Economy

Today's semisocialist welfare state grew up originally as a reaction against the oligarchy of land-owning corporations that long dominated the economy. The reaction resulted in the passage of scores of regulations aimed at protecting workers and small-scale businesspeople from the concentrated power of the large estates. For example, restrictive zoning has preserved uneconomical agricultural land—and dwindling agricultural jobs—that could be put to more productive use.

The old business oligarchs are either gone or remain as shadows of their former selves. In their place is the oligarch government and its union bosses. It's a kind of runaway populism that replaced the old-time paternalism.

—SETH LUBOVE ("REPUBLIC OF HAWAII: HAWAII IS A NICE PLACE TO VISIT BUT YOU WOULDN'T WANT TO DO BUSINESS THERE." *FORBES,* JUNE 16, 1997)

An Observation

Jack Burns, Hawai'i's Second Governor

He certainly was not the most intelligent man I ever met, he wasn't the sweetest man I ever met, he wasn't the most ingenious man, nor the shrewdest man or anything else I ever met. I've asked myself what was uncommon about this essentially common man. I believe the uncommon thing about him was a great inner sense of direction, a very strong personal sense of what was right and wrong. I think that Jack was able, in the course of defeats that would have discouraged other people, to still feel that his own sense of direction was right and to hold to it, and in the end to rally people around him and win respect.... [That is what] separated him from people more highly intelligent, more able, more everything else than he might be.

—A.A. "BUD" SMYSER (*JOHN A. BURNS THE MAN AND HIS TIMES*)

Island Colors

Did you know each island has an official color? If not, here they are:

>**Island of Hawai'i:** Red
>**Maui:** Pink
>**Kaho'olawe:** Grey
>**Lāna'i:** Orange
>**Moloka'i:** Green
>**O'ahu:** Yellow
>**Kaua'i:** Purple
>**Ni'ihau:** White

For the most part, the colors match each island's official flower, except for those of Moloka'i and Kaho'olawe. Their flowers are white, which is Ni'ihau's color. Moloka'i's flower is from the kukui nut tree, so their color—green—is the color of the kukui nuts. Kaho'olawe's flower is that of a ground shrub that has silvery gray leaves.

Why each island needs an official color is anyone's guess. Since the official flowers are for making leis, maybe the colors are for feather leis. Or perhaps the politicians didn't have anything better to do that day.

"The only good thing about leaving Hawai'i is that you *really* appreciate it when you return."

—John Richard Stephens, author/editor

The Great Makahiki Festival

A Real Celebration

The ancient Hawaiians really knew how to celebrate. Their big festival of the year, Makahiki, lasted a good portion of the rainy season—three months for most commoners and four months for the ali'i, although farmers only got three weeks off. It was a combination harvest and New Year's celebration, but it was sort of like all of our holidays and summer vacation all rolled into one.

Dedicated to Lono—the god of peace and agriculture, among other things—all war and fighting stopped, heiau ceremonies stopped, and the kapus were lifted. Everyone feasted, danced, sang, played games, gambled, and participated in or watched a wide variety of sports. The only work done was what was absolutely necessary, such as preparing food.

But First They Collect Taxes

The festival began when the constellation Pleiades rose above the horizon and ended when it set, which varied from island to island depending on how far north they were. Usually this was in October or November. Tax collectors lead by a pole with an image of Lono at the top circled clockwise around the island collecting taxes and offerings from each district. The taxes were in the form of produce, animals, decorative feathers, and other items. Much of it was surplus food that was perishable and had to be consumed. The ali'i took what they wanted from the taxes, then the kāhuna, and then the lower chiefs. In return, the gods—through the chiefs—blessed the people for the coming year. Once this was done and a district was blessed by Lono, the celebrations in that district began.

The festival ended when a tax canoe laden with offerings to Lono was taken out to sea by the ali'i and set adrift. A mock battle was fought between Lono's attendants and those of the king. The king's men would win, and Lono was symbolically killed, enabling the king to reassume control of the island, and then Kū's heiaus would reopen for business.

Captain Cook Arrives

It was during this festival in 1778 that Captain Cook arrived at Kealakekua Bay, south of Kailua-Kona on the Big Island, where they happened to have a major heiau dedicated to Lono. According to Hawaiian mythology, Lono sailed away from the islands in a large boat, promising to return. Cook's arrival near the temple during Lono's festival may have made the Hawaiians believe Cook was Lono—scholars argue over that point—but the behavior of Cook and his men wasn't what they expected. And his return after the end of the festival and after Lono had symbolically been killed was not taken lightly by the Hawaiians and may have contributed to Cook's death.

Did you know...

Banana plants grow up to 30 feet tall, but they are not trees. They have one bunch of bananas, then they put out a new shoot and die.

Did you know...

It's believed the Kuʻemanu Heiau about five miles south of Kailua-Kona on the Big Island was dedicated to surfing and is where the ancient Hawaiians prayed for good surfing conditions. It had a pool for rinsing off salt water on exiting the ocean.

Fictional Description of Real Life

What's to Eat (Lū'au Style)

The mat, almost hidden under fresh leaves, ferns, and flowers, was laden with fruits and vegetables of every kind the lands of Oahu could offer. From far and near they were gathered in: coconuts, sugarcane, pineapples, oranges, watermelons, guavas, bananas, mangoes, bowls full of red prickly pears of the cactus plant, freed of their spiny skins and bathed in their blood-colored juices; pyramids of baked taro, sweet potatoes, white potatoes, and breadfruits, of raw cabbages, love apples [tomatoes], onions both green and round, chili peppers, radishes, alligator pears [avocados], and wooden bowls holding a dozen different kind of seaweeds.... Already awaiting each of us were a huge calabash full of poi; platters of dried beef, dried fish, and dried squid; a coconut-shell cup holding crystals of red salt; another full of that delectable relish prepared by mixing fragments of baked kukui nutmeats with rock salt and crisp red seaweed; a silver fingerbowl with yellow 'ilima flowers floating upon the water; a nest of sparkling glasses to hold any drink we might choose....

Now, coming before us almost on their knees, a long line of servers brought in bowls and trenchers of hot meats, still steaming from the earth-ovens in which they had been cooked: tender flesh of pig, dog, beef, veal, mutton, and lamb, rich with gobbets of fat and flakes of crusted skin; convoys of whole chickens, pigeons, and plovers arranged around native ducks and geese. Then came the provender of the sea: raw or cooked, baked or steamed, whole or broken, they were more numerous than were the meats and fowls: mullet, 'opelu, kawakawa, aholehole, 'opakapaka, 'a'awa, ulua, and papio, several kinds of tunas, mahimahi, eels, squid, crabs, lobsters, 'opihi, pipipi, wana, sea cucumbers, even that new and costly delicacy, salted salmon imported from Oregon. Never in my whole life had my nose been treated to so many enticing aromas, my stomach to so many assaults upon its strength.

—O.A. Bushnell (*Ka'a'awa*)

The Hawaiian Cowboy

A Hawaiian cowboy is called a paniolo, which is Hawaiian for Español. In 1832, Spanish vaqueros from Alto California—California still being part of Mexico at that time—were brought over to teach the Hawaiians the skills required for ranching and handling cattle. Since the Hawaiian language doesn't have an "S" and consonants are always followed by vowels, *Español* became paniolo.

Paniolo on the Range

The image of a Polynesian wearing chaps, spurs and a ten-gallon hat, riding the range, roping calves, and breaking broncos seems incongruous to a visitor caught off guard. Rodeos in the Paradise of the Pacific? Cowboys wearing a flower lei, driving cattle to palm-lined beaches and into a rolling surf to swim to waiting ships. For transport to the stockyards? Stock Hollywood versions of the western cowboy run smack up against a paniolo, the rugged men and women who tend Hawai'i's ranchlands.

How It All Began

Hawai'i's cattle industry dates back to 1792 when Captain George Vancouver, the British navigator who followed Cook, presented horses and cattle to King Kamehameha I who, in turn, placed a kapu, or taboo, on the animals. So successful was the royal protection that in a short thirty years the cattle had formed tough, wild herds ranging throughout the island, destroying ground vegetation and endangering lives. Kamehameha III, himself capable of hunting down and roping wild cattle, lifted the kapu from the herds. Hawai'i's cattle industry became a reality when Spanish-speaking vaqueros were brought from Mexico to teach Hawaiians to ride the range on horses, to master the Mexican saddle, and to braid lariats. The California Spanish vaquero became the Hawaiian paniolo.

When Hawaiian cowboys drive cattle, they have to tie the cows to boats, which in turn, tow them out to waiting ships. These 1926 photographs of a Parker Ranch cattle drive were taken on the Big Island's northwest coast at Kawaihae Harbor. They also flew cattle on airplanes. BAKER-VAN DYKE COLLECTION

The Big Island's Parker Ranch

Then in the 1850s, John Palmer Parker—a thirty-year resident of Hawai'i—acquired 1,640 acres of pasture land in the cool highlands of Waimea. After leasing the entire Waikoloa ahupua'a land subdivision, running from the mountain to the sea, the Parker Ranch became the largest in the islands, and is now run by a charitable trust. The Parker dynasty transformed Waimea into rolling green pastures that seem incongruous alongside the lush jungles and barren lava of the Big Island. The Polynesian paniolo in time gave Waimea its reputation as a "cowboy town."

Hawaiian Rodeos

A rodeo in modern Waimea reflects Hawai'i's multiculturalism. Hawaiians, Caucasian, Japanese, Chinese, and Portuguese names are listed among the riders. Across the grass-covered lava hills of Waimea, on the slopes of Mauna Loa, Mauna Kea, Hualalai, and Kohala, a small but intensely proud breed of paniolo, whether riding horses, pick-up trucks, helicopters, or motorcycles, carry on a hundred-year-old tradition. They have adopted the trappings of the American "wild west," but always with a distinctive Hawaiian flair.

—GLEN GRANT (*FROM THE SKIES OF PARADISE: THE BIG ISLAND OF HAWAII*)

From Personal Experience

The Kula Cowboy Life

Speaking in 2002 about his life as a paniolo in Kula on Maui, Henry Silva explained, "You know, it's a real good life. It's a good fun life. It's a little hard on your butt sometimes! But it's good, it's good."

Horsewomen of Honolulu Plain

At the eastern extremity of Woahoo [O'ahu] is an extinguished volcano: there are many others in the island, but none of them have been in action within the memory of man. Between the one at the east end and the town is a wide plain about four miles long. Here the natives ride every evening after the heat of the day has subsided; on Saturday, their favourite day, Rotten Row is not more gay and lively than this plain.

The wyheenes, as the women are called, riding à l' Amazone decked out in all the colours of the rainbow, with the gaudy maro twisted round their legs, and sweeping to the ground; their pretty little straw hats covered with ribands, or their uncovered heads, with their black hair streaming in the wind, confined only by a wreath of fresh orange flowers; their laughing faces and merry voices all seem so graceful, so good-humoured, and so purely natural, that it is impossible not to be delighted with them. They are fearless riders; and although the horses are not what we should term thorough-bred, they are made to gallop at such speed that it is not an easy, though very amusing, matter to keep up a running flirtation with their dusky propellers.

—HENRY J. COKEN (*A Ride Over the Rocky Mountains to Oregon and California*)

Old-School Lū'au

Ancient Luaus

In ancient times, a luau could last for days. Each type of luau had strict rules dictating what could be eaten and by whom. As soon as it was certain that a young woman was to have her first child, the father began raising a pig for the 'Aha'aina Mawaewae feast that was celebrated within twenty-four hours after the child was born. Mullet and taro leaf were required, along with shrimp, seaweed and crab; each being instrumental in the health and well-being of the child.

The First-Birthday Baby Luau

The next really big event was the 'Aha'aina Palala; what we now call the first-birthday baby luau. This had strict ceremonial rules and ceremonial foods as well. If the baby was the first-born of the ruling chief, gifts of great value were stored away for the child. Feasting and dance honored the baby. Chants or haku mele, honoring the name of the child, were composed with great diligence in the belief that they might influence the life of the child. Some of these beautiful mele, or songs, are still sung today, combined with hula that has been handed down across the generations....

A Blending of Cultures

By the late 1700s, however, the luau menu had already begun to change from just traditional dishes. The missionaries are credited with the addition of cake. The whalers brought in salted fish that we now call lomilomi salmon. The Chinese gave us chicken long rice. White rice and sushi came from the Japanese. Over the years, the luau has continued to change, mirroring the melting pot of cultures that flavor modern Hawaii.

(*A Hawaiian Lū'au with Sam Choy and the Mākaha Sons*)

A Bird Writes About Hawai'i

Isabella Arrives

Isabella Bird (1832-1904), the first woman fellow of the Royal Geographical Society, began her travels in her early twenties in search of health. During half a century, she toured not only the United States and Canada, but also Japan, the Malay Peninsula, Korea, China, India, and the tablelands of Tibet. Already middle-aged when she voyaged to Australia and New Zealand in 1872, she arrived in Honolulu in January 1873, and spent nearly seven months in Hawaii in the critical year just after Kamehameha V had died without naming an heir and the ill-fated Prince "Bill" Lunalilo was elected to ascend the throne a fortnight before the lady's arrival.

Off to Hilo

Bird spent little time in Honolulu but sailed to the Big Island, where she enjoyed Hilo, described the Kīlauea district during a volcanic outburst, and rode astride to the almost inaccessible Waipi'o and Waimanu valleys on the Hāmākua Coast. In March she toured the vast crater of Haleakalā on Maui, and later spent a month in the serene valleys of Kaua'i. She was welcomed both in the mission stations as well as in the huts of Hawaiians on wet, lonely trails.

Bird's Books

Her book about Hawaii, *The Hawaiian Archipelago: Six Months in the Sandwich Islands Among Hawai'i's Palm Groves, Coral Reefs, and Volcanoes* is outstanding even among such other volumes of her writing as *A Lady's Life in the Rocky Mountains* and *Unbeaten Tracks in Japan* (London: John Murray, 1879; 1880). It consists of more than thirty letters written to her sister in far-off Scotland. The tone is inevitably cheerful, even in describing her plight when passing the night in a crowded, grass-roofed shack on a trail where few white women had ever ventured.

The first 1875 edition was popular, and when a new printing was needed, Miss Bird added material. A number of other editions and reprints followed.

—A. GROVE DAY (*BOOKS ABOUT HAWAII: FIFTY BASIC AUTHORS*)

From Personal Experience
Lavish Luxuriance

When Isabella Bird visited Hilo, on the windward side of the Big Island in 1873, she wrote:

> I cannot convey to you any idea of the greenness and lavish luxuriance of this place, where everything flourishes, and glorious trailers and parasitic ferns hide all unsightly objects out of sight. It presents a bewildering maze of lilies, roses, fuchsias, clematis, begonias, convolvuli, the huge granadilla, the purple and yellow water lemons, also varieties of passiflora, both with delicious edible fruit, custard apples, rose apples, mangoes, mangostein guavas, bamboos, alligator pears, oranges, tamarinds, papayas, bananas, breadfruit, magnolias, geraniums, candle-nut, gardenias, dracaenas, eucalyptus, pandanus, ohias, kamani trees, noni, and quantities of other trees and flowers, of which I shall eventually learn the names, patches of pine-apple, melons, and sugar-cane for children to suck, kalo and sweet potatoes.
>
> In the vicinity of this and all other houses, chili pepper, and a ginger-plant with a drooping flower-stalk with a great number of blossoms, which when not fully developed have a singular resemblance to very pure porcelain tinted with pink at the extremities of the buds, are to be seen growing in "yards," to use a most unfitting Americanism. I don't know how to introduce you to some of the things which delight my eyes here; but you must try to believe that the specimens of tropical growths which we see in conservatories at home are in general either misrepresentations, or very feeble representations of these growths in their natural homes. I don't allude to

flowers, and especially not to orchids, but in this instance very specially to bananas, coco-palms, and the pandanus. For example, there is a specimen of the *Pandanus odoratissimus* in the palm-house in the Edinburgh Botanic Gardens, which is certainly a malignant caricature, with its long straggling branches, and widely-scattered tufts of poverty-stricken foliage. The bananas and plantains in the same palm-house represent only the feeblest and poorest of their tribe. They require not only warmth and moisture, but the generous sunshine of the tropics for their development. In the same house the date and sugar-palms are tolerable specimens, but the cocoa-nut trees are most truly "palms in exile."

—Isabella Bird (*The Hawaiian Archipelago*)

Nostalgia

Memories

President Barack Obama, in his memoir *Dreams From My Father*, wrote:

> I still remember how, one early morning, hours before the sun rose, a Portuguese man to whom my grandfather had given a good deal on a sofa set took us out to spear fish off Kailua Bay [on O'ahu]. A gas lantern hung from the cabin on the small fishing boat as I watched men dive into inky-black waters, the beams of their flashlights glowing beneath the surface until they emerged with a large fish, iridescent and flopping at the end of one pole. Gramps told me its Hawaiian name, humu-humu-nuku-nuku-apuaa, which we repeated to each other the entire way home.

Similar Deities

In a general way, the gods and goddesses of the ancient Hawaiians roughly correspond to classical gods of ancient Greece and Rome. While the matches aren't exact, for those familiar with the classical gods, this chart provides an easy way to identify and understand some of the major Hawaiian gods and goddesses.

Realm	Hawaiian	Greek	Roman
Gods			
Great God	Kāne	Zeus	Jupiter
Peace and Agriculture	Lono	Kronos	Saturn
War	Kū	Ares	Mars
Ocean	Kanaloa	Poseidon	Neptune
Goddesses			
Earth mother	Papa	Gaia	Terra
Women	Haumea	Hera	Juno
Love and beauty	Hina	Aphrodite	Venus
Destruction	Pele	Nemesis	Invidia

Of course that is just one aspect of Pele, the "earth-eating woman" and the goddess of volcanos and molten lava. She has her positive side, as well.

In the Middle of a War

Impending War

In 1935 Honolulu, almost no one's thoughts were on impending war. Yet as events across the Pacific began to unfold militarily and diplomatically, war went from remote to possible to probable.

War workers and soldiers began to pour into Honolulu in the late '30s as project after project—many of them labeled Top Secret—came online. Few planners considered an attack by air. Most were concerned with defending against a naval bombardment followed by an enemy invasion. Others feared sabotage from O'ahu's huge concentration of resident Japanese.

Top Secret

One project that did guess right about bombs from the air—the construction of twenty enormous underground fuel tanks inside a mountain—was not finished by the day of the attack. Luckily, the tanks were not needed, thanks to a rare error by Admiral Yamamoto, who would not allow his begging pilots to return to Pearl in a third wave to destroy the existing above-ground tanks. Had he done so, according to U.S. Admiral Chester Nimitz, the ensuing damage could have "extended the war between two and ten years."

The other new project, a radar station at Ka'ena Point, actually worked perfectly but the images were discounted by higher-ups and ignored. Most of the other fixed defenses never fired a shot.

—MacKinnon Simpson (*A Century of Aloha*)

Quayle Knows Hawai'i
(only vaguely)

Dan Quayle, who was the U.S. vice president under George Bush, was not known for being particularly erudite. In response to a question about universal healthcare in 1992, he said, "Hawaii is a unique state. It is a small state. It is a state that is by itself. It is a—it is different from the other forty-nine states. Well, all states are different, but it's got a particularly unique situation."

During a visit to Hawai'i in 1989, he said, "Hawaii has always been a very pivotal role in the Pacific. It is *in* the Pacific. It is a part of the United States that is an island that is right here."

Uncommon Knowledge
Flying the King's Flag

The Hawaiian state flag was designed for King Kamehameha I in 1816 by British captain George Beckley. It was originally intended to signify that the Kingdom of Hawai'i was under the protection of the British Empire, even though Hawai'i was never officially a protectorate of Great Britain. The British flag design in the top corner is made of three styles of crosses of the patron saints of England, Scotland, and Ireland. The eight horizontal stripes represent each of the main islands of Kamehameha's kingdom. No one knows for sure what his original flag looked like, but it most likely looked like today's flag. The Hawaiians' had no flags before this one, although Kamehameha did allow Captain Vancouver to fly the British flag above his royal residence in 1794. Instead of flags, the ancient Hawaiian's flew cylinders of feathers.

Pele's Curse

Horrible Things Happen

Just about everyone's heard about Pele's Curse—that if anyone takes lava rocks from the islands, some really nasty things will happen to them. And every day, rocks are shipped back from all over the world because people's lives took a significant downhill turn after they took home a bit of lava.

Finding a Cause

When bad things happen in someone's life, it's natural to try to find a cause. When none are obvious, people tend to lean toward the supernatural. It's hard to imagine that really significant things can be random and without meaning. People do become convinced Pele's anger caused their marriage to break up, or the loss of their job, or their child to die. But with a little research one finds that Pele's Curse has nothing to do with the ancient Hawaiian religion. It was all invented in 1946 by Narou Tovley, a park ranger at the Hawai'i Volcanoes National Park on the Big Island, because he got tired of being ignored when he told tourists it was against the law to take the lava from the park.

Cursed Rocks and Stuff

The threat of a curse turned out to be very effective, but now they have to maintain a group of volunteers to deal with all the rocks that are shipped to them. People now believe it applies to all lava taken from anywhere in the islands. They ship rocks, sand, and shells back to hotels, the Mauna Loa Observatory, or to anyone they know in Hawai'i, usually accompanied with letters describing the misfortunes they've suffered. One ranger told RoadsideAmerica.com, "People mail things that aren't even from Hawai'i. We looked at something and it was slag from a furnace." The ranger added that they've also received "ceramic tiki heads and bottles with things in them." Some businesses hire kāhuna to bless lava rocks before offering them for sale or shipping them out of the state so their customers won't worry.

Apparently the museum in the park had a display showing some of the rocks sent to them, along with some letters. There is a similar display at the Petrified Forest National Park of letters from people who believe they were cursed for taking chunks of the petrified trees. The Uluru, or Ayers Rock, national park in Australia also receives packages of so-called cursed rocks that were once taken from there. This would indicate the belief is not Hawaiian in origin. In fact, the cursed rock display at the Kīlauea volcano was taken down because some Native Hawaiians said that since there are no curses in their culture, the display was misleading and reflected badly on them.

Asking Permission

Like the Native Americans, Hawaiians were brought up believing that one has to ask before taking anything from nature. To take a rock without first asking Pele and/or the rock for permission is considered disrespectful to Pele and to their culture. But whether they believe someone is jinxed or doomed for not doing so probably depends on who one talks to about it. Some Native Hawaiians have come to accept idea of the curse and feel it's disrespectful to their culture if one *doesn't* warn someone of the curse.

It Makes No Sense at All

Now if one really thinks about it, the curse doesn't make any sense. Here on Hawai'i, people often use lava as a building material. Chunks are broken off and shaped to make fences. It's ground up to lay in flower beds, or as roads and driveways. Looking at it from Pele's perspective, who would she be mad at? Who is being disrespectful? Those who grind up her "babies" so they can walk or drive on them, or those who take one home as a cherished treasure to remind them of what a wonderful place Hawai'i is?

The Target Isle

Kahoʻolawe was the most heavily bombed island of the Pacific War, but it was the United States that bombed itself. The Army and Navy used Kahoʻolawe for target practice throughout World War II. After the war ended, they went right on bombing and didn't stop until 1990. This is why Kahoʻolawe is called the Target Island. As Hawaiians protested the bombings, Admiral John Hyland said, "I think the island is of very little use for anything else."

The Navy also bombed South Kona's Kaunā Point on the Big Island from 1959 to 1970, while in the 1960s the Pentagon tested chemical weapons, such as the deadly serin nerve gas, in the Upper Waiakea Forest Reserve, southwest of Hilo.

TOP: *Five hundred tons of high explosives were stacked on the shore of Kahoʻolawe for the first of three explosion damage tests in 1965. Note the technician partially visible on the right side. The odd-looking pile was 17 feet high and 34 feet in diameter. The ship was one of three subjected to this test. The other two were further out. All three ships were fully manned during this explosion.* U.S. Navy

BOTTOM: *The shock wave from the explosion passes the test ship and creates a vapor cloud. The three tests left a crater near Hanakaniʻa Bay that is 165 feet across.* U.S. Navy

Hawai'i and the Censors

Risqué Hawai'i

In the 1950s, movies about infidelity were all the rage. It was considered a very risqué topic at the time and was quite controversial. Two of the biggest films featuring Hawai'i from that period emphasized cheating in relationships—*From Here to Eternity* and *The Revolt of Mamie Stover*. Remember, this was a time when ideal families were portrayed on television, and even in the movies, married couples slept in separate beds. Illicit sex was definitely a taboo topic.

Kapus

What the movie industry was doing with these films was bucking against the moral censorship guidelines of the Roman Catholic Church's National Legion of Decency and the Motion Picture Production Code developed by Presbyterian elder Will H. Hays, which restricted what could be shown in movies from 1934 to 1968. The Hays Code prevented the depiction of such things as "ridicule of the clergy" and the use of "the words 'God,' 'Lord,' 'Jesus,' 'Christ' (unless they be used reverently in connection with proper religious ceremonies)." While "special care" was required when showing "the use of firearms...theft, robbery, safe-cracking, and dynamiting of trains, mines, buildings, etc. (having in mind the effect which a too-detailed description of these may have upon the moron)." Basically the censors only wanted Hollywood to make movies for morons.

Fighting Censorship

Neither the film makers nor much the general public cared for these restrictions. As audiences became more accepting of adult themes, the censors continued to severely limit what was allowed in movies. Indirect censorship by the Motion Picture Association of American—consisting of the heads of the major studios—continues today in the form of motion picture ratings, which often force film makers to delete scenes or dialogue in order to be awarded the more profitable PG rating or to avoid the financially harmful NC-17 rating.

Paradise in the Battle Against Suppression

Despite the fact that the studio execs support the censorship system, those who make the movies try to get around it. Back then, they found it a bit easier to squeak by the censors with films set in exotic locals with racy reputations, such as the South Pacific and Hawai'i, which at that time was still a territory.

One of the Code's eleven big no-nos was interracial sex and marriage. As early as 1935, filmmakers pushed against this boundary with *Mutiny on the Bounty*, where Hollywood's most popular male star at the time, Clark Gable, falls for a Tahitian beauty—played by Hawai'i's Mamo Clark—causing him and the men of the *Bounty* to toss Bligh and his breadfruit plants overboard so they can return to their topless Tahitian girlfriends—covered by carefully placed tresses and leis. This theme was continued in the 1962 remake starring Marlon Brando.

Did you know...

Originally, Jimmy Stewart and Julie Andrews were partners in Mac-Farms of Hawaii.

From Here to Mamie Stover

Montgomery Clift, Burt Lancaster and Frank Sinatra. Both Clift and Lancaster were nominated for Oscars for Best Actor, but neither of them won. Sinatra did win for Best Supporting Actor and it relaunched his flagging career. COLUMBIA PICTURES

From Here to Eternity

Following the destruction, horrors and struggles of World War II, people were ready for films with mature themes. Also, the studios were adjusting to changes in the movie-going public brought on by the introduction of television. The Academy Award-winner for best picture in 1953 was *From Here to Eternity*—a war movie set at Oʻahu's Schofield Barracks just prior to the bombing of Pearl Harbor.

The film was based on the gritty novel of the same name by James Jones, which in turn was inspired by his own experiences in the Hawaiian Division's 27th Infantry. It included depictions of military sadism, explicit sex, and references to homosexuality, although the publisher cut much of the gay sex and four-letter words from the manuscript before it was published. It was immensely popular and is considered by some to be one of the great novels of the twentieth century.

Fights, Betrayal and Love

The film has three story arcs. Montgomery Clift plays an army grunt and champion amateur boxer who now refuses to fight in the ring. His commanding officer and most of the company severely harass him, trying to force him to change his mind. Meanwhile he falls in love with a prostitute played by Donna Reed.

Burt Lancaster is a hard-nose first sergeant who is strictly by the book, except when it comes to his affair with his CO's wife (Deborah Kerr), whose marriage hit the rocks when, while giving birth, her drunken husband returned from a tryst and passed out. Unable to get to a hospital, the baby died and she lost the ability to have children. Lancaster's character tries to steal her away from her husband and his CO, but is unable to follow through, refusing her demand that he become an officer.

Frank Sinatra is another army grunt who battles against racism and his own stupidity, ending up dead. Clift's non-fighting boxer avenges his death by murdering a sadistic sergeant (Ernest Borgnine), but he, too, is killed after refusing to halt for a soldier on picket duty right after the attack on Pearl Harbor.

On Location

Much of this movie was filmed on location at the Schofield Barracks, including strafing scenes by Japanese Zeros during the surprise attack. Planes from the Hawai'i Air National Guard's 199th Squadron were used as the Zeros, along with authentic footage of the attack. Scenes were also filmed at Diamond Head, Waikīkī Beach, the Royal Hawaiian Hotel, the streets of Honolulu, and the Wai'alae Golf Course. The famous scene of Burt Lancaster and Deborah Kerr kissing in the surf was shot at Hālona Cove, below Koko Crater. The Motion Picture Association of America later banned the production company from using publicity photographs of this scene, as they were deemed to be too erotic.

This movie was awarded eight Oscars. It established Montgomery Clift as one of the first anti-heroes of the Fifties struggling against authority. What makes the film great is that it avoids the black and white, good versus evil pigeon-holes of most Hollywood movies, instead presenting the characters in the shades of gray of real life. But, like Sodom and Gomorrah, punishment from the skies rains down upon them in the end, which no doubt mollified the censors.

The Revolt of Mamie Stover

Based on the controversial novel of the same name, *The Revolt of Mamie Stover* is about a Honolulu prostitute dur-

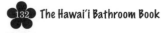

ing World War II, who struggles against the men and women in her life who treat her like dirt. Called a "dance hostess" in the movie, Stover is played by Jane Russell. On her way to Honolulu, she falls in love with a writer named Jim, but later discovers he already has a girlfriend. Getting a job at a night-club, she becomes a popular attraction. When Jim finds out, he strongly disapproves, but she convinces him to continue their affair.

After Pearl Harbor is attacked, Jim enlists in the army and convinces her to quit her job, saying he'll marry her when the war is over. Because of circumstance, she continues working and soon rises to the top of her profession, becoming one of Hawai'i's richest women. Jim is wounded and, before he returns to Honolulu, discovers Mamie is still working. He dumps her, and, in an ending added by the censors, she ends up back where she started, saying she gave away her fortune and is returning to her hometown.

On Location Again

Almost all of the exterior shots were filmed in and around Honolulu, featuring Waikīkī Beach, the Punchbowl, Ala Moana Park, the Wai'alae Country Club, the Pali, a view from Kamehameha Heights, and the terrace of the Halekūlani Hotel.

Where's a Copyeditor When You Need One?

In *From Here to Eternity*, Deborah Kerr's character says seductively, "On the other hand, I've got a bathing suit on under my dress." To which Burt Lancaster responds, "Me, too," with a big smile.

Music of the Heart

- **King David Kalākaua**—words for national anthem, "Hawai'i Pono'ī"; also "Koni Au," Hawaiian drinking song.
- **Queen Lili'uokalani**—"Aloha 'Oe"; also "Hawaiian National Anthem," 1866, sung for some 20 years.
- **Princess Likelike**—"'Āina-hau."
- **Prince Leleihōku**—"Kāua I Ka Huahua'i," love song familiar now as "Hawaiian War Chant."
- **Rev. Lorenzo Lyons**—"Hawai'i Aloha," a favorite missionary hymn.
- **Captain Henry Berger**—leader of Royal Hawaiian Band from 1872; arranged many songs, including "Hawai'i Pono'ī" and "Hilo March."
- **Charles E. King**—collected hapa-haole songs (English with Hawaiian words and phrases), arranged and published over 200 songs, including "Song of the Islands" (second most popular) and "Kamehameha Waltz."
- **Harry Owens**—"To You, Sweetheart, Aloha" and "Sweet Leilani," sung by Bing Crosby and winner of an Academy Award, 1937.
- **R. Alex Anderson**—"Lovely Hula Hands," 1940, and "The Cockeyed Mayor of Kaunakakai."
- **Alfred Apaka**—"Greatest voice Hawai'i ever produced"; theme song "Here in This Enchanted Place."
- **Tony Todaro**—"Keep Your Eyes on Hands" and "Somewhere in Hawai'i," sung by Apaka.
- **Don Ho**—"Biggest in the history of Hawaiian show business"; popularized "Tiny Bubbles."
- **Kui Lee**—Chinese-Hawaiian; composed, played guitar, sang, chatted briskly in pidgin; popular in 1960s; wrote and sang "Lahainaluna," "I'll Remember You," "One Paddle, Two Paddle."
- **Danny Kaleikini**—leader and master of ceremonies at today's Hawaiian shows; sings, chats, cracks jokes; Hawaiian, Chinese, Korean, Irish, and Italian origin.

—LaRue W. Piercy (*Hawai'i This and That*)

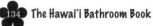

Ghostly Warriors

When They March

Akua, the fourteenth night of the moon when it separated from earth and became a god, is the night all Hawaiians are on the alert for Ka Huaka i a ka Po, the Marchers in the Night. They are the spirits of the dead chiefs and warriors, au akua (guardian gods of the living) and the gods themselves.

The Hawaiian knows that the marchers are most apt to be seen just after sunset until about sunrise. He knows that he must hide, for to be seen by the marchers is certain death.

March of the Gods

There are several types of Marchers. The gods may be distinguished by a wind that blows through the forests or shrubbery. The wind snaps off branches of great trees to clear the path for the gods.

The march of the gods is led by a row of six who carry blazing red torches. Three of the torch carriers are females and three are males. The sound clearly heard within their ranks is the chanting of their names and chants of praise.

The march can be seen at great distances because the torches are so bright. Inevitably there are thunder, lightning and a sudden downpour of rain and heavy surf.

The Procession of Ali'i

Kane is the night on which the Marchers in the Night most often consist of dead chiefs, chiefesses, priests and their close attendants. Again, a Hawaiian conceals himself for it is death to be seen by the Marchers.

Often the chiefs were accompanied by aumakua of the living. They are in the march to protect any of their living children who might be caught in the path of the march. Many Hawaiians have seen the march of the mighty chiefs and have been saved by their aumakua.

The dead chiefs may be carried in a manele (string hammock) just as the chief had been carried in life. The manele creaks as it sways on the carrying sticks.

The chief's procession are lighted by torches, but the light of the torches is not as great as that of the gods. A warlike chief is apt to march in the procession between two warriors.

In all these processions, a man who had held a similar position in life, marches at the head of the column calling kapu to warn the living to get out of the way. It is his duty to execute any living being caught in the path.

Strip Naked

A wise Hawaiian who finds himself in the path of a procession will tear off his clothes and lie face down in the dirt hoping that by his prostration he may be saved.

Near the Temple Ruins

These processions are most apt to be seen near the old heiau (temples) of ancient Hawaii.

Many Hawaiians have never seen the processions but they have heard the music of the flute, the beating of the drums and the chanting which goes on at the heiau at the end of a procession. Sometimes the procession of chiefs will end on a level piece of ground which in ancient days served as a place for sports tourneys. There the chiefs and attendants play their favorite old games to the loud sound of laughing and cheering.

Ancient Hawaiians knew just where the paths were located which were the favorite courses of the Marchers in the Night.

Although the favorite nights for the Marchers are Akua and Kane [the 14th and 27th night of the lunar month], Marchers have been seen during the Ku nights [the 3rd through the 6th] and on the nights of Lono [the 28th night]. [Note: In the Hawaiian lunar months, the moon was dark on the 2nd night and the full moon was on the 19th night.]

—CLARICE B. TAYLOR (*HAWAIIAN ALMANAC*)

An additional note: Similar accounts can be found in other cultures. In the U.K. it's usually marching Roman soldiers that are seen. In the Eastern U.S., it's soldiers from the Revolutionary War or the Civil War.

Great Things about Hawai'i

Billboards are illegal.

There is no daylight savings time. Schedules aren't disrupted twice a year, as in most states.

Hawai'i has extra holidays. There are three official state holidays—Prince Jonah Kuhio Kalanianaole Day (Kuhio Day, for short), King Kamehameha I Day and Statehood Day (marking Hawai'i's admission as the 50th state). Other unofficial holidays include Lei Day and Chinese New Year, along with Girl's Day and Boy's Day, which were both imported from Japan. Then there's Makahiki and the Aloha Festivals.

Hawaii's ethnic and cultural diversity brings together the best of many different traditions.

Flavorful and delicious fresh fruit is everywhere, including many exotic ones, such as poha berry and dragon fruit. And don't forget the lilikoi (passion fruit) cheesecake.

Sweet Hawai'i

JOHN RICHARD STEPHENS

Want a truly amazing desert? Here is a Tahitian Black Pearl at Mama's Fish House Restaurant in Pā'ia, Maui. With cookie clamshells about the size of your hand (it's sitting on a large dinner plate), hinged with whipped cream, the dome-shaped chocolate mousse with a vanilla center is coated with a chocolate ganache and rests on a bed of chopped macadamia nuts, all sitting on a puff of whipped cream and a starburst of chocolate and lilikoi syrups. Hawai'i is home to some of the best chefs in the world.

More Things to Love about Hawai'i

A bird shopping at Harvest Market in Hanalei, Kaua'i. JOHN RICHARD STEPHENS

There are birds everywhere that serenade you with their singing all day long.

In many places you never have to close your windows, except on the rare occasions when there's wind *and* rain. In fact many restaurants and bars are open air lanai-style... always—even when it rains. They don't have windows so you can enjoy the fresh air and fantastic views, while the birds wander about under the tables. They fly around in the fanciest restaurants and never seem to bother anyone. Surprisingly, bugs aren't a problem. Perhaps the birds eat them.

There are flowers just about everywhere and they're blooming year around, making Hawai'i very colorful. Plants also grow like crazy.

You can always wear sandals or go barefoot, unless your job requires boots or shoes.

All beaches are open to the public.

You can swim in the ocean year round without a wetsuit.

Hawai'i has incredibly spectacular sunsets. On some islands, conditions are excellent for seeing the green flash.

You can swim or lay out on the beach *most nights* and still be comfortable, even in December.

You get fresh fruit in your drinks.

Spirits of Aloha
History of the Mai Tai

The Mai Tai didn't originate in Hawai'i, but it was quickly adopted as one of the most popular drinks on the islands. Two people claim they invented it. Donn Beach, a.k.a. Don the Beachcomber and a slew of other names, said he created the Mai Tai Swizzle in 1932 or 1933, but the drink quickly faded away and was off his menu within a few years.

Trader Vic Bergeron claimed he invented the Mai Tai in 1944, saying, "I was at the service bar in my Oakland restaurant. I took down a bottle of 17-year-old rum. It was J. Wray Nephew from Jamaica; surprisingly golden in color, medium bodied, but with the rich pungent flavor particular to the Jamaican blends. The flavor of this great rum wasn't meant to be overpowered with heavy additions of fruit juices and flavorings. I took a fresh lime, added some orange curacao from Holland, a dash of Rock Candy Syrup, and a dollop of French Orgeat, for its subtle almond flavor. A generous amount of shaved ice and vigorous shaking by hand produced the marriage I was after. Half the lime shell went in for color... I stuck in a branch of fresh mint and gave two of them to Ham and Carrie Guild, friends from Tahiti, who were there that night. Carrie took one sip and said, 'Mai Tai—Roa Ae' [actually it's 'Maita'i roa a'e']. In Tahitian this means 'Out of This World—The Best.' Well, that was that. I named the drink 'Mai Tai.'"

Perhaps they both invented similar drinks by the same name. Perhaps Trader Vic took Donn Beach's cocktail and improved and popularized it. Perhaps one of them made up their story to take a poke at the other. Both were leading figures in the Polynesian restaurant and bar business that lead to the explosion of popularity in the tiki culture from the 1940s through the 1960s. After extensive research, mixologist Jeff "Beachbum" Berry came to the conclusion that Donn Beach's cocktail is a different drink with the same name and that Trader Vic copied and improved upon a drink called the Q.B.

Cooler, unknowingly giving it the same name as Donn's old drink. But that's just educated speculation.

There are many recipes for the drink—even Trader Vic modified his recipe a couple of times—but here are the two original recipes.

Mai Tai Swizzle (1932-1933?)

by Donn Beach

Pour the following into a cocktail shaker with ice:

> 1.5 oz. Myer's Plantation rum
> 1 oz. Cuban rum
> 0.75 oz. fresh lime juice
> 1 oz. fresh grapefruit juice
> 0.25 oz. Falernum (or sugar syrup like Rock Candy Syrup)
> 0.5 oz. Cointreau
> 2 dashes Angostura bitters
> 1 dash Pernod
> Shell of squeezed lime
> 1 cup of cracked ice (with chunks about the size of a dime)

Shake for one minute and serve in a double old-fashioned glass filled. Garnish with four sprigs of mint and a spear of pineapple. Sip slowly through mint sprigs.

Mai Tai (1944)

by Trader Vic

Pour the following into a cocktail shaker over shave ice:

> 2 oz. 17-year-old J. Wray & Nephew Rum
> Add juice from one fresh lime.
> 1/2 oz. Holland DeKuyper Orange Curaçao
> 1/4 oz. Trader Vic's Rock Candy Syrup
> 1/2 oz. French Garnier Orgeat Syrup

Shake vigorously. Pour into a glass and top with a sprig of fresh mint.

Royal Hawaiian Mai Tai

by the Mai Tai Bar at the Royal Hawaiian Hotel

No matter who invented the drink, it was Waikīkī that made it popular. In 1953 the Matson Steamship Lines asked Trader Vic to establish a drink list for the bars at their Royal Hawaiian, Surfrider, and Moana Hotels. The Mai Tai quickly became the best known of all the tropical drinks and one of the most popular cocktails in the world—particularly in Hawai'i.

Since it was the Matson hotels on Waikīkī that made the drink famous, here is their Hawaiian recipe.

Combine the following ingredients in this order in an Old Fashioned-style glass over shave ice.

> 1 oz. dark rum
> 1 oz. light rum
> 1 oz. orange Curaçao
> 2 oz. orange juice
> 0.5 oz. lime juice
> A dash of orgeat
> A dash of simple syrup (bar syrup)

Stir with a swizzle stick and garnish with a slice of pineapple and a maraschino cherry pierced with a toothpick stuck into the top of the pineapple. It is now common to float the dark rum on top and to use a toothpick umbrella.

In the 50s and 60s, bartenders tried to use the best quality ingredients in their cocktails. This was lost in the 70s and umbrella drinks were disparaged and looked down upon—they became foo foo drinks—but now they are making a resurgence as bartenders work hard to make their versions stand out. For some truely amazing Mai Tais, visit the Don the Beachcomber Mai Tai Festival every August in Kailua-Kona on the Big Island. This is where bartenders from around the world compete to create the ultimate Mai Tai.

A Bit of Old Hawai'i in Waikīkī

It's Exciting!...Really

No single creation in Waikīkī caused more excitement or brought more recognition to Hawai'i's tourist industry than the International Market Place. It was the brainchild of Donn Beach and his friend George "Pete" Wimberly of Wimberly Allison Tong & Goo Architects, conceived on wrapping paper in the back of the old Moana Cottages.

Donn's vision was to create a replica of old Hawai'i in a five-acre space in the heart of Waikīkī. The original structures typical "grass shacks" lived in by ancient Hawaiians. Appropriately surrounded with coconut palms, the grounds were defined by carved "tikis" placed strategically, representing Hawaiian gods. Outrigger canoes with simulated warriors paddling them provided a feeling of vitality. Bridges with koa-wood railings were built over contrived streams and gullies to create a feeling of exploration to the different sectors of the village. Waterfalls attracted tourists with cameras.

Going Native

At the very center was a grass area where Hawaiian women in native dress sat on woven mats to work on native arts and crafts for the delight and benefit of the visitors. This was a daily feature that always drew crowds for observation and picture-taking.

Merchandise sold in the original complex was mostly arts and crafts from the Pacific and Orient. Each shop was required to submit plans to the firm of Wimberly Allison Tong & Goo, which maintained rigid standards as to shop décor and signage. Everything was coordinated to create an atmosphere of Hawai'i and the Pacific.

A Tree-House Restaurant

An unusual feature of the Market Place was the use of tree houses. Several magnificent banyan trees were situated near the front entrance. With his vivid imagination, Donn even built a small restaurant in the limbs of the trees with table settings on them, covered by nipa-grass roofs. Winding stairways climbed up to the platforms where gourmet meals were served, allowing the view of activities below.

The Downward Slide

The International Market Place remained for many years the premier attraction in Waikīkī. As tourism grew, however, and both Donn and Pete Wimberly devoted their time to other projects, the standards deteriorated. The area became increasingly crowded as the owners sought to fill every square foot of space with revenue-producing shops. New stalls were jammed into open spaces without regard to density. A new breed of shopkeeper, who spoke little or no English, took over the Market Place, selling everything from junk jewelry to slippers and clothing made overseas in Taiwan and Hong Kong. The International Market Place, as it was conceived, deteriorated and today bears no resemblance to its original concept. But the ideas and images conceived by Donn Beach live on in the restaurants, nightclubs, and other venues in present-day Hawai'i, adding the exotic flavor of tropical romance that we have come to know as paradise.

— Arnold Bitner and Pheobe Beach (*Hawai'i's Tropical Rum Drinks and Cuisine by Don the Beachcomber*)

A Fond Reminiscence

Marlene Dietrich's Accident

The tiny Don's Beachcomber bar was often filled to overflowing capacity with motion picture stars, directors and producers, all of whom had heard about the place, thanks to Neil Vanderbilt, a roving reporter from the New York Tribune.

Just after eleven o'clock one evening following the completion of a film, Marlene Dietrich arrived at the Beachcomber's establishment with more than a dozen friends. People were already jammed around the little bar watching the original drunken mynah bird "Rajah" eat whiskey-soaked pieces of apple, in the end falling off his perch and stumbling while trying to walk along the bar. The Beachcomber had trained "Rajah" to say, "Give me a beer! Give me a beer! Give me a beer, stupid!"

Marlene took one of the empty stools the Beachcomber had reserved for her and her director. She watched intently while the Beachcomber began to mix what became her favorite drink, the "Beachcomber's Gold," in which he used 30-year-old Jamaican rum. When finished, the drink was poured over shave ice that had been tossed into a champagne glass and formed into the shape of a fan. The Beachcomber's Gold was simply exquisite, according to Marlene. As the Beachcomber handed Marlene her favorite drink, someone bumped her and the contents of the ice-cold drink spilled down the plunging neckline of her elegant gold-lamé gown.

There was no restroom in the Beachcomber's little bar. Customers had to go outside and through the hotel lobby, up a flight of stairs and down a hallway to get to one. And the restroom wasn't of proper size or a real ladies room at that. The Beachcomber quickly grabbed a towel and Marlene's arm, whisking her out of the bar and into the "Ladies Lounge." With the door open, he sat her down and handed her the towel, then turned to close the door to leave.

"For Christ's sake help me!" she said. "I can't get my gown off!" Standing in the wide-open doorway and feeling like an idiot, the Beachcomber began to gently pull her gown off her shoulders, when she suddenly grabbed the straps from his hand and yanked it down to her waist. She looked at him and said, "Don, dry me off, quickly!"

The Beachcomber took the bar towel from her lap and started very gingerly to dry, as he told it, "each of her beautiful, pearl-shaped breasts."

When she looked up and saw his face, she began to laugh, saying, "Don, you look like you've just seen a ghost."

"I have," he thought to himself. "And never a lovelier pair at that."

— Arnold Bitner and Pheobe Beach (*Hawai'i's Tropical Rum Drinks and Cuisine by Don the Beachcomber*)

Rise of the Tiki Culture

Romance of the Islands

Around the 1800s, embellished travel accounts started to appear, picturing Edenic islands, where natives lived in natural innocence, deities hid in carved statues, and graceful women danced with undulating hips.

When, in 1819, the Hawaiian religion collapsed and statues crumbled, when, soon after, the missionaries came and tried to suppress cultural traditions, including the hula, the early images of a simple, exotic paradise lingered in America. Hawai'i became a symbol of all that felt easy, romantic, carefree, good.

Vacation Paradise

In 1898, the United States claimed Hawai'i as a Territory, and, with it, its sultry myth—now within reach as a vacation paradise. Burdened under prohibition, an economic depression, and a heavy work ethic, Americans in the 1920s and 1930s ignited their fantasies with a popular culture based loosely on Hawaiiana ways.

Tourism in Hawai'i gradually took off, actively pushed by the Hawai'i Promotion Committee and its successors....Statehood in 1959 propelled pop culture into a mania.

Adopting Tikis

Stifled by the gray sobriety of their own country, striving for the Hawaiian neo-myth, hungering for a more passionate life, middle-class America adopted and adapted the image of the carved tiki, not in the least worried by its spiritual significance. In *The Book of Tiki*, an exuberant celebration of the tiki cult that evolved in America in the mid-1900s, author Sven A. Kirsten points out that Tiki, the god of creation, metamorphosed into Tiki, the god of recreation.

Tikis Invade the Mainland

Across America, jolly jungle establishments mushroomed—festive drinking holes resembling grass huts, adorned with

kapa, lauhala, glass balls, fish nets, coconuts, pineapples, hula dolls, and shell-studded lamps. Polynesian weapons, fearsome masks and flaming tiki torches added island passion. Tiki bowling alleys. Tiki hotels. Self-respecting people owned tiki stuff and celebrated at the tiki bar. They listened to tiki music in a tiki costume, and indulged in tiki foods and drinks. The new, happy-go-lucky tiki god reigned a good thirty years, and he was huge. Ubiquitous, modern tiki statues watched.

—Sophia V. Schweitzer (*Tiki of Hawai'i*)

Who Would Have Guessed
An Island Wedding

Billionaire Microsoft co-founder Bill Gates rented the entire island of Lāna'i for his wedding to Melinda French in 1994. He rented all 349 rooms in the three hotels, every golf course, and every helicopter on Maui to prevent the press from disrupting the ceremony. Their 15-minute wedding took place at the Manele Bay Hotel golf course on the 12th tee. Among the approximately 130 wedding guests were billionaire Warren Buffet, Microsoft co-founder and billionaire Paul Allen, Nextel billionaire Craig McCaw, Washington governor and U.S. senator Dan Evans, and *Washington Post* publisher Katharine Graham. Willie Nelson played at the reception. The whole shebang cost Bill more than a million bucks, which, of course, is pocket change to him.

Did you know...

Lāna'i used be called the Pineapple Island, but the pineapple plantation closed, so now they call it the Secluded Island or the Private Isle.

Hawaiian Crops
(2009)

Sugarcane, pineapples, and mac nuts are definitely associated with Hawai'i. So who would have expected Hawai'i's biggest crop by far to be genetically modified corn seed? With the other crops in decline, corn is taking over. While they can only grow one crop a year on the mainland, in Hawai'i they grow four.

Crop	# of Farms	Acreage Used	Amount Sold
Seed crops (96% of this is corn seed)	10	> 6,010[a]	$222,560,000
Flowers and nursery products	1,010	—[b]	$80,092,000
Pineapples (land used for pineapple)	40	Withheld[c]	Withheld[c]
Sugarcane, unprocessed (Maui and Kaua'i)	2	39,600	$44,200,000
Macadamia nuts	570	17,000	$29,400,000[d]
Coffee	830	8,000	$27,840,000[e]
Fruits, excluding pineapples	1,577	3,900	$25,373,000
Vegetables and melons (harvested acreage)	548	2,300	$22,410,000[f]
Taro	110	—[b]	$2,440,000
All other crops	Not given	20,700	Not given

[a] The state did not list this figure and they included the seed acreage under "all other crops," so this figure is from the USDA for the 2007-2008 season. For 2009, the number would be greater.

[b] This acreage is included under "all other crops."

[c] The state government withheld these to avoid disclosing the figures for a large operation.

[d] This number is for in-shell macadamia nuts only.

[e] This number is for parchment coffee only.

[f] This number includes ginger root and herbs, but the numbers for farms and acreage don't.

The Ghostly Woman of Makapu'u Beach

Glen Grant spent many years collecting supernatural accounts from people in Hawai'i. This excerpt from his book, *Chicken Skin Tales,* is about a mermaid-like spirit or a ghost that people claim they've seen at Makapu'u Beach, on the southeast corner of O'ahu. Makapu'u means "bulging eye."

The Woman in White

Several people have reported that as they were driving in the early hours of the morning along the road that winds past Makapu'u, they have seen a woman wearing a white dress along the side of the road. Sometimes she has been seen with a white dog. Then, just as you pass by her, she dashes in front of your car, vanishing right in front of your eyes.

Other people have seen her running along the Makapu'u Beach. As she runs along the wet shoreline, she leaves no footprints in the sand. On some occasions, she has been seen naked in the waters of Makapu'u, calling out into the night the name of the lone fisherman casting out his lines—calling him into the still, cold darkness of the sea, enticing him to join her in the realm of death and mystery.

She Attacks

One late night in the 1950s, four Farrington High School friends were walking along the shoreline at Makapu'u. As three of them ran off ahead, the fourth friend lagged behind looking for crabs that scurried across the sand at night. A piercing scream suddenly broke the stillness of the night, as the three young men turned around to watch horrified as their buddy was literally floating in the air! His body was being lifted up and into the sea as waves suddenly engulfed him, his screams now drowned out as he was pulled down into the dark waters of Makapu'u. Then an instant later, a crashing wave delivered him up, drenched and gasping to the beach.

"Where in the hell is that wahine?" he was screaming as he struggled to his feet. "I'll kill her! Where is she?"

"What lady?" his stunned friends replied.

"The one that dragged me into the ocean! I'll kill her. Where in the hell did she go?"

It took an hour of arguing to convince their very wet and frightened friend that there had been no woman on the beach that night. Still he insisted that a young Hawaiian girl in a long white dress had suddenly come out of the surf, grabbed him from the shoreline, lifted him up and thrown him into the crashing surf, and then tried to pull him down into the water. Fortunately an in-coming wave helped him break free of her grip, carrying him to safety on the beach.

—GLEN GRANT (*CHICKEN SKIN TALES*)

Say *What?!!*

Origins

The Book of Mormon says that in about 600 BC, a group of Jews (Nephites) sailed to the Americas, becoming the Native Americans, and that the Native Americans then populated the South Pacific. This would mean Native Hawaiians are Jewish. So far, the evidence points against this.

Eddie Would Go

You've seen the bumper stickers and the T-shirts that say, "Eddie would go." What does that mean?

Edward "Eddie" Ryan Makua Hanai Aikau was the first lifeguard hired to patrol the North Shore beaches, famous for their huge waves. He was fearless, heading out into thirty-foot waves for a rescue...but he was also supremely strong and skilled. No lives were lost on his watch.

Eddie Went

In 1978, Eddie joined the crew of the *Hōkūle'a*, a modern replica of the ancient Hawaiian voyaging canoes. They planned to sail from the Hawaiian Islands down to Tahiti, using only traditional navigation techniques. The canoe set out on March 16th and ran into bad luck the very same day. One of the hulls leaked and the canoe capsized south of Moloka'i. The crew clung to the capsized canoe all night, lighting flares, hoping that passing ships would see them. By mid-morning the next day, things were looking desperate. The *Hōkūle'a*, was drifting further and further from land. Eddie volunteered to paddle his surfboard to the island of Lāna'i, which he estimated as only twelve miles away. He thought he could make it in five hours or so.

The crew's officers were reluctant to let him risk his life, but Eddie insisted. He set off on his surfboard, a life jacket tied around his waist. He was never seen again.

The rest of the crew were lucky. They were spotted, and saved, by a Coast Guard cutter. The state mounted a giant air-sea search for Eddie, to no avail.

The Eddie

More than thirty years later, Eddie's heroism is still remembered. A prestigious surfing contest, the Quicksilver Big Wave Invitational in Memory of Eddie Aikau (the Eddie, for short) is held in Waimea Bay in years when ocean swells reach a minimum of twenty feet. It's said that the phrase "Eddie would go" comes from the first Eddie, when the waves were so high that organizers thought of calling off the competition. Surfer Mark Foo looked out at the monster waves and said, "Eddie would go." The Eddie was held and the phrase, "Eddie would go," testament to his courage, became an island catch-phrase.

—KAREN LOFSTROM

Chickens at the Beach

In Hawai'i, even chickens go to the beach. This couple prefers Anini Beach on North Shore Kaua'i. JOHN RICHARD STEPHENS

Humpbacks and Spinners

Hawai'i's Humpback Whales

In Hawaiian waters you can find more than twenty species of whales and dolphins, but generally only two are seen—spinner dolphins and humpback whales. The humpback whales migrate to the Northern Pacific, so they are only here for part of the year. A few begin to arrive in October and a few remain in April. Their population around Hawai'i peaks at about 10,000 in January and February. This is where they mate and have their babies.

The average humpback is about as large as a city bus, but at forty tons, it weighs a lot more than a bus, which weighs around twelve tons. A humpback whale's heart by itself weighs about 430 pounds, while its lungs are the size of a Volkswagen. Whale calves weigh three tons when they are born and are around sixteen feet long. They drink an amazing 75 gallons of milk a day, causing them to double in size within a year. Adults, when they're at their feeding grounds near Alaska, will eat one to three tons of plankton, krill, and small fish a day.

Spinner Dolphins

Spinner dolphins are here year round and are generally seen in sandy bays during the day. At night they dive for fish and squid, sometimes reaching depths up to 3,000 feet. It's so dark down there that they can't see and have to use echolocation to find their snacks. Like birds, when they sleep, only part of their brain goes to sleep, so they remain partially awake to watch for predators even when they're asleep. Groups of males are called "alliances," while groups of females are called "parties." Seven is the highest recorded number of spins made by a spinner while flying through the air.

At the Movies

O'ahu on the Silver Screen

Most of the movies and TV shows made in Hawai'i are made on O'ahu. These are some of those films and shows:

- *Battleship* (Liam Neeson; 2012)
- *The Descendants* (George Clooney; 2011)
- *Avatar* (Sam Worthington, Sigourney Weaver; 2009)
- *Princess Ka'iulani* (Q'orianka Kilcher; 2010)
- *Hawaii Five-O* (Daniel Dae Kim; 2010 TV series)
- *Jurassic Park III* (Sam Neill, Tea Leoni; 2000)
- *Lost* (Jorge Garcia; 2004 TV series)
- *Pirates of the Caribbean: On Stranger Tides* (Johnny Depp, Penélope Cruz; 2011)
- *Journey 2: The Mysterious Island* (Dwayne Johnson, Michael Caine; 2012)
- *Rise of the Planet of the Apes* (James Franco; 2011)
- *The Time Machine* (Guy Pearce; 2001)
- *Forgetting Sarah Marshall* (Kristen Bell; 2008)
- *Jurassic Park* (Sam Neill, Laura Dern, Jeff Goldblum; 1993)
- *Pearl Harbor* (Ben Affleck, Kate Beckinsale; 2001)
- *Pirates of the Caribbean: At World's End* (Johnny Depp; 2007)
- *Underwater* (Jane Russell and Gilbert Roland; 1955)
- *Along Came Polly* (Ben Stiller, Jennifer Aniston; 2004)
- *The Old Man and the Sea* (Spencer Tracy; 1958)
- *Twilight for the Gods* (Rock Hudson, Cyd Charisse; 1958)
- *The Rundown* (Dwayne Johnson, Christopher Walken; 2003)
- *The Master* (Philip Seymour Hoffman, Joaquin Phoenix; 2012)
- *Point Break* (Patrick Swayze, Keanu Reeves, Gary Busey; 1991)
- *Paradise, Hawaiian Style* (Elvis Presley; 1966)
- *Blue Hawaii* (Elvis Presley; 1961)
- *Baywatch* (David Hasselhoff, Pamela Anderson;

1989 TV series)

- *The Informant!* (Matt Damon; 2009)
- *Tears of the Sun* (Bruce Willis; 2003)
- *Godzilla* (Matthew Broderick; 1998)
- *Snakes on a Plane* (Samuel L. Jackson; 2006)
- *Gidget Goes Hawaiian* (James Darren; 1961)
- *Blue Crush* (Kate Bosworth; 2002)
- *Sphere* (Dustin Hoffman, Sharon Stone; 1997)
- *Magnum, P.I.* (Tom Selleck; 1980 TV series)
- *Hawaii Five-O* (Jack Lord; 1968 TV series)
- *Mighty Joe Young* (Bill Paxton; 1997)
- *Don Juan DeMarco* (Johnny Depp, Marlon Brando, Faye Dunaway; 1994)
- *You, Me and Dupree* (Kate Hudson, Owen Wilson, Matt Dillon; 2006)
- *Windtalkers* (Nicolas Cage; 2002)
- *The Karate Kid, Part II* (Pat Morita, Ralph Macchio; 1986)
- *The Final Countdown* (Kirk Douglas, Martin Sheen; 1980)
- *Tora! Tora! Tora!* (Martin Balsam; 1970)
- *From Here to Eternity* (Burt Lancaster, Montgomery Clift, Deborah Kerr; 1953)
- *The Big Bounce* (Owen Wilson, Morgan Freeman; 2004)
- *The Shaggy Dog* (Tim Allen; 2006)
- *Above the Law* (Steven Seagal, Pam Grier; 1988)
- *The Caine Mutiny* (Humphrey Bogart, José Ferrer; 1954)
- *Mutiny on the Bounty* (Marlon Brando, Trevor Howard, Richard Harris; 1962)
- *In Harm's Way* (John Wayne, Kirk Douglas; 1965)
- *Mister Roberts* (Henry Fonda, James Cagney, William Powell; 1955)
- *Krippendorf's Tribe* (Richard Dreyfuss; 1998)
- *Operation Pacific* (John Wayne; 1951)
- *Picture Bride* (Youki Kudoh; 1994)
- *The Wackiest Ship in the Army* (Jack Lemmon: 1960)
- *The Big Lift* (Montgomery Clift; 1950)
- *In the Navy* (Bud Abbott, Lou Costello; 1941)
- *Diamond Head* (Charlton Heston; 1963)
- *Feet First* (Harold Lloyd; 1930)

- *Pearl* (Angie Dickinson, Dennis Weaver, Robert Wagner; 1978 mini-series)
- *The Revolt of Mamie Stover* (Jane Russell 1956)
- *The Don Ho Show* (1976 TV series)

Movie Theaters of Old Honolulu

Off to the Picture Show

The moving pictures, or ki'i 'oni'oni, came to the islands in February 1897, when a few short vignettes were screened at the old Honolulu Opera house. By 1906, Honolulu had its first movie theater, the Orpheum. By the 1920s, films from the new Hollywood film industry were being shipped by boat from Los Angeles to Hawai'i, where they played in the movie theaters that were springing up everywhere: large towns, small towns, suburbs, and military bases. The large island immigrant population also enjoyed films imported from China, Japan, and the Philippines.

Movie Palaces

The biggest, fanciest movie palaces were built in downtown Honolulu, then the largest shopping, dining, and entertainment venue in the islands. (Hard to believe, now that it's all business and skyscrapers.)

One of the largest of these theaters was the Hawaii Theatre, opened in 1922 on the site of the old Bijou Theater. The owner, Consolidated Amusements, had spared no expense: the neoclassical building featured gilded columns, decorative grilles, and hand-painted murals. It played to large crowds for many years, but by the 1970s and 1980s, television had thinned movie audiences and the aging theater ceased to turn a profit. It was closed in 1984 and was rumored to be slated for demolition. Local citizens sprang to its defense. Surely this piece of Honolulu history should be saved from the wrecking ball! After several years of determined fund-raising, enough was raised to buy the theater and later to carry out a $22 million renovation. It re-opened as a performing arts center in 1996.

Another well-known downtown theater, the Princess Theatre, was one of the first in the U.S. to offer stadium seating: the floor sloped toward the screen, so that those in back had a better view. It opened in 1922, on the site of the old Orpheum Theater. Hawaii Pacific University now stands on the site.

King Theater, on King Street between Smith and Fort Streets, is said to have been one of the high-class theaters. It also is long gone.

Japanese Theaters

The old Toyo Theater, on College Walk, is still standing. This Japanese-style building was modeled on the Tōshō-gū shrine in Nikko. It opened in 1938 and showed Japanese movies. By the late 1960s, it was reduced to showing adult movies and in imminent danger of demolition. Scenic Hawaii, Inc. raised enough money to purchase and preserve it. It is now used for meetings and stage shows.

Another Japanese cinema, remembered as "the old Kokusai" used to stand next to the Toyo. Some time in the 1930s the Kokusai moved to a site at Beretania and Nu'uanu, where locals knew it as "the new Kokusai." Later the theater was modernized, renamed the Empress, and switched to Chinese martial arts movies. The building was eventually sold to a church; it is still standing.

More Honolulu Cinemas

Other downtown theaters included the States, Aala, and Palama; the Liberty and Golden Harvest, which showed Chinese movies; the Nippon, with Japanese movies; and the Zamboanga, which showed Filipino cinema.

There were theaters all over O'ahu and the Honolulu suburbs in the pre-television days; most of them have been torn down or repurposed. Three that deserve mention are the Pawaa, the Varsity, and the Waikiki.

The Pawaa, at South King and Punahou, opened in 1929. In 1962, it was remodeled for wide-screen films and renamed the Cinerama. Many Honolulu old-timers remember standing in line to see the *Star Wars* movies there. The theater closed in 1999; it is now an auto parts store.

The Varsity, on University Avenue, opened in 1939 as a single-screen theater. In the 1980s it was divided in half, becoming a two-screen theater. Several generations of University of Hawai'i students knew it both as an occasional lecture hall and as an art cinema. It was shut down in 2007.

The old Waikiki Theater on Kalākaua Avenue, in Waikīkī, opened in 1936. It featured a spacious courtyard entry, with a large fountain. Inside, a rainbow curved over the proscenium arch and fake coconut palms lined the walls. The theater served tourists—most of them wealthy, in those days before trans-Pacific air traffic—and locals who wanted a night out in luxe surroundings. Rising real estate prices doomed the theater. It was closed in November of 2002 and demolished in 2005, to be replaced by a shopping center.

—KAREN LOFSTROM

Way Back in the Day

Honolulu's Plague of Horses

The first horses in Hawai'i were given to King Kamehameha I in 1803 and he was not quite sure what to make of them. By 1854 they were becoming a problem. A committee of the Royal Hawaiian Agricultural Society submitted a report that said:

> In making up a report on horses the first thing we wish particularly to call attention to, is the lamentable increase of the miserable creatures to be seen every day in the streets of Honolulu and in all the horse breeding districts on the Islands. Horses are evidently fast becoming a curse and nuisance to the country and to most of their owners, especially to the lower classes of natives.

> About one-half of the horses on the Island are never used for any purpose but multiplication—are never bitted or backed—are born, live and die without being of any advantage to anyone, or having served any purpose, useful or ornamental, but the impoverishment of the land, and the propagation of the nuisance.

The Singing Fighter Pilot

R. Alex Anderson (1894-1995). FROM
A CENTURY OF ALOHA, ANDERSON FAMILY

Shot Down and Captured

Born in Honolulu in 1894, R. Alex Anderson graduated from Punahou School and Cornell University before becoming a fighter pilot in France during World War I, where he was wounded during a dog fight over enemy territory.

Describing how he was shot from behind by German in a Fokker biplane, he recounted, "Something stung me in the back and a red hot needle pierced my left knee. Over my shoulder I caught sight of him directly on my tail. He was so close that I thought he would run me down. An instant later I was diving under him. Vertically down I fell. As in a nightmare I saw the ground rush at me."

After crash landing, he was captured by the Germans, but eventually escaped, sneaking through Belgium to safety. He went on to become a successful businessman, introducing both elevators and air conditioners to the Hawaiian Islands.

Writing Popular Songs

Anderson is best known for the songs he wrote. He had no formal training, but that didn't stop him from writing almost 200 of them. Some were recorded by his friend and frequent golf partner, Bing Crosby. Crosby sang Anderson's "Mele Kalikimaka" with the Andrews Sisters on the flip side of the 1949 remake of his "White Christmas" single. Anderson's other songs include "Christmas in Hawaii," "The Merriest Hawaiian Christmas," "Lovely Hula Hands," "Lei of Stars," "Blue Lei," "I'll Weave a Lei of Stars for You," "I Will Remember You," "On a Coconut Island," "Hula Moon," and "The Cockeyed Mayor of Kaunakakai." In 1939, Mary Pickford said to him, "I never heard a song for this flower," so he wrote "White Ginger Blossoms" for her.

He died in 1995, just short of his 101st birthday, but he'll always be remembered through his classic Hawaiian songs.

What Does it Mean?

Hybolics

Hybolics is one Pidgin word, short fo' da english hyperbolic, or da use of hyperbole—da exaggerated form of speech. Long time ago wen Pidgin to da Max came out, da ting wen define hybolics as "to talk like one intellectual-kine haole." Built into dis definition is da assumption dat only Caucasian people talk standard english and standard english automatically means mo' intellectual. By taking da name Hybolics wot we tryin' fo' do is reclaim da word and make da statement dat you can use Pidgin jus as well fo' express da kine intellectual ideas.

—LEE TONOUCHI

Mix and Match

Laughter

Here in Hawaii we laugh at ourselves more than most people do in other places. Hawaii is a chop suey nation—Portagee, Pake, Buddhahead, Sole, Yobo, Kanaka, Haole, all mixed up. Nobody is in the majority here. We are all part of at least one minority group. Some of us are part of several minority groups. And we all laugh at ourselves. This is healthy.

—FRANK DELIMA

Misunderstanding Hula

Two Different Views

The hula was never as risqué as early prudish visitors claimed, or perhaps hoped for. The fact that the first Western audiences were sailors didn't help. To begin with, the captains of the ships insisted the dances only be performed for their men at night. In a way this makes sense. They needed the sailors to work during the day and the best time for relaxation was in the evening. Unfortunately this made the dances seem more suggestive. It was also unfortunate that the captains insisted that only the women dance. Perhaps this was because, having been cooped up with a bunch of men for the long voyages, they just didn't want to watch men dance. Perhaps they weren't really interested in the dancing at all and just wanted to watch topless women. If so, the Hawaiians would never have realized this. Nudity, particularly when swimming, was a common everyday occurrence, but to sailors coming from a repressive society, it would have been salacious. Remember, at that time most people in Western society considered it indecent if a woman exposed her ankles to view.

It's too bad that something that had great meaning to one people, would have been seen in such a completely different light by those from another culture. The sailors and early visitors just didn't get it. They totally missed what makes hula significant. The missionaries were even further off mark, and that's one of the reasons why they banned it. Even today many people think only women dance the hula, which is sad considering that the men are just as talented as the women.

Synchronicity

Mark Twain may have realized this—he was more perceptive than most—but as a satirist and humorist, he was playing along with Western expectations when he wrote,

> "At night they feasted and the girls danced the lascivious hula hula—a dance that is said to exhibit

the very perfection of educated motion of limb and arm, hand, head and body, and the exactest uniformity of movement and accuracy of 'time.' It was performed by a circle of girls with no raiment on them to speak of, who went through an infinite variety of motions and figures without prompting, and yet so true was their 'time,' and in such perfect concert did they move that when they were placed in a straight line, hands, arms, bodies, limbs, and heads waved, swayed, gesticulated, bowed, stooped, whirled, squirmed, twisted, and undulated as if they were part and parcel of a single individual; and it was difficult to believe they were not moved in a body of some exquisite piece of mechanism."

Literary Masters

Swimming as a Spectator Sport

In 1866 Mark Twain visited Captain Cook's monument in Kealakekua Bay on the Big Island. After checking out the nearby ruins of Hikiau Heiau, he wrote:

> At noon I observed a bevy of nude native young ladies bathing in the sea, and went and sat down on their clothes to keep them from being stolen. I begged them to come out, for the sea was rising and I was satisfied that they were running some risk. But they were not afraid, and presently went on with their sport. They were finished swimmers and divers, and enjoyed themselves to the last degree. They swam races, splashed and ducked and tumbled each other about, and filled the air with their laughter. It is said that the first thing an islander learns is how to swim; learning to walk being a matter of smaller consequence, comes afterward.
>
> —MARK TWAIN

The Things, They are a Changin'
Paul Theroux on Hawai'i

Although many of its birds and flora have been wiped out by humans or alien species, Hawaii's other Edenic attributes are just about indestructible. I keep telling myself that no one can taint the orchidaceous air, or flatten the gigantic sea cliffs, or still the great waves, or obliterate the rainbows.

—PAUL THEROUX

The Adventure Continues
The Future of the Islands

The Hawaiian Islands are very slowly eroding away. Wind, rain, waves, all take their toll on the isles, but it is slow. As U.S. Geological Survey Director Marcia McNutt pointed out, "The inevitable fate of the Hawaiian Islands millions of years into the future is seen to the northwest in the spires of French Frigate Shoals and the remnants of other once mighty islands, ancestors of today's Hawaii, but now sunken beneath the sea through the forces of waves, rivers, and the slow subsidence of the seafloor."

But by then, new islands will have formed to the southeast.

Did you know...

The opening scene in the movie *Die Another Day*, where James Bond and two companions surf in on monster waves, was filmed at Jaws on Maui's North Coast.

Early Contact

First Western Contact

If Captain Cook was not the first of European navigators to discover the Hawaiian Islands, he was at least the first to chart and make their existence known to the world. It has been pretty satisfactorily established that Juan Gaetano, the captain of a Spanish galleon sailing from the Mexican coast to the Spice Islands, discovered the group as early as 1555. But he did not make his discovery known at the time, and the existence of an old manuscript chart in the archives of the Spanish government is all that remains to attest his claim to it.

After Cook

The first to arrive after the death of Captain Cook were the English ships *King George* and *Queen Charlotte,* and the same year a French exploring squadron touched at Maui. In 1787 several trading vessels visited the group, and the natives began to barter provisions and sandal-wood for firearms and other weapons of metal.

Captain Vancouver

In 1792, and again in 1793, Captain Vancouver, of an English exploring squadron, touched and remained for some time at the islands. He landed sheep, goats and horned cattle, and distributed a quantity of fruit and garden seeds.

Discovery of Honolulu

The harbor of Honolulu was first discovered and entered by two American vessels in 1794, and it soon became a favorite resort for the war, trading and whaling vessels of all nations.

—ROLLIN MALLORY DAGGETT (U.S. CONGRESSMAN AND MINISTER TO THE HAWAIIAN ISLANDS IN 1882)

An Island Treasure

Duke on Aloha

In Hawai'i, we greet friends, loved ones or strangers with aloha, which means with love. Aloha is the key word to the universal spirit of real hospitality, which makes Hawai'i renowned as the world's center of understanding and fellowship. Try meeting or leaving people with Aloha. You'll be surprised by their reaction. I believe it and it is my creed. Aloha to you.

—DUKE KAHANAMOKU

Did you know...

Duke Kahanamoku competed in four Olympics from 1912 to 1932, setting three world records, while winning three gold medals, two silver, and one bronze.

"Well, at least it took Tarzan to beat me."
—Duke Kahanamoku, commenting on his second place finish to Johnny Weismuller at the 1924 Paris Oympics

Traditional Saying

O ke aloha ke kuleana o kāhi malihini.

("Love is the host in strange lands." In the old days, Hawaiians greeted everyone, even strangers, and offered them food. Generosity is highly valued in Hawaiian society.)

Who Needs Snail Bait

Snail Hunters

While most caterpillars are vegetarian, Hawai'i is the only place in the world where carnivorous caterpillars hunt snails. These rare caterpillars track down their prey and wrap it up in silk so it can't escape or shut itself inside its shell. They then begin to eat the snail alive, gradually crawling up into the shell until the snail's entire body is consumed, leaving an empty shell. Once this feast is over, they undergo a metamorphosis, turning into moths.

Picky Eaters

Of course they only do this as juveniles. Once they become adults they presumably progress to a liquid diet, like most other moths and butterflies. But as young caterpillars, they are picky and refuse to eat anything but snails. They will even starve to death rather than eat a salad. Sound familiar?

Gourmet Caterpillars

With roughly 150,000 known species of moths and butterflies, there are only two that do this, and both live in Hawai'i. One species was initially found in the Makawao Forest Reserve on Maui, but has since been seen on Moloka'i, among the rocks of fresh lava flows on the Big Island, and in forests on the slopes of Mauna Kea. Amazingly these two species evolved this predilection independently of each other. Snails and caterpillars live together throughout the world and there is definitely no shortage of vegetation on the islands, so scientists are hard at work trying to discover why only gourmet Hawaiian caterpillars have abandoned their leafy greens for *escargot au naturel.*

Snails' Revenge

Snails that Harpoon Fish

There is a sea snail that hunts fish by shooting it with something like a harpoon that injects poison. It paralyzes the fish, which it then spends up to two weeks eating. These are cone snails and they can be found throughout the Indian and Pacific oceans, usually around coral reefs. The tops of their shells are found on Hawai'i's beaches and are known as puka shells. The waves break off most of the shell, leaving just the tops. Often the tip is worn off so the puka shell has a hole in the middle. Puka shells generally come from smaller cone snails, but there are many others. In Hawai'i there are more than 33 kinds, only some of which are venomous.

How It Works

Cone snails are usually active at dawn and dusk, but some are nocturnal. Their harpoons are actually a modified barbed tooth that is sometimes serrated with which they inject their venom. Called a radula, it looks very much like a harpoon. They probe the water with their long, tube-like proboscis until they encounter their prey. Their proboscis can extend to more than twice the length of its body. They use it like a blow-gun to shoot the harpoon at around 400 miles per hour. In comparison, that's more than half as fast as the speed of sound—about 700 mph depending on the temperature—and much faster than a Lamborghini, which tops out at 220 mph.

As soon as the snail harpoons its prey, it starts pumping in venom and then reloads with another harpoon. It's much wider tube-like mouth engulfs the prey, which is usually too large to bring inside its shell.

Just Don't Back Them into a Corner

They don't usually attack people unless they feel threatened. Fortunately the deadliest one—*Conus geographus*—is *not* found in Hawai'i. Each of those snails can carry enough venom to kill ten people and it can kill someone within five minutes. It's said there are people in Guam who, when stung, will immediately chop off their arm or leg with a machete in order to save their lives.

The Weirder and the Wilder

No Killer Snails on These Islands

Tangling with Snails

There are snails that kill people, but they are not found in Hawai'i. There are some in Hawai'i that can make you ill, but chances are extremely slim that a snail will kill you. Perhaps if you're weak, have health issues, or are allergic to snail venom, then you might want to be careful. Still, chances of encountering one are very rare. For the most part, the people who tangle with poisonous cone snails are scuba diving, collecting shells with the critters still in them. There don't seem to be reports of any deaths here, but on rare occasions people get sick.

Getting a Taste of Snail Venom

An interesting account of a severe case can be found in the August 1, 1956, issue of the *Hawaiian Malacological Society Shell News*, which was written by a friend of someone who was stung in western O'ahu:

"He was diving off Nanakuli seeking shells in the sand bottom. Noticing a shell half buried in the sand he picked it up, when almost immediately the cone stung him on his middle finger. Despite sucking the wound to draw out any poison, within fifteen minutes he developed a bad headache. During the next twelve hours at home he was extremely nauseated, followed by painful stomach cramps through the night. He stated that shortly after the initial sting he experienced a noticeable shortness of breath, almost, as he described it, as if someone was sitting on his chest. By the next morning these symptoms had ceased but the wounded finger continued to pain him."

First Aid for Snail Stings

Even this seems to be unusual. A Hawaiian first aid book called *All Stings Considered* notes, "Most cone snail punctures in Hawaii are not dangerous, and require no specific treatment other than thorough scrubbing of the wound." Although if any symptoms, like those of that diver develop, they recommend going to the emergency room. If possible, bringing the offending snail along too, being particularly careful not to be stung again. It's best to put cone snails in a wood, metal, or glass container, as they might harpoon you through anything else. Hawaiians shake shells when they pick them up in order to confuse the creature, just in case it's a cone snail. That way they won't be stung right away.

Benefits from Venomous Snails

On the positive side, researchers at the University of Hawai'i are using cone snail venom to develop new pain-killing drugs, one of which "is 1,000 times more potent then morphine, with no development of addiction, tolerance or major side effects." They are also using the venom to develop new pesticides.

Did you know...

Ancient Hawaiian traditions tell of snails that sing, whistle, or chirp, which is unlikely since they don't have vocal chords, ears, or enough lung capacity, but you never know.

James Michener's *Hawaii*

Many visitors to the islands get their first taste of Hawaiian history before they even leave home with James Michener's 1959 novel, *Hawaii.* Released the same year Hawai'i achieved statehood, Michener's dramatic novel begins thirty million years ago with the volcanic origin of the Hawaiian Islands, then takes readers through Polynesian settlement, the arrival of American Protestant missionaries, the era of sugar plantations, mass immigration, Pearl Harbor, and the years leading up to statehood.

Although a work of fiction, *Hawaii*'s characters and events are based on reality, and placed within the context of actual history. In the years since *Hawaii* was first published, numerous historians have criticized Michener's subjective interpretations of Hawaiian history—particularly his scorching portrayal of the stern, unyielding missionaries. Yet more than half-a-century after it first hit bookstores, Michener's *Hawaii* is still a national favorite and continues to be one of the most-read dramatic depictions of the Hawaiian Islands.

—CARRIE CHING (*THINGS HAWAI'I*)

James Michener and Hawai'i

In the South Pacific

James Albert Michener (1907–1997) first came to the islands during WWII, when he served in the navy. He traveled widely in the Pacific and after the war ended, published a book of stories inspired by his travels. *South Pacific* became a best-seller and Michener became a full-time writer.

A Novel about Hawai'i

He returned to the islands in 1958, planning to write a novel about Hawai'i. The novel wouldn't just be *set* in the islands; it would be an episodic novel *about* the islands, from their volcanic birth to Polynesian settlement to Western contact and present-day island society. He interviewed, read tirelessly at the Hawaiian Mission Children's Society Library, typed hundreds of pages, and listened and rewrote when local friends criticized.

The book was published in 1959 and despite its daunting size (937 pages in hardcover), it was an immediate success. The book is still in print, still read, and has sold millions of copies. It has been translated into thirty-two languages and has been dramatized in two movies: *Hawai'i,* 1966, with Max von Sydow and Julie Andrews, and *The Hawaiians,* 1970, with Charlton Heston.

Critics Trashed It

Critics panned the book; it was full of cardboard characters, they said, and humdrum journalistic prose. There were other critics right here in the islands: they felt that he had been unfair to their own versions of Hawaiian history and society. The Protestant missionaries who arrived in 1820 were depicted as intellectually limited, and culturally insensitive (if hard-working and brave); some of the Asian characters were less than noble; many of the missionary-descendent characters from the last chapter, set in the 1950s, were pompous and self-serving.

Against the Establishment

Michener did arrive in the islands with a definite point of view. He was a Democrat, while the white island establishment was staunchly Republican. He believed in multi-culturalism, while the establishment believed in keeping Asians in their place. His experiences here only strengthened his views. His Japanese-American wife, Mari, experienced even more discrimination here than she had faced on the mainland, which surprised and upset him.

A Refreshing Change

Michener's book was published in the same year that the islands achieved statehood. In the following years, Democrats took over state government, anti-Japanese prejudice dwindled, and Hawai'i became more and more like the cosmopolitan melting-pot he believed it could be.

—Karen Lofstrom

What Does the Future Hold?
The New Century

When I worked in Hawai'i, over a period of some twelve years, 1950-62, my wife and I lived part of the time in a cliffside house atop a rise in Pupukea overlooking O'ahu's north shore, and there in the evenings after quitting the typewriter, I would sit on the lanai and study the ocean waves as they thundered on the beach. I saw storms bend palm trees and tides sweep inland to engulf the roads, but also I saw times when the ocean was as calm as the surface of a mirror with stars and a rising moon dancing on the waters. In those quiet times I often speculated on what the future of these heavenly islands might be. Seventy years from then, in the middle of a new century, would Hawai'i still represent the acme of what can be accomplished when men and women who love beauty and know how to protect it, and how to discipline themselves and their society? Or would it deteriorate to a bruised land, overcrowded, scarred with junk and devoid of beauty? I saw then that its future could develop in either direction, depending on the will of the people to protect the wonders they had inherited, and I could not decide what the chances were for beauty to prevail.

—James A. Michener (A. Grove Day, Mad About Hawai'i)

Legend of the *Maneki Neko*

This Maneki Neko holds a gold coin that says "one million ryo," which is an extremely large sum of money.
JOHN RICHARD STEPHENS

There's a legend that in the 1600s, there was an impoverished temple in Tokyo's Setagaya ward that was in the care of a starving monk who had a cat named Tama. One day Lord Ii Naotaka, the second lord of Hikone Castle near Kyoto in the Shiga Prefecture, was returning from a falconry trip when rain caused him to seek shelter under a tree near the temple. From there he spotted Tama at the entrance to the temple's grounds, beckoning him to come inside. The sight was so strange that he began to follow the cat. As he did, the tree was knocked down by lightning. He credited the cat with saving his life and he became the temple's patron. The temple prospered and statues of the *Maneki Neko* were placed around the grounds, while paintings of Japanese Bobtail cats decorated the walls. In 1697 it was renamed Gōtokuji Temple. When Tama died, he was buried in the temple's cat cemetery, while Lord Ii Naotaka's grave is nearby in the human cemetery.

Maneki Neko figures are still sold there today, while on display are many *Maneki Neko* that have been donated to the temple as thanks by owners who believed they had been served well by their Lucky Cats.

Destroying the System

King Kamehameha II. Hawai'i State Archives

The End of the Kapu

It's believed the kapu system began with the arrival of the second wave of Polynesians between 1000 and 1300 AD from Tahiti. It lasted until October 1819 when Liholiho, who, when he became king, took the name Kamehameha II, sat down to eat dinner at the women's table, under the influence of his mother and his father's queen. By eating with the women and giving them forbidden food, the kapu was broken. This happened in Kailua-Kona on the Big Island and was largely the result of power struggles following the death of Kamehameha I and the women's desire to be treated equally.

Facing the Wrath of the Gods

Breaking the kapu was not an easy thing for King Kamehameha II to do, as he really wasn't sure whether the gods would strike him down. He had to drink quite a bit of alcohol to calm his nerves and build up the courage to sit at the women's table.

Liholiho's Real Name

A quick side note: Actually it's not quite correct that Liholiho took the name Kamehameha II on assuming the throne. It's a bit more accurate to say that he took the name Kalani Kalei'aimoku o Kaiwikapu o La'amea i Kauikawekiu Ahilapalapa Keali'i Kauinamoku o Kahekili Kalaninui i Mamao 'Iolani i Ka Liholiho, but they called him Kamehameha II for short.

 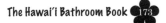

Birds in Flight and Underground

Both the 'Ua'u and the 'A'o birds—pronounced "oo-ah oo" and "ah oh"—were given their names because of the sounds they make when laying their square eggs. Just kidding.

Call Them 'Ua'u

A long time ago, the sky would turn dark when a flock of 'Ua'u birds took flight. Now there aren't many left. Some call them Hawaiian Dark-Rumped Petrels, but probably not to their face. These birds nest in holes in the ground, which are mainly found on Kaua'i and Haleakalā—Maui's largest mountain. They spend almost their entire lives in flight, except when underground. Sometimes utilizing existing crevices and lava tubes, their nesting chambers can be up to thirty feet deep.

Kīlauea Lighthouse on northeast Kaua'i. JOHN RICHARD STEPHENS

Birds with Their Own Sound System

'A'o birds faintly resemble seagulls, but are black with a white undercarriage. Also known by the less interesting name of Newell's Shearwater, they also nest in burrows. They used to be common on all the islands, but now they're an endangered species and only have their chicks high in the mountains of Kaua'i. This is primarily because when they try to raise their babies elsewhere, they get eaten by introduced animals, such as rats, dogs, cats, and mongooses. Also, lights from urbanization tend to blind them at night causing them to crash into things, particularly the ground, so they pretty much stick to Kaua'i. In order to encourage them, the Kīlauea Point National Wildlife Refuge set up a sound system that plays 'A'o noises throughout the night so the 'A'os feel like there are more of them than there actually are.

Going, Going, Gone
The Road to Extinction

A good many other bird cries are now not heard at all. In *The Redbook of Rare and Endangered Fish and Wildlife of the United States,* almost half the species listed are Hawaiian. Of all the birds in the world that have gone extinct in modern times, about 15 percent are Hawaiian. The state bird, the nēnē, the Hawaiian goose, has been brought back from the edge of extinction by most laborious effort over the last decade or so. But every time a mangrove swamp is filled, a Hawaiian fishpond drained and dredged for a marina, a housing subdivision, a golf course—every time a military road is cut through an upland forest and half-tracks grind a habitat to pieces, it becomes just so much harder to be a Hawaiian plant or bird or animal.

—GAVAN DAWS (*A HAWAIIAN ANTHOLOGY*, ED. JOSEPH STANTON)

Traditional Saying

The prayer of the Kahuna (priest) is like a worm, it lies in the dust until the day it moves on.

Did you know...

Maui is known as the Valley Isle, the Magic Isle, and the Hunchbacked Island, because its shape on a map resembles an old hunchbacked person.

Literary Masters
The Spirit of Aloha

Hawaii and the Hawaiians are a land and a people loving and lovable. By their language may ye know them, and in what other land save this one is the commonest form of greeting, not "Good day," nor "How d'ye do," but "Love?" That greeting is Aloha—love, I love you, my love to you. Good day—what is it more than an impersonal remark about the weather? How do you do—it is personal in a merely casual interrogative sort of a way. But Aloha! It is a positive affirmation of the warmth of one's own heart-giving. My love to you! I love you! Aloha!

—JACK LONDON (STORIES OF HAWAII)

Did you know...

The ancient Hawaiians placed lei on their chiefs as a sign of affection.

Jack London

John Griffith London (1876-1916), adventurer and popular author, sailed his self-designed ketch *Snark* from San Francisco to Honolulu in 1907, and with his wife, Charmian, spent five months touring the islands before embarking on a two-year cruise of the South Seas.

Jack learned to ride a surfboard at Waikīkī, was entertained by Prince Jonah Kuhio and the deposed Queen Liliuokalani, and rode around O'ahu. He and Charmian visited Haleakalā Ranch on the island of Maui and Jack wrote a graphic chapter in *The Cruise of the Snark* (New York: Macmillan, 1911) concerning their trip through the "House of the Sun," the dormant crater of Haleakala. They stayed at the celebrated Parker Ranch on the Big Island and watched the bubbling fire pit of Halema'uma'u at Kīlauea Volcano. A visit to the isolation colony on Moloka'i elicited another chapter about the leper residents there. Three of the six stories in his *The House of Pride* (1912) concern leprosy, and his hosts in Hawai'i chastised him for dwelling heavily on this aspect of island life.

Two stories in *The House of Pride* are outstanding. "Koolau the Leper," a fictionized version of an actual episode in 1893, gave London a chance to show a strong personality eventually defeated by all the forces of law. "Chun Ah Chun," deriving from his knowledge of the noted Afong family of Honolulu, is a charming story concerning the sagacity of a wealthy Oriental paterfamilias of a large brood of marriageable daughters.

—A. GROVE DAY (*BOOKS ABOUT HAWAII: FIFTY BASIC AUTHORS*)

 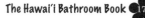

Words of Love and Romance

Eighteen Ways to Say, "I Love You"

1. Aloha. ("Love.")
2. Aloha kāua. (Used as a greeting to one person. It means, "May there be friendship or love between us.")
3. Aloha kākou. (This greeting means the same thing but is addressed to a group.)
4. Ko'u aloha ("My Love.") or Ia iho ke aloha. ("To my love.")
5. Ku'u Lei. ("My beloved.")
6. Ku'uipo. ("Sweetheart.")
7. Kipona aloha. ("Deep love.")
8. Nau ko'u aloha. ("My love is yours.")
9. Aloha nui loa. ("All my love.")
10. Na'u 'oe. ("You're mine.")
11. Ia iho ke aloha. ("To my love.")
12. Me ke aloha pumehana. ("With the warmth of my love.")
13. Ka honi mai me ke aloha. ("And with love is a kiss.")
14. Ma'ane'i no ke aloha. ("For love is here and now.")
15. Ko aloha makamae e ipo. ("Sweetheart, you are so precious.")
16. 'O ku'u aloha no 'oe. ("You are indeed my love.")
17. Aloha no au ia 'oe. ("I truly love you.")
18. Aloha aku no, aloha mai no. ("I give my love to you, you give your love to me")

Wedding Sentiments

- Male 'ana. ("Wedding.")
- E hoomau maua kealoha. ("May our love last forever.")
- No kau a kau. ("For eternity.")
- No keia la, no keia po, a mau loa. ("From this day, from this night, forever more.")
- I ho'okāhi kāhi ke aloha. ("Be one in love," or be united by affection.)
- Pilialoha. (To be in the bond of love.)
- Ua hilo 'ia i ke aho a ke aloha. ("Braided with the cords of love.")

- Ua ʻuo ʻia a paʻa. ("Tied fast together," as in marriage. ʻUo refers to tying feathers together when preparing to make a lei.)
- Awaiāulu ke aloha. ("Love made fast by tying together," referring to marriage.)
- Male ana e pili mai aloha kaua. ("We two will cling to love in marriage.")
- Hoʻi hou ke aloha. ("Let us fall in love all over again.")
- Ua ola loko i ke aloha. (Love gives life within, meaning love is essential for physical and mental well-being.)
- I ka noho pu ana a ʻike i ke aloha. (It's only after living together than one learns the meaning of love.)
- Pili kau, pili hoʻoilo. ("Together in the dry season, together in the wet season.")
- Koʻekoʻe ka pōhoa ʻole. ("Nights are cold without a mate.")

Romantic Expressions
- Honi. ("Kiss.")
- Nou no ka ʻiʻini. ("I desire you.")
- Paʻipunahele. (An expression of love for a favorite lover.)
- ʻOno kāhi ʻao lūʻau me ke aloha pū. ("A little taro green is delicious when love is present," meaning that something plain tastes delicious when you're in love.)
- Ua kaʻa niniau i ka wili wai. ("Swirled about by the eddying waters." This refers to the feeling of being madly in love, but it can also mean someone is intoxicated or drunk.)

Did you know...

As an actor, Duke Kahanamoku appeared in fifteen films. His roles include an Indian chief, a pirate captain, and the "Devil-Ape."

Making Sugar

The following interesting account of the inner workings of a sugar mill was written by J. M. Lydgate in 1918:

Boyhood Experiences in Hilo

My first boyish acquaintance with the sugar business began, I should say, in the fall of 1864. We had landed in Honolulu, our family and that of Alex Young, from Vancouver Island, in April, 1864, and after a short stay in Honolulu moved to Hilo [on the windward side of the Big Island], where the firm of Lydgate and Young inaugurated a small ironworks to minister to the needs of the sugar plantations along the Hilo coast.

Immediately back of Hilo, on the Pu'ueo side, was the Amaulu Plantation owned by Chinese. The mill was about half a mile from town, and naturally an inquiring boy was not long in finding it and in developing a good deal of interest in it.

The Crusher

It was, of course, a very primitive affair. The crusher was water driven, by means of a large overshot water-wheel, I should say about 20 feet in diameter, which rattled and groaned and splashed mightily, like some weary Hercules. The rollers were iron ones, about fifteen inches in diameter, by perhaps two and a half feet long. The cane was fed into the mill by hand, from the pile in the yard, over an apron; a very circumspect feed carefully delivered, lest the mill be choked and some accident happen. There was no fly-wheel to act as a reservoir of power, though the water-wheel itself served that purpose in a measure, and of course there was no provision for reversing, a very necessary expedient in such a mill.

The Boiling House

From the mill a scanty stream of juice ran in an open spout to the boiling house, which stood by itself some little distance away. Here was installed the open train, a series of four or five pots, five or six feet in diameter, diminishing in size somewhat to the final one of the series. These pots were shaped somewhat like an opihi shell, or like the Chinese rice pots comparatively shallow and wide flaring, and were coupled, lip to lip, by bolts through an intervening flange, the whole forming a range, set in brick walls, within which, and under the pots, a fierce fire was kept going. For this purpose the bagasse was insufficient and had to be reinforced by wood, and the liveliest job on the plantation was that of stoker, a poor unfortunate who was always being pai-pai-d or stirred up, in language as forcible as it was sometimes profane. The fierce fire kept these pots in a state of violent ebulition, while a Hawaiian attendant, nearly nude and sweating like a Turk, stood by with a long sweep to sweep off the scum from the top of the foaming juice. The vision through the open doorway into the dim interior with the dusky naked figures silhouetted against the great volumes of steam that rolled up into the dark recesses of the open rafters, and hung there to trickle back in large drops of sugar sweetened rain, would have been worthy the brush of a modern Rembrandt.

Meanwhile, as the density was somewhat increased by the rapid evaporation, the liquid was baled over into the next pot, where further cleaning and further evaporation went on, until finally, in the last pot it was boiled to "proof," the density necessary for graining. This point in the process was determined by the Chinese sugar boiler, who, with a long thin stick dipped into the pot, took out a proof, and trailed off a slender little stream into a large opihi shell full of water. And then taking the sample between thumb and finger, and holding up to the light he judged of its fitness for "strike." When that point was reached, the mass in this last pot was bailed out into a spout, that by the necessary connections, conveyed it away to the coolers, where it was allowed to remain for weeks, or until it had grained up from the bottom, leaving, however, a lake of molasses over the shallows of grained sugar below. In this lake many roaches, and an occasional mouse or even a rat came to an untimely end.

Drying the Sugar

In due time the grained mass was dug out with spades, and shoveled into tubs, and slid along on skids to the centrifugals. The centrifugal, at least as a sugar-drying device, was a Hawaiian invention, the work of D. M. Weston of the Honolulu Iron Works, of a few years before, and had, I fancy, been pretty generally adopted by the few mills on the islands.

Those at Amaulu were very primitive affairs, small brass-screened tubs built onto the end of the upright shaft of a turbine water-wheel, operating in a pit under the floor. They probably wouldn't dry more than twenty-five pounds at a charge and as there were only two of them at Amaulu, the daily output was not very large.

Packing and Shipping

The sugar resulting was packed in kegs...For every purpose, except perhaps refining, this keg package was very much superior to our modern bag package. It was cleaner, more secure against waste and wet, against rats and pilfering hands, and against all the wear and tear of transportation. The one thing against the keg was its cost; that and perhaps its inconvenience in transportation. Of course those were the days when all our sugar went into the open market, and must be sold as grocery grades, and the looks of it went a long way; anything like mussiness, or any suggestion of floor sweepings was fatal. The daily output was finally carted to the landing storehouse whence, from time to time, it was shipped to Honolulu by schooner.

—J. M. Lydgate

Did you know...

The main valley on Maui is called the Valley of Sugar because of its fields of sugar cane.

The House of the Sun

Ancient and Modern Astronomy

Haleakalā Observatory is a very important site for astronomy, since Haleakalā's peak has the fourth finest viewing conditions in the world. There is very little light pollution from cities or towns, and it is usually above the clouds. Occasionally they get some fog at night and rarely they get a little snow.

The ancient Hawaiian royalty, religious leaders, and astronomers would go up there to observe the stars, just as astronomers do today. Young navigators also went there to learn to navigate by the stars. Using the stars was just one of the ways they navigated their ships around the Pacific. They also studied the winds, waves, ocean swells, cloud formations, birds and fish. They named the mountain Haleakalā, which means "House of the Sun." This is particularly appropriate today, since it has become one of the top sites for studying the sun.

The domes on the left are the Pan-STARRS 1 and 2 telescopes. The complex on the right is the Maui Space Surveillance Complex, which contains observatories operated by the U.S. Air Force and the University of Hawai'i. The largest building in the middle is AEOS—which tracks and identifies man-made objects, such as satellites and ballistic missiles—and to the right is GEODSS. JOHN RICHARD STEPHENS

Dangers from the Sun

At the Mees Solar Observatory, the University of Hawai'i studies solar flares and solar radiation, which can affect the earth and disrupt satellites, such as knocking out your cell phone. By providing warning of solar activity, the satellites can be oriented so their shields will protect them and you can keep on talking, blissfully unaware that disaster was averted.

Killer Asteroids

Pan-STARRS stands for Panoramic Survey Telescope and Rapid Response System, which will consist of four 1.4 billion pixel cameras on six-foot telescopes taking high-resolution pictures of the entire sky every week. At the time of writing, only one of the four cameras is operational. Their primary purpose is to search for potential killer asteroids and comets by making repeated surveys of the sky. By comparing surveys, Pan-STARRS has the ability to find moving and variable objects. The scientists hope to catalog up to 10 million asteroids.

Past Asteroid Blasts

Above a remote area of Indonesia in 2009, an asteroid about the size of a 30-foot bus exploded in the sky with a force roughly equivalent to 50,000 tons of TNT. That's about three times the destructive power of atomic bomb the U.S. blew up over Hiroshima. Fortunately no one was hurt in the Indonesian blast, but it highlights the danger people face when large rocks drop down from outer space. The object that caused the Tunguska blast in Siberia in 1908 was about 50 meters long. That happens about once a millennium. Impacts, like the one in Indonesia, happen about once a decade.

Early Warning of Asteroid Impacts

With Pan-STARRS, scientists should be able to spot just about all dangerous asteroids that are about half-a-mile wide and many of those that are 1,000-feet wide—ones that could cause global and regional catastrophes. They will then be able to predict where and when an asteroid or comet will hit with extremely high accuracy. For an asteroid that could wipe out a city, they should be able to provide enough notice for people to evacuate. For larger impacts that could be catastrophic, the earth can't be evacuated. Blowing the object up won't work because the earth would still be hit by the pieces. The best option is to nudge it off its trajectory so it will miss the earth.

Tracking Basketballs in Space

GEODSS, or Ground-Based Electro-Optical Deep Space Surveillance, is a U.S. Air Force observatory that, along with one in New Mexico and one in the Indian Ocean, monitor man-made objects that are pretty far out there. Consisting of three telescopes, this system is able to track a basketball-sized object that's more than 20,000 miles away, and a chair at 35,000 miles. As a reference, the Kármán line, which is generally considered to be the boundary of outer space, is only 62 miles above us. For them to track a hypothetical basketball in space, it could be up to one-twelfth the distant to the moon or a third as high as the highest satellites. At least, that's the declassified capability. Chances are, the actual capabilities are much better than that. Still, that's a long way off to be able to see a basketball.

Shipwrecked in a Field

Why is this boat sitting in the middle of this field in Kīlauea on Kaua'i. Perhaps it was tossed there by Hurricane Iniki. JOHN RICHARD STEPHENS

"Mele Mele" Mango Memories

You Guys are Missing Out

I really don't know if it's my place to say so or not, but I sometimes want to tell our children, "Hey, look, you guys are missing out. Maybe you don't need to have fancy cars, a certain kind of hairdo, or a lot money in your pocket to find the identity you're searching for. Maybe you need to appreciate what we have here in Hawai'i. Maybe you need to give the islands a chance."

As kids, I remember we'd have fun just walking along the beach early in the morning looking for glass balls, or walking in the mountains—smelling the beautiful rain coming off of the trees and being sheltered by the leaves. We knew where ice cold spring water came gushing out of the mountain. I thought that was the highest high you could get. Sometimes, the simple things in life are the most amazing.

Waiting for Mango Season

The tropical seasons offered us variety. Mango season was a big thing for us. Everybody would go out to look for mangos up in the hills in back of Laie. We had our own names for these common mango groves, like Kakiyama and CPC. We'd send out search parties that would come back with their reports. "Ready?" "No, not ready. Still green yet." When the mangos ripened, we'd throw rocks at the branches to knock the fruit down. We were always making up our own slang, and, for some reason, "mele-mele" [i.e. yellow] came to mean a really-really ripe mango. If we spotted a mele-mele mango, about ten guys would be throwing rocks trying to get the ripe fruit.

Obtaining the Plunder

I was too short and chunky to climb the trees, but some of the kids would climb up to the top of the branches and shout down to the kids below, "Ready?" "Ready!" we'd shout back. Then they'd start swinging and shaking the branches. "Whoo-hahh..." And all these mangos would rain down on us. We'd pick up the mangos and sit by the side of the canefield road, peeling and eating them....

Don't Lose Out

Those are just some of the wonderful memories I have of the way we grew up. I realize we can't turn back the hands of time, and sometimes it doesn't help to dwell on things we can't control. However, there are still many wonderful aspects of Hawai'i that we tend to neglect. It's a matter of priorities, I guess. But when we don't give these islands a chance, I think we really lose out.

(WITH SAM CHOY: COOKING FROM THE HEART)

"And everywhere, there were piles of fruit for sale—oranges and guavas, strawberries, papayas, bananas (green and golden), cocoanuts, and other rich, fantastic productions of a prolific climate, where nature gives of her wealth the whole year round. Strange fishes, strange in shape and colour, crimson, blue, orange, rose, gold, such fishes as flash like living light through the coral groves of these enchanted seas, were there for sale."

—Isabella Bird

(THE HAWAIIAN ARCHIPELAGO, 1875)

Did you know...

Pineapples have nothing to do with pines or apples, neither do they—as some mainlanders are led to believe by their name—grow on trees.

Local Grinds

Growing up in Hawaii is all about the food.

You get together with family a couple times a week and everybody brings everything.

The white rice and mac salad are a given. Then there's the full multiethnic local style spread that covers every square inch of the table top. There's chow mein, Spam musubi, kalua pig, spaghetti, adobo, lau lau, fried chicken, hot dogs, salad drenched in ranch dressing and chili with undrained ground beef ('Ah, no worry boy. Jes' stir 'em in. Da's wat make dat ing tase good, da fat!' is what the uncles used to say.)

Same thing goes for the lau lau with the big ol' chunks of pork fat ("'Eh, no take out da 'aila. Das da bes' paat. Give 'em to me. I eat 'em. No waste boy.'").

—KEONI SUBIONO (*HONOLULU STAR-BULLETIN*, APRIL 28, 2007)

Kuhio Grill

The Kuhio Grill on King Street was Mō'ili'ili's landmark dining and drinking establishment. In its heyday, local customs and multicultural values of reciprocity were the norm. Late-night drinkers never got a printed menu. The waitress provided an abundance of sashimi, fried shrimp, catch-of-the-day, chopped and grilled steaks, teriyaki chicken, and more. Customers left their money on the table and she collected for the drinks. At the end of the evening patrons calculated how much food had been consumed, its value, and what tip to give the waitress. This informal arrangement worked because regular customers knew their level of generosity would determine the quantity of food brought out the next time they paid a visit to the Kuhio Grill, where waitresses had excellent memories!

—GLEN GRANT (*HAWAI'I LOOKING BACK*)

Top Secret

The Unknown Mine

The men deep inside the hill in 1941 knew well the meaning behind those words, for they lived them each day, seven days a week, in round-the-clock shifts. Their job was to carve twenty huge fuel tanks—each far larger than Aloha Tower—out of solid rock under a mountain. In total secrecy.

Many were miners, recruited from the tunnels of Appalachia or the American West. They were used to bragging about digging sixteen tons of coal a day or prying a giant nugget from the bowels of the earth. At Red Hill they couldn't brag, and those lucky enough to have wives or girlfriends couldn't even share where they worked. Others were builders of giant dams and bridges whose creations bragged for them. A big secret hole in the ground didn't say much.

Liquid Gold

Fuel was a weak link in the Pacific War. It had to be shipped everywhere. O'ahu needed fuel storage, as the Pacific Fleet was based here, and battleships and aircraft carriers traveled only a few feet per gallon!

Called simply "The Underground" by those who built it, the twenty huge tanks held a total of 252 million gallons of fuel—enough in those days to power the Navy's entire Pacific Fleet for a year. Red Hill was being hollowed out to replace the white fuel tanks that dotted Pearl Harbor. These had only one-fourth the capacity and were extremely vulnerable to enemy attack. Navy engineers found the perfect site in the ridgeline of volcanic rock called Red Hill. The ridge was deep enough to fit the tanks and still have the protection of more than a hundred feet of rock on top.

The Secret Landmark

The Red Hill Project is a National Historic Civil Engineering Landmark, putting it in some pretty impressive company: the Golden Gate Bridge, Hoover Dam and the Panama Canal.

One of the most complex engineering jobs in the world, the novel concept for building it was created on a cocktail napkin at the Halekūlani Hotel in 1940 by a young hydraulics engineer, James Growden. Most underground fuel tanks are horizontal, as Red Hill's were planned to be, making removal of "mush" (excavated material) extremely slow. Growden had the novel idea to flip them vertical, put an endless conveyor out of the mountain beneath them and let gravity take care of the rubble. He presented it to the project manager at dinner in Waikiki one night. It was accepted and construction officially started on December 26, 1940. It continued nonstop, with just two Christmas Days off, until September 28, 1943.

Unnoticed

Driving 'ewa up Red Hill on Moanalua Road today, you will see no evidence that the ridgeline on your right has been hollowed out. Or that the tanks still hold millions of gallons of fuel for ships and airplanes. Or that a small underground railway from Pearl Harbor still brings shift changes for those working there. A large, innocuous, light-blue water tank high on the ridge is all that signals the area.

—MacKinnon Simpson (*A Century of Aloha*)

Did you know...

Before the United States bought Pearl Harbor in 1887, it was called Pearl River Lagoon. The Navy changed the name to its current less attractive, but more official sounding designation.

Visiting Father Damien

In 1888 Edward Clifford visited Father Damien, who at that time had been at Kalaupapa on Moloka'i for almost sixteen years. He wrote about how Father Damien discovered he had Hansen's disease:

Discovering He was Infected

It was after living at the leper settlement for about ten years that he began to suspect that he was a leper. The doctors assured him that this was not the case. But he once scalded himself in his foot, and to his horror he felt no pain, till he put his hand into the pail and felt how hot the water was. Anaesthesia had begun, and soon other fatal signs appeared.

No Longer a Threat

Hansen's disease is caused by a bacterial infection. While it's not usually contagious, it's thought that it can be transmitted though respiratory droplets. Today it is treatable, although most people are naturally immune. It does not cause body parts to fall off, but it does damage the immune system, allowing other infections to cause lesions, deformities, and damage to limbs, skin, nerves, and eyes.

When Edward Clifford visited Father Damien, neither of them realized that it was the last year of Father Damien's life.

Spending Time with Father Damien

After dinner we went up the little flight of steps which led to Father Damien's balcony. This was shaded by a honeysuckle in blossom. A door from it led into his sitting-room—a busy-looking place, with a big map of the world—and inside it another door opened on his bedroom.

Some of my happiest times at Molokai were spent in this little balcony, sketching him and listening to what he said. The lepers often came up to watch my progress, and it was pleasant to see how happy and at home they were. Their poor faces were often swelled and drawn and distorted, with bloodshot goggle eyes; but I felt less horror than I expected at their strange aspect. There were generally several of them playing in the garden below us.

I offered to give a photograph of the picture to his brother in Belgium, but he said perhaps it would be better not to do so, as it might pain him to see how he was disfigured.

He looked mournfully at my work. "What an ugly face!" he said; "I did not know the disease had made such progress."

Looking glasses are not in great request at Molokai!
—EDWARD CLIFFORD

Father Damien about six weeks before he died. WILLIAM BRIGHAM.

Honolulu's Hotel of Sorrows

Picture brides often had to work in the fields along with the men, but for lower wages.

In the early 1900s, there was a hotel near the wharf in Honolulu that some called the Hotel of Sorrows. It was said that if you walked by this particular hotel on certain evenings, you could hear sobs emanating from the rooms.

Picture Brides

The lamentations occurred only on nights after a ship had arrived bringing "picture brides" to Hawai'i from Asia.

By the 1880s, Hawai'i's large sugar and pineapple plantations needed workers. Lured by hopes of a better life and decent wages, men were recruited from around the world—Portugal, Japan, Korea, China and other countries.

Many of the plantation workers were unwed Asian men who came hoping to earn money and eventually return to their own countries. But after years on the plantation and realizing they might never go home, some asked families and friends to send them wives. Prospective brides and grooms exchanged photos—the blurry sepia images of early cameras—and chose mates without ever actually meeting.

Deceptions

Arranging "picture bride" marriages became an avocation for matchmakers in Asia and a business for entrepreneurs in Hawai'i. Matchmakers received a handsome fee for their services. And the photographer who snapped photos of plantation workers might even rent them suits so that they could appear more prosperous. Occasionally, a middle-aged or homely man might be concerned that no woman would choose him.

Rather than take a chance on finding a match, he might ask a younger or better-looking man to stand in for him in the photograph. The photos were sent off to relatives and matchmakers in the homeland.

In many parts of Asia, women were an expendable commodity and had no choice in the matter. Families would arrange the marriages for a variety of reasons. Some simply hoped for better lives for their daughters. They had been led to believe that anyone who lived in Hawai'i was prosperous.

In truth, most plantation workers endured long, sweltering hours in Hawai'i's pineapple and sugar fields for low wages—and they expected their new wives to also work in the fields while still caring for a house and family.

Arriving in an Unknown Land

The grooms, and sometimes the matchmakers, stood on the O'ahu docks, awaiting the ships. Each man, holding his bride's picture, peered into the faces of the women demurely leaving the ship. Sometimes the couples recognized each other and smiled shyly. Sometimes they were so unlike their pictures that the matchmaker had to introduce them.

Mass marriages often took place right at the dock. Some couples went immediately to their new homes, small wooden camp cottages provided by plantation owners; others rushed to a nearby hotel, nicknamed the Hotel of Sorrows, to consummate their marriage. It is said that on those nights, from inside the wooden building, the soft sound of the brides' weeping could be heard, mixing with the mournful wails of ocean birds.

Sorrow and Disappointment

Why did the women weep?

Some cried from homesickness. They had left home, relatives and friends and might never return. Others sobbed because after an exhausting sea journey they had been too quickly bedded by their eager husbands.

Many a bride was confronted at the Honolulu docks by someone who looked nothing at all like the picture she had been pressing to her heart. Her new husband was older or homelier, poorer or uglier. She must spend the rest of her life with someone she was sure she would never love.

Leading New Lives

Most picture brides eventually adjusted to life in Hawai'i, loving their husbands, raising numerous children, caring for plantation homes and also working in the fields. These strong couples, merging lives in such a less-than romantic way, raised children who became leaders in Hawaii business, education and politics.

—TONI POLANCY (*HAWAI'I IN LOVE*)

Fictional Description of Real Life

Gannen Mono
First-Year Men

In his novel *The Stone of Kannon,* Bushnell described the hope-filled arrival of the first Japanese contract laborers in 1868. Here they are about to reach shore in what they call Tenjiku, which means heaven.

> The best part about arriving in Tenjiku, they agreed, was the fact that it brought them nearer to the time when they would begin to work for those rich sugar planters. Thoughts of all the honorable money they were going to earn, visions of all the estimable gold they would save and all the respect they would receive when they returned home comforted them for the hardships they had endured during the voyage, strengthened them for the work that lay ahead. The discovery that this place was not really like the Lord Buddha's Tenjiku did not dismay them. Paradise must wait. In this world a man must do the best he can, to bear the life the gods have arranged for him...

—O.A. BUSHNELL (*THE STONE OF KANNON*)

 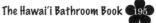

Plantation Life

My father was assigned as a field laborer on a sugar cane plantation...on Maui. He quickly learned that the recruiting agents in Madeira had misrepresented both working and living conditions on the plantation. He knew nothing about farming, and had a difficult time completing his three-year contract. After three months of laboring in the cane fields, his hands and feet ached constantly. Luckily, the plantation manager, Mr. Henry P. Baldwin, learned that father was a shoemaker, and transferred him from the fields to the plantation stables to be head stableman and harness maker....Father continued as head stableman and harness maker for the plantation until his three-year contract ended. The period had been a difficult one; plantation life was hard with long days of rough work and low pay and few opportunities for economic and social advancements. Furthermore, the only two children born to this family on the plantation also died there....Father moved from Hamakuapoko and opened his own leather shop, and earned an improved living making shoes, saddles, bridles, harnesses and other articles for whoever needed them. Mother supplemented the family's income: being a professional dressmaker, she converted a spareroom into a dressmaking shop."

—NETTIE DO REIS *(PEOPLE AND CULTURES OF HAWAI'I, A PSYCHOCULTURAL PROFILE)*

The field or ordinary labor on our plantations is done by Hawaiian, Portuguese, Chinese and Japanese. All these classes make good all-round plantation laborers. The Portuguese, who come from Madeira and the Azores, are the best for heavy work; the Hawaiians make good teamsters, and the Chinese and Japanese excel for factory work. The Japanese are good workers, but are not so easily managed as Chinese, and where there is a large number of them on a plantation they are apt to combine and make trouble in various ways.

H.P. BALDWIN *(THE SUGAR INDUSTRY IN HAWAII, 1894, OVERLAND MONTHLY 25)*

The Not-So-Sacred Gulch

'Ohe'o Gulch and its twenty-two pools in Haleakalā National Park on Maui were renamed "Seven Sacred Pools" in 1946 to attract visitors even though no one considered them sacred and there's fifteen additional pools, but in 1979 Hawai'i's Lieutenant Governor ordered the state to stop calling it that and the national park followed suit in 1995. But most people still call it Seven Sacred Pools, which is more in line with the majestic beauty of the location than 'Ohe'o Gulch.

Two of the non-sacred pools at 'Ohe'o Gulch. ELAINE MOLINA.

Ku'u Pua I Paoakalani

Queen Lili'uokalani wrote this song in 1895 while being falsely imprisoned under house arrest at 'Iolani Palace. It is one of more than 160 poems, songs, and chants written by her. During her imprisonment, each day John Wilson would bring her flowers from her garden at Paoaokalani in Waikīkī. By wrapping them in newspaper, he gave her access to the news she wasn't allowed to read.

Ku'u Pua I Paoakalani
E ka gentle breeze e pā mai nei
Ho'ohāli'ali'a mai ana ia'u,
E ku'u sweet never fading flower
I bloom i ka uka 'o Paoakalani.

Hui:
'Ike mau i ka nani o nā pua
O ka uka o Uluhaimalama
'A'ole na'e ho'i e like
Me ku'u pua i ka la'i o Paoaka-lani.

Lahilahi kona ma hi'ona
With softest eyes as black as jet
Pink cheeks so delicate of hue
I ulu i ka uka o Paoakalani.

Nane 'ia mai ana ku'u aloha
E ka gentle breeze e waft mai nei
O come to me ka'u mea e li'a nei
I ulu ika uka o Paoakalani.

My Flower in Paoakalani
O gentle breeze that waft to me
Sweet, cherished memories of you
Of my sweet never fading flower
That blooms in the fields of Paoakalani.

Chorus:
I've often seen those beauteous flowers
That grew at Uluhaimalama
But none of those could be compared,
To my flower that blooms in the fields of Paoakalani.

Her face is fair to behold
With softest eyes as black as jet
Pink cheeks so delicate of hue
That grew in the fields of Paoakalani.

Now name to me the one I love
Gentle breezes passing by
And bring to me that blossom fair
That blooms in the fields of Paoakalani.

—Queen Lili'uokalani

Queen Ka'ahumanu

The statue of Ka'ahumanu in the Queen Ka'ahumanu Shopping Center in Kahului on Maui. It's said she was an excellent surfer. (JOHN RICHARD STEPHENS)

The Feminist Queen

Six feet tall, bold, fiery and beautiful, Ka'ahumanu has no equal in Hawai'i's feminist history. Her wisdom and strength guided the islands in a period of major transition for the Hawaiian people, and her actions profoundly affected the course of Hawaiian history.

Ka'ahumanu married Kamehameha I, Hawai'i's most celebrated ruler, when she was in her early teens and he was in his 20s, and she soon became his favorite. A handsome woman, she enhanced her appearance in the Hawaiian way by tattooing her legs, hand and tongue. The royal couple spent long hours together, talking, smoking pipes and surfing. More importantly, Kamehameha carefully listened to the counsel of this strong-willed and uncommonly intelligent woman throughout the turbulent years of his ascendancy and rule.

Declaring Herself Co-Ruler

After Kamehameha I died in 1819, Ka'ahumanu declared herself kuhina nui, or co-ruler, with the new young king, Liholiho, also known as Kamehameha II. Greatly disturbed by the restrictions of Hawaiian religion, she persuaded Liholiho to break the kapus.

 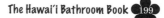

New Laws

In 1824 while in Lahaina, Ka'ahumanu thought she was dying. In an effort to help her people before she died, she proclaimed a code of law for the island of Maui, prohibiting murder, theft, gambling, and the profaning of the Sabbath.

From the time of Kamehameha II's departure for England in 1823 until her death in 1832, Ka'ahumanu essentially ruled the kingdom, for Liholiho died abroad, and his brother Kauikeaouli, or Kamehameha III, was only 12 years old in 1825, when he was proclaimed king.

—GAIL BARTHOLOMEW (*MAUI REMEMBERS*)

Traditional Saying

Pipili no ka pīlai i ke kumu kukui.

("The pīlai gum sticks to the kukui tree." This is said of someone who maintains a close relationship with a relative, such as a grandchild with their grandparent.)

Did you know...

In 1881 King Kalākaua became the first reigning monarch to travel all the way around the world.

Did you know...

Queen Lili'uokalani was the only woman to rule the Kingdom of Hawai'i on her own.

Hula's Struggle to Survive

Vital or Idolatrous?

Master hula dancers held positions of high honor in ancient Hawai'i, for their art and its rituals were vital to the fabric of society. Far more than just a diversion, the dance was interwoven with religion, poetry, music, and drama.

Men, women and children rendered hula in a wide variety of styles, but the missionaries did not discriminate—they condemned all renditions. In 1823, missionary William Ellis reacted to a hula he observed in Lahaina. "Six women, fantastically dressed in yellow tapas, crowned with garlands of flowers...began their dance. Their movements were slow, and though not always graceful, exhibited nothing offensive to modest propriety....The music ceased: the dancers sat down:...I preached to the surrounding multitude with special reference to their former idolatrous dance, and the vicious customs connected therewith."

Regulating It

There is no question that certain dances were suggestive and therefore quite popular with boisterous whalers on shore leave in Lahaina. In an effort to regulate such hula, commercial performances required licenses, which were available only for the whaling centers of Lahaina and Honolulu. Fortunately, missionaries and their followers did not totally silence the sounds of the native dance. Hula schools in all Maui districts kept traditions alive despite official disapproval. An informant in 1864 complained, "There is much hula dancing at Halehaku...the police should watch at the place mentioned, because these people are doing it all the time."

—GAIL BARTHOLOMEW (*MAUI REMEMBERS*)

The Show is Canceled

In 1935—the same year Shirley Temple and Minnie Mouse danced—in Washington, D.C., the Speaker of the House of Representitives, Joe Byrnes, told reporters that he had stopped a hula dance in the House Office Building because he thought it unwise to convert the Congressional caucus room into a dance hall. The entertainment had been arranged by the delegate from Hawaii, Samuel Wilder King, as part of "Hawaiian Night" for the secretaries of Congressmen. The next day one of the Washington newspapers published the following doggerel:

> "It will not do," the Speaker said,
> "she cannot dance the hula.
> From Plymouth Rock the moral shock
> would spread to Ashtabula.
> The solid South, the Golden West
> —from Portland to Missoula—
> would be surprise and scandalized,
> if she should dance the hula.
> In private hall, if danced at all,
> must be Hawaii's hula.
> In Washington you may have fun,
> but the hula is tabula."

—Jerry Hopkins (*The Hula*)

California Punch?

Hawaiian Punch was invented in a garage in Fullerton, California, in 1934 by A.W. Leo, Tom Yates and Ralph Harrison. Originally it was a syrup to pour on ice cream. Eventually people started adding water to it, so the company began selling it as a drink in 1950. Five years later they turned it into a frozen concentrate and it quickly became a national brand. There is nothing Hawaiian about Hawaiian Punch.

The Man Who Invented Baseball...Sort of

The Vague History of Baseball

Alexander Cartwright, Jr. (1820-1892), is said to be the man who founded modern baseball. In 1953, the U.S. Congress went so far as proclaiming this to be true. In spite of what Congress says, whether it really is true is a matter of debate. No one knows when or how baseball began, but it appears to have evolved from the bat-and-ball games of England. We do know that the game became very popular in New York in the 1850s.

The earliest reference to baseball in America is a 1791 law against it—preventing it from being played near the Pittsfield town hall in Massachusetts. The first organized club in New York was the Gotham Base Ball Club, which was founded in 1837. Then in 1845, former members of this club formed the Knickerbocker Base Ball Club. This is where Cartwright comes in. He belonged to the Knickerbocker Club and was part of a committee that wrote down the rules for the game that are thought to be the basis for today's rules. As near as anyone can tell, the earliest game they played under these rules was at Hoboken, New Jersey, in 1846, although it's likely there were some in 1845.

Fighting Over History

Apparently Cartwright was promoted as "the father of modern baseball" by an early group of baseball historians to counter claims that the game was invented in 1839 by Abner Doubleday at Cooperstown, New York. There was a lot of fighting over this for many years, but it's now known that the Cooperstown story is false. So Cartwright was inducted into the Baseball Hall Fame at Cooperstown as one of several people who had a hand in establishing the rules of baseball, a few of which are still used today. At least, that's what is now generally accepted. This too is controversial and it's said that at least one of those who helped write the rules in 1845 insisted Cartwright didn't have anything to do with it. When documentation is scarce, establishing history can sometimes be a messy business.

The Honolulu Baseball Team of 1910. Hawaiian baseball was probably racially integrated from its beginning, although it also had teams formed by ethnic groups. This picture was taken 37 years before Jackie Robinson was allowed to play for the Brooklyn Dodgers in 1947. On a related note, in 1941 Jackie Robinson was forced to leave UCLA before graduating because of financial hardship, so he moved to Honolulu to play football with the semi- professional Honolulu Bears, which was also an integrated team. This was cut short when America entered the war and Robinson joined the Army, serving as a second lieutenant. He then when on to become a national hero for breaking mainland baseball's race barrier. Perhaps his short time in Hawai'i encouraged him by showing him how things could be.

Seeking a Fortune, Finding Hawai'i

In 1849, Cartwright took off for California, hoping to make a fortune in the Gold Rush, but he was only there for a short time. He came down with dysentery and was told Hawai'i was an excellent place to go for one to recover their health. Once he felt better, he intended to return to New York by way of China, but he ended up spending the rest of his life in Honolulu. He brought with him a baseball and the rules he probably helped write, but it is not known whether he had a role in establishing Hawaiian baseball, but the game did become popular here in the 1860s.

Cartwright in Honolulu

Cartwright helped form Honolulu's first volunteer fire department and in 1850 was appointed as Chief Engineer by King Kamehameha III. The king also joined in as a volunteer fireman whenever there was a fire. Cartwright went on to became an advisor to Queen Emma and was the executor of her will. He was also a financial advisor to King David Kalākaua and was on the public library's board of directors and was its president for many years. In addition, he helped establish the Queen's Hospital, the Pacific Club, and was an acting grand master in the Freemasons. He died in 1892 and is buried in the Nu'uanu Valley Cemetery. Many people have paid their respects at his grave, including Babe Ruth.

An Island Treasure

Don Ho

From Hawaiian descent, born in the small Honolulu neighborhood of Kaka'ako in 1930, Don Ho took his local-boy talents from a small cocktail lounge in Kāne'ohe to Duke Kahanamoku's in Waikiki in 1962 to add his resonant voice to the blossoming rage of exotica. With his backup gang, the Ali'i, equipped with guitars, xylophones, and drums, he emerged as a suave entertainer, Hawai'i's own show biz man. The audience adored his sing-alongs. By 1966, Ho had two albums out. That year he released "Tiny Bubbles," the song that would propel him to national fame. When tiki exotica faded, the Don Ho show and his motto "Suck 'em up" remained.

—Sophia V. Schweitzer (*Tiki of Hawai'i*)

Did you know...

Instead of smoking peace pipes, when ancient Hawaiian chiefs wanted to make peace, they sat down together to weave leis.

Alice Cooper is Our Homie

Maui Nō Ka 'Oi

For many years *Condé Nast Traveler* readers have consistently voted Maui as the best island in the world, so it's not surprising that many of the rich and famous would own homes here. For the most part, Maui is not very exclusive, so someone who works as a busboy might live within walking distance of Alice Cooper's house. He's lived here since the early 1970s. A bit to the south is Clint Eastwood's second house—his main home being in Carmel, California—while Brittany Spears owns a home nearby. (One has to wonder if Clint invites Brittany over for barbeques.) Steven Tyler owns a beautiful place that sits on a rocky shoreline next to a popular snorkel spot. Also nearby is where Richard Chamberlain used to live. Speaking of Alice Cooper and Clint Eastwood, they are both part owners—along with several others—of the Māla Restaurant at the Wailea Beach Marriott Resort.

Oprah

The one celebrity that people seem to be the most interested in is Oprah Winfrey. She has a vacation house about five miles up Haleakalā in Maui's Upcountry. Actually she owns a lot of ranchland there—about 1,000 acres—and an additional 165 acres on the windward side of Maui, near Hāna, with a red-sand beach. She has at least six other estates and houses throughout the U.S. and in the Caribbean, but this one is worth checking out at http://www.oprah.com/home/Oprahs-Hawaiian-Home. She also owns an exclusive, high-end bed and breakfast inn near her house.

Hanging Out and Washing Cars

Just up the road from Oprah, Mick Fleetwood has an up-country house. Actually he has two houses on Maui. This one he uses sort of like most people use their basements or garages—he plays music there, hangs out with buddies and drinks fine wines. He and his family live in his other house in West

Maui, near where Carlos Santana, Randy Travis, and Kelsey Grammar used to own homes. Mick is involved in many charitable events on the island and you can even have him wash your car at some fundraisers.

Home of the Stars

A Casual Atmosphere

Some celebrities prefer the rustic/surfer/hippy ambiance of Pā'ia, on Maui's North Shore. This is where you'll find Woody Harrelson, Owen Wilson, Walter Becker of Steely Dan, Willie Nelson, and surf champion Laird Hamilton. Willie Nelson is a long-time resident of Pā'ia and he's often seen, and occasionally plays, at Charley's Restaurant and Saloon there. Former-NBA coach Don Nelson has a beach house in Pā'ia, while also owning one of the town's buildings with shops and an art gallery, along with 22 acres of farmland upcountry where he grows flowers and olive trees.

More Rock Stars

Sammy Hagar owns two homes on Maui—one of them on the North Shore. He also owns Sammy's Beach Bar and Grill in the Maui International Airport. He has seven of these restaurants around the country.

George Harrison also lived on Maui's North Shore for many years and would occasionally join local musicians on stage in Pā'ia.

In addition, Pat Simmons of the Doobie Brothers lives on Maui, while Eddie Vedder lives in a remote location on one of the small neighboring islands.

Sighted

It's often said that Helen Hunt has a house on Maui. It wouldn't be surprising as she's been vacationing here since she was fourteen. She's often seen in South Maui and has said that Hawai'i feels like home to her. Her daughter is named Makena'lea, but is not named after the South Maui community. The name has something to do with a friend's dream and means "many flowers from heaven."

Hawai'i Nō Ka 'Oi

These people could live anywhere in the world they wanted to. It's nice to know that out of all the interesting and exotic places they've visited around the globe, they've chosen Hawai'i as their home.

Pet Pigs

While people all over the U.S. keep pigs as pets, those in Hawai'i have a particular fondness for their porkers. They often keep one in their tiny backyards and at least one woman takes hers for walks on a leash in a residential neighborhood of Pa'ia on Maui. JOHN RICHARD STEPHENS

The Wettest Spot

World Record Rain

Kaua'i gets a lot of rain. In fact, the east side of Wai'ale'ale, which is in the center of Kaua'i, is or was one of the wettest spots in the world. It rains at this remote location just about every day of the year. So far the record for a single year, measuring the year from August 1860 through July 1861 which includes parts of two rainy seasons, is 1,042 inches—almost 87 feet—in Cherrapunji, India, but that was very unusual and largely because they received 366 inches during the last month of that period. Rainfall records for Kaua'i don't go back that far, so we don't know what was happening then on Wai'ale'ale. When you compare Wai'ale'ale's annual average of 460 inches over 32 years from 1931 to 1962 with Cherrapunji's average from 1931 to 1960, Cherrapunji falls short at 455 inches. Measurements from 1851 to 1960 drop Cherrapunji's average to 445 inches, but we don't have that data for Wai'ale'ale. To put it in perspective, 460 inches is 38 feet, 4 inches of rain.

When It Rains, It Dumps

Could Kaua'i hold the world record for average annual rainfall, as many guidebooks say? Probably not, but it's difficult to determine because of variations in the measuring methods used and the different time periods covered by the measurements, so in a way it's like trying to compare mangos and papayas. Measurements from 1941 to 1979 place Mawsynram, which is about ten miles west of Cherrapunji, at 467 average inches per year. There's even more competition from Lloró, Colombia, which some put at 524 inches, but this is just an estimate.

Problems with the Data

Annual averages for Wai'ale'ale vary considerably depending on the time period covered. Various sources give differing amounts, such as 451 inches and 510 inches. You can get 359 inches (1949-2004), 407 inches (1961-1990), 396 inches (1971-2000), or 423 inches (1981-2010). Perhaps there were some particularly heavy storms during the 1931-1962 period when the oft cited average of 460 inches was calculated.

Initially the rain gauge was a large metal barrel that could hold 900 inches of water which entered through an opening on top, and once a year a U.S. Geological Survey crew would climb the mountain to see how much water was in there. Now, of course, it's all done electronically.

Wind can influence how much rain makes it into the gauge and evaporation takes some of it back out. Sometimes backup gauges at a location show different amounts of rainfall. Also, one should keep in mind that the data is incomplete. In fact, there is no data at all for more than twenty-one years scattered throughout the 1949 to 2004 period and many of the years are missing data for at least one month, so even calculating the average for a single year can be challenging. Various methods of adjusting for the missing data, the varying length of months, and differences in collection times can give you different results, so the figures aren't as straight forward as they seem.

Why Wai'ale'ale?

There are several reasons why Wai'ale'ale is so wet. Because it is cone-shaped, it doesn't matter which direction the wind comes from. Once the winds hit the mountain's steep sides, the air is rapidly pushed upwards more than 3,000 feet in less than half a mile. If the slope were gentler, the rain would be spread out over a wider area and the amount of rainfall would drop. As the air shoots up the mountain, it suddenly expands and cools causing the moisture to condense into clouds. When the clouds become saturated, it rains. With a peak at 5,148 feet, this is Kaua'i's second highest summit and right below the trade wind inversion layer at 6,000 feet, which creates something of a ceiling for the clouds. The rain dumps right on the peak. And because Kaua'i is the northernmost of Hawai'i's main islands, it is more exposed to frontal systems. Because of all this rain, the three-mile-wide flat top of the mountain is essentially a bog that extends five miles down its northwest slope.

Maui's Wet Spots

It Pours on Big Bog

Maui also has a wet spot, which appears to be as soaked as Wai'ale'ale. Called Big Bog, it's up the windward side of Haleakalā above Hāna. Haleakalā rises 10,020 feet above sea level so its summit is well above the inversion layer and resembles a high desert. Big Bog is a lower bog of a series of bogs on the side of the mountain. At 5,413 feet, Big Bog is below the cloud ceiling and only 265 feet higher than Wai'ale'ale's summit. Measurements put Wai'ale'ale's average rainfall at 393 inches with an error range of plus or minus six inches (1950-2011) and Big Bog's at 404 inches plus or minus nine inches (1993-2011), so they're pretty close.

Maui's Other Wet Spot

Maui has another place with very heavy rainfall. This is West Maui's Pu'u Kukui mountain. High up the slope from Wailuku and Kahului, at the very remote upper end of 'Īao Valley, the cliffs rise abruptly to the peak at 5,788 feet. Measurements at the summit show a cumulative average rainfall of 366 inches plus or minus eight inches (1928-2011). Not quite as drenched as the other two, but still quite damp. In 1980 its average for the year was close to 500 inches. We don't know what it was that year for Big Bog, but its yearly high so far is 551 inches for 1992—the first year it was measured. The highest for Wai'ale'ale was 666.17 inches in 1983. That's about 55.5 feet of water.

The Wettest Town

Hilo, on the Big Island, gets the most rain of Hawai'i's towns, but the amount varies widely from around 130 inches near the shore to about 200 inches on the inland side. Just six miles upslope from Hilo's city limits is the wettest spot on the Big Island, where the annual rainfall can be greater than 300 inches. In comparison, Washington and Oregon—the rainiest spots in the contiguous 48 states—average under 130 inches a year. Seattle gets only 38 inches on average, while Honolulu gets 20 to 100 inches depending on how far up the mountain you are.

Getting Wet

No matter how you measure it, Hawaiʻi has at least three of the rainiest places on earth. If you want to see these wet spots, you can hike to the summit of Waiʻaleʻale, but it takes one to two days to get there and one to two days to get back. Hiking to the sites on Maui is prohibited, but you can see all these spots by helicopter.

Backyard Cows

Some people even keep cattle in their backyard. Perhaps they were just mowing the lawn. These happy cows live comfortably near Hāna on the Windward Side of Maui. JOHN RICHARD STEPHENS

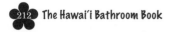

Native Hawaiian Houses

Homes of the Rich and Poor

The dwellings of the masses were constructed of upright posts planted in the ground, with cross-beams and rafters, and roofs and sides of woven twigs and branches thatched with leaves. The houses of the nobility were larger, stronger and more pretentious, and were frequently surrounded by broad verandas. It was a custom to locate dwellings so that the main entrance would face the east, the home of Kane. The opposite entrance looked toward Kahiki, the land from which Wakea came.

Types of Buildings

The homes of well-conditioned Hawaiians consisted of no less than six separate dwellings or apartments: 1st, the heiau, or idol-house; 2d, the mua, or eating-house of the males, which females were not allowed to enter; 3d, the hale-noa, or house of the women, which men could not enter; 4th, the hale-'aina, or eating-house of the wife; 5th, the kua, or wife's working-house; and 6th, the hale-pe'a, or retiring-house or nursery of the wife [menstrual house]. The poorer classes followed these regulations so far as their means would admit, but screens usually took the place of separate dwellings or definite apartments.

—ROLLIN MALLORY DAGGETT, U.S. CONGRESSMAN AND MINISTER TO THE HAWAIIAN ISLANDS IN 1882

Gold-Dust Day Geckos

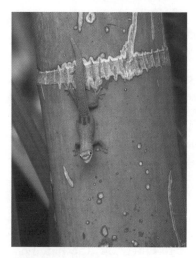

A Gold-Dust Day Gecko in Keal-akekua on the Big Island. JOHN RICHARD STEPHENS

Inhabiting Oʻahu, the west side of Maui, the Hilo and Kona districts of the Big Island, a small area on Kauaʻi, and in Kaunakakai on Molokaʻi, these bright-green geckos with tiny golden-yellow spots sprinkled over their shoulders and reddish spots on their lower back—usually in three tear-drop shapes—and their bright-blue eye-shadow, are arguably the most beautiful of Hawaiʻi's lizards. There are both males and females. Some gecko species, such as Hawaiʻi's tree geckos and mourning geckos are all female and reproduce parthenogenetically.

Did you know...

Hawaiʻi's endemic Happy Face Spider has what looks like a smiling face on its back.

Did you know...

After converting to Christianity, the Queen of Kauaʻi, Deborah Kapule, turned the former sacred site, Malae Heiau, into a cattle pen.

That's Why They Call Him "The Brain"

"Hawaii's the 50th state? I thought it was a suburb of Guam."

—Bobby "The Brain" Heenan
(A FORMER PROFESSIONAL WRESTLING MANAGER
AND COMMENTATOR WHO WAS INDUCTED
INTO THE WWE HALL OF FAME)

Obviously they don't teach geography at wrestling school. So, do you think he might have been taunting a Hawaiian wrestler or do you think he really didn't know? Wait...you don't need to answer that.

Uncommon Knowledge

What Does It Mean?
(Lānaʻi)

- **Lānaʻi (island, district) and Lānaʻi City (town):** perhaps "day of conquest"; possibly "hump" or "swell" because of the island's shape.

- **Pālāwai (basin):** bottom lands, or pond scums.

The Dry Spot

The driest spot in Hawai'i and in all Oceania is Puako on the Big Island which receives an average of less than nine inches of rain each year. While Puako may not get much rainfall, it's hardly desert. There is literally tons of water just inches away in the form of the Pacific Ocean.

What Good is a Dry Spot?

So what do you do with a place that is a huge lava field and gets almost no rain? On Hawai'i they put in resorts. After all, you can expect it to be sunny year around, while the ocean helps keep the temperature moderate. Because of this, Puako sits between the Waikoloa Beach Resort and the Hapuna Beach Resort, just a short drive up the Queen Ka'ahumanu Highway from the Kailua-Kona airport.

What Else is it Good For?

And what do they have there, besides some really beautiful resorts? Golf courses. There's the Waikoloa Beach Course, the Waikoloa King's Course, the Mauna Lani North and South Golf Courses, the Mauna Kea Golf Course, and the Hapuna Golf Course. Don't like golf? Then go shopping at the Queen's MarketPlace or swim with dolphins or do a couple hundred other things.

Escaping the Dryness

So what do you do if you get tired of the sun and you really want some rain? Drive two hours east from the driest spot in the islands to Hilo, the wettest town in the islands. In between you can stop in cattle country. Hawai'i's microclimates are pretty cool.

Kapu
(The Sequel)

Rules and Restrictions

The tabu was the most ingenious and effective of all the inventions that has ever been devised for keeping a people's privileges satisfactorily restricted.

It required the sexes to live in separate houses. It did not allow people to eat in either house; they must eat in another place. It did not allow a man's woman-folk to enter his house. It did not allow the sexes to eat together; the men must eat first, and the women must wait on them. Then the women could eat what was left—if anything was left—and wait on themselves. I mean, if anything of a coarse or unpalatable sort was left, the women could have it. But not the good things, the fine things, the choice things, such as pork, poultry, bananas, cocoanuts, the choicer varieties of fish, and so on. By the tabu, all these were sacred to the men; the women spent their lives longing for them and wondering what they might taste like; and they died without finding out.

The Death Penalty Again

These rules, as you see, were quite simple and clear. It was easy to remember them; and useful. For the penalty for infringing any rule in the whole list was death. Those women easily learned to put up with shark and taro and dog for a diet when the other things were so expensive. [Note: Actually other sources indicate women weren't allowed to eat dog either.]

It was death for any one to walk upon tabu'd ground; or defile a tabu'd thing with his touch; or fail in due servility to a chief; or step upon the king's shadow. The nobles and the King and the priests were always suspending little rags here and there and yonder, to give notice to the people that the decorated spot or thing was tabu, and death lurking near. The struggle for life was difficult and chancy in the islands in those days.

—Mark Twain

Kapu: A New Beginning

Burning Down the House

After ending the kapu system in 1819, the new king—Kamehameha II—figured if the old gods existed, then he had already pissed them off royally and it was too late to go back, so he might as well go all the way. Therefore he had the kāhuna and the people destroy the icons and set the heiaus on fire. The ancient Hawaiian religion officially came to an end, although some continued to carry it on in secret. Oddly, this was a revolution led by those at the top of society, some of whom—like the high priest, Hewahewa—had the most to lose. Apparently they realized that it was in everyone's best interest to cast their entire religion aside. On the other hand, it freed up the workforce from rituals and offerings, so they could work on producing goods and sandalwood that the chiefs could trade for Western items. It also freed the ali'i and kāhuna from their many rituals and kapus.

Welcoming a New Religion

It was about a year and a half later that the first missionaries arrived and were embraced by the favorite wife of Kamehameha I—Queen Ka'ahumanu. The missionaries quickly set about teaching the Hawaiians a different set of restrictions. They banned surfing, hula dancing, and speaking Hawaiian in schools. Working on Sundays, including building a fire, was against the law and people were arrested for it. For the Hawaiian commoners, their workload increased. Besides their traditional domestic duties and growing or catching their own food, they were now required to cut sandalwood or raise nontraditional crops for the chiefs to trade for Western goods. Along with attending church services and religious instruction, the missionaries put them to work building increasingly larger churches, meeting houses, schools, and missionary housing. The introduction of land ownership in 1848 once again restricted most people from entering specified areas. And, of course, there were the usual restrictions on drinking, gambling, horse racing, most forms of sex, and several forms of marriage.

Uncommon Knowledge

The Hawaiian Planet

A Bit About Our Planets

You probably didn't know that our solar system has a Hawaiian planet. Actually it's a dwarf planet, but it's still a planet.

Our solar system has as least five dwarf planets. Pluto lost its full-planet status because of its low mass, so it is now a dwarf planet. Eris, the largest dwarf planet, is larger than Pluto and about a fourth the mass of the Earth. It's distance from the sun is about three times that of Pluto. All of the dwarf planets are out beyond Neptune, except Ceres, which is in the asteroid belt.

Just Like Pele's Mother

Now, Haumea is the Hawaiian dwarf planet. It's named after Pele's mom—the goddess of fertility and childbirth. Its two moons, Hiʻiaka and Namaka, are named after two of Haumea's other daughters. In mythology, her daughters were born through different parts of her body. It is believed that the two moons were formed from parts of the dwarf planet. In addition, there are ten other small objects associated with Haumea that currently aren't considered moons or dwarf planets. The entire group is referred to as the Haumea family. So far, it is the only known family out beyond Neptune.

What's It Look Like?

The planet has an oblong shape—it's twice as long as it is wide—and sort of resembles an egg, which is probably caused by its rapid rotation. Astronomers think that this spin was caused by a collusion with a larger object at least a billion years ago. A day on Haumea is only 3.9 hours long, but a single year on Haumea is equal to 285 Earth years. It's thought this and perhaps additional collusions created all the objects in Haumea's family.

Pictures of it aren't very clear because it's so far away—about fifty times farther from us than the sun—but photographs by the Pan-STARRS telescope on Haleakalā, Maui, show Haumea has a reddish spot near one end.

The element that is associated with Haumea the goddess is stone, so it's appropriate that observations suggest Haumea the planet is made almost entirely of rock, covered with a crust of pure ice. This is unusual for objects in the Kuiper Belt. Perhaps the ice is shave ice with a spot of shark's blood.

O'ahu's Space Observatories

Ever wonder what they're doing up on that mountain?

The observatories that can be seen on the top of Kaena Point on the western coast of O'ahu are mainly a satellite tracking station operated by the Department of Defense. Here there is equipment for tracking and communicating with vehicles in the military's space programs and for detecting and tracking nuclear missiles that might be launched against the United States by Russia, the People's Republic of China, or North Korea. There are two radomes, which is short for radar domes that protect microwave or radar antennas from the weather. The locals call them golf balls.

The Kaena Point Solar Observatory—formerly the Palehua Solar Observatory before it was moved—is one of five electro-optical observatories operated by the U.S. Air Force for detecting solar flares and warning of solar activity which can damage satellites and disrupt communications. The other four of these observatories are in New Mexico, Massachusetts, Italy, and Australia so that someone is watching the sun around the clock. The observatory has four radio telescopes with antennas that measure from three to twenty-eight feet.

The 1873 Hawaiian Lifestyle

Isabella Bird was sickly as a child in Britain. As she grew older, she found her health greatly improved when she traveled, so she became a travel author and natural historian in order to finance her long excursions to remote and exotic places around the world. Sailing from San Francisco to New Zealand, she got off the ship in Honolulu in January of 1873 and ended up staying for six months, touring the islands. On visiting Hilo, on the windward side of the Big Island, she wrote:

Why Work?
The melon and halo patches represent a certain amount of spasmodic industry, but in most other things the natives take no thought for the morrow. Why should they indeed? For while they lie basking in the sun, without care of theirs, the cocoanut, the breadfruit, the yam, the guava, the banana, and the delicious papaya, which is a compound of a ripe apricot with a cantaloupe melon, grow and ripen perpetually. Men and women are always amusing themselves, the men with surf-bathing, the women with making leis—both sexes with riding, gossiping, and singing.

Every man and woman, almost every child, has a horse. There is a perfect plague of badly bred, badly developed, weedy looking animals. The beach and the pleasant lawn above it are always covered with men and women riding at a gallop, with bare feet, and stirrups tucked between the toes. To walk even 200 yards seems considered a degradation.

Everyday Luaus
The people meet outside each others' houses all day long, and sit in picturesque groups on their mats, singing, laughing, talking, and quizzing the haoles, as if the primal curse had never fallen. Pleasant sights of out-door cooking gregariously carried on greet one everywhere. This style of cooking prevails all over Polynesia. A hole in the ground is lined with

stones, wood is burned within it, and when the rude oven has been sufficiently heated, the pig, chicken, breadfruit, or kalo, wrapped in ti leaves is put in, a little water is thrown on, and the whole is covered up. It is a slow but sure process.

The Dark Side
Bright dresses, bright eyes, bright sunshine, music, dancing, a life without care, and a climate without asperities, make up the sunny side of native life as pictured at Hilo. But there are dark moral shadows, the population is shrinking away, and rumours of leprosy are afloat, so that some of these fair homes may be desolate ere long. However many causes for regret exist, one must not forget that only forty years ago the people inhabiting this strip of land between the volcanic wilderness and the sea were a vicious, sensual, shameless herd, that no man among them, except their chiefs, had any rights, that they were harried and oppressed almost to death, and had no consciousness of any moral obligations.

Now, order and external decorum at least, prevail. There is not a locked door in Hilo, and nobody makes anybody else afraid.

—ISABELLA BIRD (*THE HAWAIIAN ARCHIPELAGO*)

Note: It sounds like she was describing what was left of the Makahiki festival, which was abolished in 1819, although some elements probably continued informally. She arrived in Hilo in January, which would have been towards the end of the ancient festival that was formally abolished 54 years earlier.

Did you know...

Herman Melville, the author of *Moby Dick*, jumped ship in Honolulu in 1848 and got a job working in a bowling alley. Little did he know that one character in his novel—Starbuck, Captain Ahab's first mate—would have a string of coffee shops named after him.

Celebrating Children

Keiki in Kimonos

Each year, Japanese parents dress their children in their finest formal clothes for the *Shichigosan* festival, which is an ancient tradition that began as a coming of age event, signifying the transition to middle childhood. In medieval times, aristocratic and *bushi* (warrior) families dressed up both girls at ages three and seven, and boys at ages three and five, in kimonos, then took them to the Shintō temple where priests prayed over them to drive away evil spirits and for their prosperity and long lives.

Keiki in Kimonos. BAKER-VAN DYKE
COLLECTION

Odd numbers are considered lucky by the Japanese, which is why those ages were chosen. *Shichi-go-san* literally means "seven-five-three." In the days when infant mortality was high, this festival was a celebration that the child had survived to begin the next phase of their lives. Parents also offer thanks to the kami—the spirits or natural forces—for protecting their child. This practice spread to the common people by the mid-1800s.

Dressing Up for Candy

Today the age of the child no longer matters. All children take part, and it now usually occurs on the weekend closest November 15th. Boys are no longer dressed in kimonos for the festival—just girls—while some children now wear Western-style suits and dresses. The children are given *chitose-ame*, or "thousand-year candy," signifying the wish for long, healthy lives. The wrapper of the long, thin, red and white candy features illustrations of turtles and cranes, both of which symbolize long life.

This festival is a wonderful way to celebrate the lives of children.

Growing Children

The ancient Hawaiians didn't measure time in years and they didn't keep track of a person's age. There were no birthday parties. The age of a child was only loosely tracked by the child's ability to do certain things. Here are a few of the milestones Hawaiian children passed while moving toward adulthood.

A flower beginning to unfold.	*A baby.*
The child's head is warmed by the sun.	*A toddler able to creep into the sunlight without assistance.*
One who can carry a water bottle.	*At about the age of two, children were given small gourds so they could assist in carrying water.*
One who can carry two coconuts.	*At about the age of five.*
His butt is covered with a malo.	*A boy of age five or six. Prior to this age, a boy didn't wear anything and he ate with the women. When he was old enough to wear a malo, or loincloth, he would begin to eat*

	in the men's eating house.
One who can carry a smaller child on his or her back.	*At around age ten, a child is big enough to carry a younger sibling on his or her back.*
The coffee berries aren't ripe yet.	*A child who is not old enough to be attractive to the opposite sex.*
Almost ready to make fire by holding a fire stick in his hand.	*A boy who is almost old enough for sex.*
One who is old enough to broil food.	*One who is old enough to have a mate and would likely be considered an adult.*

Did you know...

When he died, it's estimated King Kamehameha the Great had between twenty and twenty-five wives.

Introduced Species

Hawai'i has had considerable human help in becoming the wonderful paradise that it is. Many of the best things on the islands were brought here by people from all over the world. Here are a few introduced species and where they originated:

- **Brought by the early Polynesians:** coconut palms, kukui trees, mountain apples, breadfruit, bamboo, sugar cane, bananas, ginger, ti, taro, yams, sweet potatoes, bottle gourds, pigs, dogs, chickens, rats, geckos, skinks, house flies, fleas, and lice.
- **Cook Islands:** Cook's pines.
- **Australia:** ironwood and silk oaks.
- **India:** mangos, mynah (or myna) birds, and mongooses.
- **China:** lychees.
- **Asia:** banyan trees.
- **From tropical America:** bougainvilleas, plumerias, and papayas.
- **Mexico by way of Peru:** guavas.
- **Brazil:** pineapples.
- **Africa:** coffee.
- **Other recently introduced species:** horses, cattle, deer, pronghorn antelope (on Lāna'i), donkeys, mules, goats, sheep, cats, red-crested cardinals, bullfrogs (from California), cockroaches, and mosquitoes. Only three of the 30,000 species of orchids worldwide are native to Hawaii. The rest that you see have all been imported.

While some of these things have been detrimental, most have been good for the islands. Of course, the one non-native species that has had the greatest impact on the islands is *Homo sapians.*

Unfortunately some introduced species outcompete or wipe out some native species and conservation efforts are required to save them. Threatened or endangered animals include Hawaiian Monk Seals, Spinner Dolphins, a number of sea turtles, the Nēnē, several species of Booby, and the Hawaiian Hoary Bat. Looking over *Hawaii's Comprehensive Wildlife Conservation Strategy*'s "Appendix A: Wildlife (Fauna) Species of Greatest Conservation Need" also reveals some unexpected candidates for conservation. Who would have suspected that native species in need of protection include centipedes, ticks, earwigs, flies, lice, and some fleas that are found in the Northwestern Hawaiian Islands.

Did you know...

The hoary bat and the monk seal are the only two types of mammals that are native to Hawaii, although they might soon be joined by the Hawaiian kangaroo.

Did you know...

Hawaiian Monk Seals became a separate species 15 million years ago, but it's estimated are fewer than 1,200 left, so they might not be around much longer.

What Were They Thinking?

Meddling with Nature

This had been the story all along: the advance of introduced species, the retreat of the native. The Hawaiians brought one kind of rat with them. Westerners brought other kinds, then the mongoose to keep down the rat. But the mongoose, it turns out, does not care this way or that way about the rat. The two pests—one on his way home, the other on her way to work—nod politely to each other, and the mongoose goes off to eat the eggs of native birds, and in sunstruck moments gnashes at golf balls forsaken in the rough.

—Gavan Daws (*A Hawaii Anthology*)

Falling into Molten Lava

For more than four decades, Dr. Wendell Duffield studied volcanoes around the world, mainly with the U.S. Geological Survey. Three of those years were spent at the Hawaiian Volcano Observatory. He has since retired and now is a professor of geology at Northern Arizona University in Flagstaff. It's difficult to understand why anyone would leave Hawai'i for Arizona—perhaps the vog got to him—at any rate, he's written four books on volcanoes. Here he describes some close encounters of the burning kind.

Accidents Happen

As careful as we always tried to be when we worked close to active lava at Kīlauea, my friends Jeffrey Judd, Norman Banks, and fellow geologist George Ulrich went into molten lava up to the knees while working at the edge of sluggish flows. Jeffrey fell into the lava in the early 1970s, Norm in 1983, and George in 1985. Only one of Jeffrey's legs penetrated into the hot stuff. Both of George's got burned. Norm was burned the least.

Quick Medical Care

Rather incredibly, their legs were pulled from the lava flow within seconds, medical help was quickly available, and neither Jeffrey, Norm, nor George suffered any long-term debilitating effects of their third-degree burns. They can dance, run, and play tennis today. But I think that many what-ifs and other imagined possible horrors of those accidents are permanently burned into their memories.

It seems impossible that Jeffrey, Norm, and George didn't lose their legs from the knees down. George took a temperature reading of the molten rock of 2,079° Fahrenheit right before he fell in. Those limbs probably were saved by a combination of being in the lava for only a few seconds, and getting medical help quickly, first in Hilo on the Big Island and then in Honolulu on O'ahu. Their heavy field boots and the pant legs of denim jeans may also have provided some insulation to reduce heat damage to skin and flesh that might otherwise have occurred.

Fire hose lava from Kilauea pours from the side of a cliff at East Lae'apuki in 2005 after a 34-acre lava bench dropped down into the ocean. That molten stream is six feet thick. KELLY WOOTEN, USGS AND HVO.

What Helped Save Them

Jeffery reports that his pant leg started to burn away only when it was out of the lava and in the oxygen of Earth's atmosphere. Having arrived at the scene by helicopter, George was wearing a fire-retardant flight suit, even better partial protection than denim jeans alone. I suppose it's even possible that a thin insulating rind of rock solidified against legs whose temperature was way below the melting/freezing temperature of basalt. If so, the rind would probably have quickly broken off in the flurry of extracting a leg from the lava.

Learning Respect for Lava

Geologists whose research takes them to a volcano observatory such as that at Kīlauea go through an evolution of increasing comfort (or decreasing discomfort?) while working at close range with a molten rock that is bubbling off a mixture of noxious gases not recommended for the long-term health of one's lungs, if inhaled.

Respect for such a hazardous material is a natural human reaction. It would be foolish to jump into that work—figuratively or literally! My personal experience of learning to safely coexist with live lava at Kīlauea may be typical of most staff members who have cycled through a stint at the Hawaiian Volcano Observatory. But as we all know, accidents happen no matter how careful one is.

Experiencing Live Lava

My introduction to so-called live lava—geologists apply the word lava to both the solid and liquid rock—was in 1967. I sat on the rim of Halema'uma'u Pit Crater within Kīlauea Caldera and watched in awe as a lake of molten basalt sloshed, bubbled, and circulated some two hundred feet below. Having just recently earned my PhD in geology at Stanford University, I remember thinking that a description of a scene like this in a text book is a pretty feeble substitute for witnessing the real thing. Molten rock that had originated in and then intruded up from the mantle was being added as new material to Earth's surface crust right before my eyes.

Heat radiated by the lava lake was so intense that I could peek over the rim of the crater for only thirty seconds or so before retreating. Exposed skin would otherwise blister. A sulfurous rotten-egg odor of fumes bubbling off the lava stung the linings of my nostrils and produced an acrid taste in my mouth. If I stood as motionless as possible, I could feel the ground beneath my feet vibrate in what seismologists call harmonic tremor. It's a kind of earth shaking that a seismograph records as a steady sine wave of one to a few cycles per second. I supposed this tremor was caused by the continuous sloshing of lava in the crater. Whatever happened to terra firma, I wondered.

Sacrifices and Offerings

Noise from the circulating and bubbling lava conjured up an image of the bloop, bloop, bloop of a huge pot of beef stew simmering on my mother's kitchen stove. If there is any truth to the lore that some cultures have thrown humans into a lava stew to appease something or someone, death for the sacrificed would be quick. Modern Hawaiians honor Kīlauea Volcano and the resident goddess Pele by throwing offerings of food, beverage and coins into Halema'uma'u.

—Dr. Wendell A. Duffield

Did you know...

The Ironman World Championship triathlon, held every year on the Big Island, consists of a 2.4-mile rough water swim, followed by a 112-mile bike ride, and a 26.2-mile trail run—all without a break.

Did you know...

Because of the volcanic eruptions at Kīlauea, Hawai'i is the only state that is getting larger.

Fictional Description of Real Life

A Modern Lūʻau

There were around thirty people at the luau at first. George and a cousin...dug a pit and roasted a small pig wrapped in chicken wire in it for a day and a half before Christmas....Dennis was impressed by the gathering; the people did seem all of one family, huge men who shook his hand with their large, soft hands, huge women in muumuus who sat around in the shade fanning themselves and talking story with the aroma of pork escaped from the ground, and they all talked with the familiarity of a family even though, as he understood, they hadn't seen one another in a year....

The cars parked in front of the Maunawili house went... right out of sight in both directions, and both the front and back porches had an absurd profusion of slippers, shoes and high heels piled up by those who went into the house. One Waianae cousin came in a suit with a vest and gold watch chain, and Kenika found him sitting in the grass taking off his shoes before going into the house, and told the man that he really didn't have to do that, but he said, nah nah, s'okay. His hand was shaken by the meaty hands of dozens of uncles and cousins and friends, and he was mauled by huge women wearing startlingly bright muumuus, who planted kisses on his cheeks and put leis over his head until they rose all the way to his nose....

A three-man guitar and ukulele band showed up just after noon, and played Hawaiian songs as the people chattered. George and his friends drew the chicken wire-wrapped pig out of the pit in the backyard at two, but Kenika thought it surely had to be superfluous because there was so much food everywhere, heaps of little crabs, shrimp, various kinds of fish and octopus chunks, Japanese and Chinese and Filipino delicacies, little squares of coconut cake, beer, juice for the kids. But with the pig came the sweet potato, poi, lomi salmon, fried chicken, and more obscure vegetables and meats and desserts from the aunties and uncles and calabash cousins of different backgrounds and mixes of races.

—Ian MacMillan (*The Red Wind*)

Important Hawaiian Words and Phrases

Guidebooks and tourist books always contain a list of significant Hawaiian words and phrases that everyone should know. Of course it is very important to know what aloha, mahalo, kama'āina discount, and hau'oli Hanukaha (happy Hanukkah) mean. For those of you who are beyond that, here is a list that you might find useful:

- **'A'ohe ka he lohe o ko pepeiao huluhulu?** (Don't your hairy ears hear?)
- **Kulikuli!** (Shut up!)
- **Helo aku!** (Go away!)
- **Kaniali'i hūpē kole.** (Runny-nosed brats.)
- **'Ou hohono.** (You stink; particularly, but not always, BO.)
- **Pua'a.** (Pig.)
- **Hoki.** (Ass, as in "mule.")
- **Ka hyena.** (Hyena.)
- **Ka māpū, Ka papuna.** (Baboon.)
- **Ka loli.** (Slug.)
- **Ka ko'e, Ka ilo.** (Worm.)
- **'Ōpala.** (Garbage).
- **Pupule.** (Crazy or insane.)
- **Hehena.** (Barking mad or demonically possessed.)
- **Pakalolo.** (Ganja or wacky tobacky.)
- **Uwe!** (Oops! Oh, no!)
- **Pika!** (Pizza!)

More on Lucky Cats

A red Maneki Neko, such as this one, is often used to fight illness and exorcise evil spirits. JOHN RICHARD STEPHENS

The Cat Beckons

Lucky cats are very popular in Hawai'i. To those who are not Japanese, it looks like the cat is waving hello or goodbye, but it's not—it's making a beckoning or welcoming gesture. In Western culture, when we want someone to come to us, we raise our hand with the back facing out and repeatedly move the hand towards us. In Japan, they hold their hand up with the palm facing forward and then repeatedly curl their fingers down towards the palm of their hand. This is what the cat is doing. He is essentially saying, "Come on in." A few are made in Japan for export with their paw facing back, more like the Western inviting gesture.

Lucky Cat Symbolism

Most Lucky Cats are calico Japanese Bobtail cats—a breed that is very popular in Japan. They are often tri-color—black, brown, and white—which is very rare in nature and is considered especially lucky. Black Maneki Neko are kept around children to protect them from illness and evil and by women to protect them against stalkers. White ones represent purity, while gold ones bring in money and pink ones are used to attract love.

Lucky Cats are usually depicted holding one or more gold coins with an outrageous sum written on them. If there were an American version, it would be holding a billion dollar bill. The coins are all in an old-style currency which was replaced by the yen. Some hold a lucky mallet or a lucky fish. It's not known when they made their first appearance, but they were popular by the mid-1800s.

The Silver Screen
Lāna'i Flicks

These two movies had scenes filmed on Lāna'i: *The Tempest* (Helen Mirren, Russell Brand; 2008) and *Exit to Eden* (Dana Delany, Dan Aykroyd, Rosie O'Donnell; 1994).

Did you know...

Hawaii has its own time zone: Hawaiian Standard Time.

Did you know...

Jack Lord of *Hawaii Five-O* almost got the roll of Captain Kirk in *Star Trek*, but he wanted to co-produce the show, so Gene Roddenberry chose William Shatner instead.

"*Coming to Hawai'i is like going from black and white to color.*"

—John Richard Stephens, author/editor

Rich and Famous on the Road to Hāna

Hitting Warp speed on the road to Hāna. JOHN RICHARD STEPHENS

Getting There

The windward side is one of the most remote and beautiful areas of Maui. The road to Hāna is famous for being an arduous drive with its 54 miles which feature "617 hairpin turns and 54 one-lane bridges." People will tell you that it takes at least six hours to get there. Nonsense! One can easily drive from Pā'ia to Hāna in an hour and a half, and that's with a fifteen-minute stop along the way. The thing is, you'll want to make many more stops. It is extremely beautiful. The lush jungle with its many waterfalls rivals the Big Island's Hāmākua coast and Kaua'i's North Shore.

Early Hānaiians

Jim Nabors was probably the first celebrity to discover this area. While his primary home is on O'ahu, he also had a house with a mile of oceanfront land in Hāna which he bought back in the Sixties or Seventies. In the Eighties he sold some of the land to his friends, Carol Burnett and Burt Reynolds. Carol Burnett had three units of a four-unit condo there, while her friend and co-star Tim Conway, owned the fourth unit of her condo. Burnett's other co-star, Vicki Lawrence, also owned a place nearby. Richard Pryor had a place in Hāna, while Kris Kristofferson and Weird Al Yankovic both have places on Maui's windward side.

The First Christmas in Hawai'i

A New Holiday

Honolulu had never seen a celebration quite like this one. The temporary Anglican church at Pele'ula had been elaborately decorated with cypress boughs cut from the mountains, an abundance of myrtle, orange boughs and beautiful native flowers. The altar, festooned with verdant shrubs with large red cone-shaped berries, was graced with a large text reading, "The Word was made flesh." A silver candelabra lent by King Kamehameha IV cast a blazing light through the tiny church, which by midnight of Christmas Eve, 1862, was filled with joyous celebrants softly chanting the Litany in the native Hawaiian language. Thirty men and women received Holy Communion amid much singing and ritual. When the service ended at 1:00 a.m., the battery at Punchbowl fired a salute as flaming tar barrels cascaded down the crater's rim. The first official observance of Christmas in the Hawaiian Islands had begun.

This is how the Punchbowl looked from the Honolulu Prison in 1865. C. L. WEED.

An Earlier Introduction

In ancient times, the people of old had celebrated the abundance of the harvest and Lono, the god of peace, with the Makahiki, a lengthy holiday season of special feasts and games. It was a time when goodwill prevailed and thanksgiving was revered. When the first European voyagers came to Hawai'i, they often celebrated Christmas in the islands, sometimes exchanging gifts and festivities with the Native Hawaiians. The first recorded Christmas in Hawai'i was on December 25, 1786, when Captain Nathaniel Portlock of the *King George* and Captain George Dixon of the *Queen Charlotte* exchanged Yuletide pleasantries with Hawaiians at Waimea Bay, Kaua'i. On Christmas Eve the crew enjoyed roast pig and seapie and "offered our Christmas libations in punch, mixed with the juice of the coconut, toasting our friends and mistresses in bumpers of this liquor, which perhaps, pleased more on account of its novelty than from any other circumstance."

On Christmas morning, over a hundred women carrying children in their arms gathered among the foreign captains, each child receiving a small gift with delight. Later that day, the chief of the village reciprocated the presents with a present of hogs and vegetables. The first staff Christmas party and exchange of Yuletide gifts had taken place in Hawai'i with evidently much mutual pleasure....

The Anti-Christmas Christians

When the brig *Thaddeus* arrived in Hawai'i in the spring of 1820 bearing the pioneer company of American Protestant missionaries, the religious nature of Christmas celebration would take a new turn. Tracing their religious convictions to their conservative New England Puritan church, these congregationalist missionaries believed that only those religious observances specifically set forth in the Bible should be celebrated. While Thanksgiving in November, gift-giving on New Year's Eve, and feasting on the Fourth of July were observed by the missionaries, Christmas celebrations were considered a Catholic ritual not condoned by the Bible. Consequently, the day of the Lord's birth was observed with quiet prayer and "business as usual."

The powerful influence of the early missionary church prevailed in Hawai'i through half a century despite the later arrival of Catholics, Methodists and secular Americans who were embracing Christmas on the mainland as a joyous family celebration complete with home decorations, Christmas trees, and St. Nick....Perhaps the staunchest of the missionary leaders, Reverend Hiram Bingham, noted in his journals for Christmas 1841 that his children had hung out their stockings with the "ridiculous notion" that Santa Claus would leave them some small gifts! Needless to say, their stockings the next day were bare.

Reevaluation and Change

With the ascension of Kamehameha IV, Alexander Liholiho, to the throne in 1854, the young King and his part-English bride Queen Emma would lean away from Puritanism and toward British traditions. As early as 1857 the King proclaimed December 25th Thanksgiving Day in Hawai'i, an edict that allowed foreigners and natives of all faiths to honor the day, each in their own way. Finally in 1862, His Majesty openly embraced the Anglican faith, inviting a branch of the church to be introduced to the islands. Receiving baptism in the church Kamehameha IV then proclaimed that Christmas December 25 would become an official holiday in the Hawaiian islands.

The First Official Christmas

It was His Majesty King Kamehameha IV who had donated much of the floral decorations for the Pele'ula church services on Christmas Eve. He also translated into Hawaiian the Litany which was chanted. Following the beautiful display of Punchbowl crater aglow with lava-like flames, His Majesty then led an unusual procession of celebrants through downtown Honolulu. Twenty torches made of kukui wood and coconut fibers dipped in tar and standing eight feet tall followed His Majesty as the procession walked down Fort and King Streets.

Green candles were burning along the parade route with onlookers and marchers singing Christmas carols. Gathering at the fountain courtyard at the King's Palace, the processioners, numbering in the thousands, delighted in the igniting of fireworks and rockets shot into the air with the great shout of the crowd. At this point, as one reveler remembers, "We sang the grand old carol 'Good King Winceslaus' (sic); and after a glass of champagne punch we made the air right with the National Anthem, and another round of protracted Hurrahs, and so to bed."

Mele Kalikimaka had forever become a part of life in the Hawaiian Islands.

—Julie Mehta (*Mele Kalikimaka: Christmas in Hawaii*)

Did you know...

Queen Ka'ahumanu had a large pet hog that often disrupted Sunday church services.

Literary Masters

Paul Theroux on Honolulu

Ask tourists why they like the city, and they will name a hotel or a Waikiki restaurant. These people have no idea that Honolulu is a secret city, a place of beloved noodle shops, sushi bars, grocery stores; a park where a softball game is usually in progress, or a church hall is hosting an orchid-growers' club.

—Paul Theroux

"*I liked Hawaii because it was a void. There was no power here apart from landowning, no society worth the name, just a pecking order. There was a social ladder but it wasn't climbable, and the higher on it people stood, the sillier they looked, because everyone knew their secrets.*"

—Paul Theroux
("Honolulu Revealed," *Honolulu Magazine*, Aug 2001)

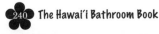

Old and New in Honolulu

British author and playwright W. Somerset Maugham, who wrote *Of Human Bondage* and *The Razor's Edge*, visited Honolulu for three weeks in 1916. Describing its multicultural atmosphere, he wrote:

> "It is the meeting-place of East and West. The very new rubs shoulders with the immeasurably old. And if you have not found the romance you expected you have come upon something singularly intriguing. All these strange people live close to each other, with different languages and different thoughts; they believe in different gods and they have different values; two passions alone they share, love and hunger. And somehow as you watch them you have an impression of extraordinary vitality. Though the air is so soft and the sky so blue, you have, I know not why, a feeling of something hotly passionate that beats like a throbbing pulse through the crowd."
>
> —W. SOMERSET MAUGHAM, 1921

Traditional Saying

He ihona, he pi'ina, he kaolo. ("A road goes down, up and level." In other words, life is like a road.)

Did you know...

Duke Kahanamoku was a descendent of King Kamehameha I, through Princess Bernice Pauahi Bishop.

What's in a Name?

(Moloka'i)

- **Moloka'i** (island, district): the name of one of the children of the goddess Hina.
- **Kalaupapa** (town): the flat plain.
- **Pali** (coast): cliff.
- **Hālawa** (valley, beach, bay, town): curve.
- **Kaunakakai** (town): the modern name for Kauna-kahakai (beach landing).
- **Mauna Loa** (mountain, town): long mountain.
- **Maunaloa** (town): long mountain.

The Weird and the Wild

Honu

There are seven species of sea turtles in the world, five of which can be found in Hawaiian waters, although only one is regularly seen. That is the honu, or Hawaiian green sea turtle. They are the only sea turtle that will crawl up onto the beach to sunbathe during nonbreeding seasons.

The Hawaiian Wahine

This is Isabella Bird's interesting description of Hawaiian women in Honolulu from her visit in 1873.

It's the Way They Dress

The women are free from our tasteless perversity as to colour and ornament, and have an instinct of the becoming. At first the holokū, which is only a full, yoke nightgown, is not attractive, but I admire it heartily now, and the sagacity of those who devised it. It conceals awkwardness, and befits grace of movement; it is fit for the climate, is equally adapted for walking and riding, and has that general appropriateness which is desirable in costume.

It's in the Way They Walk

The women have a most peculiar walk, with a swinging motion from the hip at each step, in which the shoulder sympathizes. I never saw anything at all like it. It has neither the delicate shuffle of the Frenchwoman, the robust, decided jerk of the Englishwoman, the stately glide of the Spaniard, or the stealthiness of the squaw; and I should know a Hawaiian woman by it in any part of the world. A majestic wahine with small, bare feet, a grand, swinging, deliberate gait, hibiscus blossoms in her flowing hair, and a lī [lei] of yellow flowers falling over her holokū, marching through these streets, has a tragic grandeur of appearance, which makes the diminutive, fair-skinned haole, tottering along hesitatingly in high-heeled shoes, look grotesque by comparison.

—Isabella Bird (*The Hawaiian Archipelago*

Robert Louis Stevenson

Robert Louis Stevenson (1850-1894), the world-famed Scottish author, first arrived in Hawaii with his family on his chartered yacht *Casco* in 1889 and spent five months exploring the islands, being entertained by hospitable residents of high and low degree, and writing some of his best fiction and essays. Stevenson's step-daughter, Isobel Osbourne Strong, wife of King Kalakaua's court painter, had arrived earlier, and R. L. S. and his wife, Fanny, were immediately accepted as a part of the royal circle. Stevenson chatted with Princess Kaiulani beneath her father's banyan tree at Waikiki and was inspired to write this poem for her that became treasured by residents and visitors alike.

When Stevenson returned to the islands in 1893 for a five-week stay, he found a changed political climate. Pro-American annexationists had overthrown his friend Queen Liliuokalani. In bad health, he nevertheless visited old friends and gave a memorable address to the Scottish Thistle Club. He died on his Samoan estate a year after this final Hawaii visit.

His 1889 experience resulted in much literary creation. His *Travels in Hawaii* includes ten sketches of adventures on the Kona Coast, at the City of Refuge, and on the island of Molokai, where he spent a week at the leprosy settlement guest house before circling the eastern end of Molokai by steamer and on horseback.

Two of Stevenson's best short stories—"The Bottle Imp" and "The Isle of Voices" in *Island Nights' Entertainment*—have settings in Hawaii, and the inspiration for his Pacific novel of adventure, *The Wrecker,* came from an incident reported in the Honolulu newspapers during his residence at Waikiki. The most notorious of his writings about the islands, however, was his classic piece of searing personal invective attacking Honolulu's Reverend Charles M. Hyde, who had written a letter to a California associate defaming Father Damien, who had died when Stevenson was in Honolulu.

—A. Grove Day (*Books About Hawaii: Fifty Basic Authors*)

The Royals
To Princess Ka'iulani

Princess Ka'iulani at about the time she was sent to England.

Princess Ka'iulani was the heir to the throne of the Kingdom of Hawai'i. She was the daughter of Princess Miriam Likelike and her Scottish husband, Archibald Cleghorn, who was the last Royal Governor of O'ahu. In 1889 when she was thirteen years old, her parents sent her off to school in England for four years. Before she left, she was very anxious and really didn't want to leave Honolulu, but she didn't have any choice.

In January of that year, Robert Louis Stevenson arrived in Honolulu. Stevenson was already well known for his classic tales *Treasure Island* and *The Strange Case of Dr. Jekyll and Mr. Hyde.* Over the next few months he became friends with King Kalakaua and Princess Ka'iulani. Since Stevenson was Scottish and the princess was half Scottish, they felt a connection. No doubt the princess peppered him with questions about the U.K., for which she was about to depart. Stevenson was aware of her apprehension, so he wrote the following poem in her autograph album, along with this explanatory note:

> Written in April to Ka'iulani in the April of her age; and at Waikiki, within easy walk of Ka'iulani's banyan! When she comes to my land and her father's, and the rain beats upon the window (as I fear it will), let her look at this page; it will be like a weed gathered and pressed at home; and she will remember her own islands, and the shadow of the mighty tree;

and she will hear the peacocks screaming in the
dusk and the wind blowing in the palms; and she
will think of her father sitting there alone.

—R. L. S.

Forth from her land to mine she goes,
The island maid, the island rose,
Light of heart and bright of face:
The daughter of a double race.
Her islands here, in Southern sun,
Shall mourn their Ka'iulani gone,
And I, in her dear banyan shade.
Look vainly for my little maid.

But our Scots islands far away
Shall glitter with unwonted day.
And cast for once their tempests by
To smile in Ka'iulani's eye.

—ROBERT LOUIS STEVENSON

An additional note: It's from Stevenson's poem that Princess Ka'iulani received her nickname—the Island Rose.

Traditional Saying

I mohala no ka lehua i ke ke'ekehi 'ia e ka ua.

("The Lehua blossom unfolds when the rains tread on it."
In other words, gentle words will get a better response from
someone than using harsh words.)

The Weird and the Wild

Humuhumu-nukunuku-a-pua'a

Humuhumu-nukunuku-a-pua'a. JOHN RICHARD STEPHENS

Now say that three times as fast as you can. Actually it's not as hard as you'd think, if you practice. Go ahead.

Just kidding. Now say it with a mouth full of shave ice.

Who has a Pig Nose?

The humuhumu is probably Hawai'i's favorite fish (not to eat)—at least, it's Hawai'i's official state fish. Translated, the name means "pig-nose triggerfish" and it's pronounced "who-moo who-moo new-koo new-koo ah poo-wah, ah." And in following the theme of its name, they're sometimes known to make grunting noises. They usually do this when chased by predators. Perhaps they're trying to warn others or maybe they're trying to startle the predator. We may never know. They can also spit jets of water. They do this to stir up and blow away sand to reveal things they can eat. Sometimes they'll scoop up sand and spit it out so they can look through it. The fish's pig-like nose (so they thought), grunting, and its rooting through sand, all reminded the Hawaiians of pigs. In fact, this fish was allowed to be used as a substitute for pigs in religious rituals. It's odd that they thought it had a pig-nose when it actually doesn't have a nose at all.

That's Humu for Short

The Incredible Shrinking Name

This fish's name is often shortened by English speakers to Humuhumu or just Humu. While some cultures, such as German, tend to lengthen their words. English is an odd language in that its speakers are always trying to shorten words. And if the words are already short, they shorten them more. For example, consider mag, zine, info, intro, limo, app, abs, ID, rehab, perp, Xmas, and dub (for a spoken W). Or how about dat (that), bby (baby), ne (any), and 2 (to), which shortens these short words by just one letter (or character) each. Thus, many people just call this fish humuhumu for short. That word actually refers to all triggerfish, while the full name is specific to the reef triggerfish and its less common relative, the lagoon triggerfish. Perhaps it would be better to call it the pigfish or a sea pig. Then again, that takes away some of its charm and dignity. With its yellows, golden browns, florescent blues and the little red stripe on each of its pectoral fins, it really is an amazingly beautiful fish, even with its fat lips that make it look like somebody punched it in the mouth.

The Longest Name

Some say its name is longer than it is, but there are some pretty big humuhumus. They can get up to ten inches in length. People also say this is the longest name of all the Hawaiian fish, but that's not so. If someone tells you that, just tell them they've forgotten about the lauwiliwilinukunuku'oi'oi (pronounced "laow will-ee will-ee new-koo new-koo, oy, oy"). It translates as the "long-snout, wiliwili-leaf-shape fish," but it's popularly known as the butterflyfish.

Boat Days

A Big Event

For many years the arrivals and departures of Honolulu's passenger ships were gala social events. Musicians played, hula girls swayed and visitors cried beneath a deluge of leis and paper confetti. Flags and streamers flew everywhere. Nothing else in the city's history has ever matched the frenzied excitement and celebration of Boat Days.

It is hard to imagine now in this age of jet airplane service, but during the first half of this century Honolulu's regular routine almost stopped when the big Matson ships came in. As soon as Hawaiian Electric Company's whistle sounded, people dropped whatever they were doing and hurried over to the harbor in order to welcome the newcomers.

Greetings

Canoe paddlers escorted the vessel to shore and beach boys swam out to dive for coins tossed overboard. Waiting majestically on the wharf, playing familiar island tunes, was the Royal Hawaiian Band....

As the ship rounded Diamond Head small boats filled with hotel representatives, newspaper reporters, photographers and health officials would meet the ship. While the hotel people made room assignments, the news people ran up and down the decks of the vessel looking for the passengers they wanted to interview....

When the Ships Depart

As the ship left its mooring, the Royal Hawaiian Band usually played "Aloha Oe," or "Farewell to Thee" while it steamed out of the harbor. Friends of the passengers would then jump in their automobiles and race around to the Diamond Head Lighthouse. Here they got a final glimpse of the ship before it disappeared around Koko Head.

 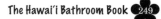

The Boat Days Come to an End

Following the attack on Pearl Harbor, the Matson Navigation Company's passenger liners were confiscated by the U.S. Government and became troop ships. They were returned to civilian service after the war but by the mid-1950s the airplane had taken over as the primary means of travel between California and the Hawaiian Islands. Boat Days were never quite the same again.

—RONN RONCK (*HAWAIIAN YESTERDAYS*)

A Fond Reminiscence

It Was Like a Masquerade

My first impression was that the town had attended a masquerade party that night before and had remained in motley to greet the steamer...The pier was a garden of gay blossoming, and the expression common to all faces was an honest smile. The confusion of landing swept everyone into swirls of laughing, crying and chattering humanity. A persistent fragrance of flowers dominated the smell of oil, wood, steam and dirt from the harbor. Flowers were everywhere, bouquets, baskets, and, most interestingly of all, garlands of flowers elaborately woven in designs of many colors. A feeling that was warm, hospitable and welcoming flowed from the crowd to the ship, enveloping stranger and friend alike...That lei, the first of many that I wore in Hawaii, will remain in my heart as long as I can remember, as a symbol of that hospitality which is Hawaii's own. It is a hospitality so generous, so splendid, that it overwhelms the visitor.

—GLEN GRANT (*HAWAI'I LOOKING BACK*)

Did you know...

At the beginning of the *Gilligan's Island* TV show, the SS *Minnow* departs on its "three-hour tour" from Waikīkī's Ala Wai Yacht Harbor.

Been Here a Long Time

Riding Along on a Conveyer Belt

The Hawaiian Islands and the Emperor Seamount Chain which stretch up to Alaska's Aleutian Islands were all formed by a single somewhat stationary volcanic vent in the ocean floor. As the tectonic plate the islands are riding on moved over the vent, the lava broke through in spots forming volcanos and the islands. This has been going on for millions of years.

What's a Million Years?

While it's difficult to imagine a million years, it's a bit easier to picture it this way: Wai'anae Mountain Range on western O'ahu arose from 3.4 to 2.7 million years ago, while the Ko'olau Mountains formed 2.5 to 2.2 million years ago. Now, the islands are moving northwest at the rate of 2.8 inches a year, so if you imagine Wai'anae blasting up out of the sea where the Big Island's Kīlauea volcano is now and slowly rolling along at the steady rate of almost three inches a year, then three million years is how long it took for Wai'anae to move from there to where it is now. That's 250 miles at the speed of three inches a year. It takes 22,629 years for the islands to move one mile. That's eleven times the 2,000 years since the times of Jesus and Julius Caesar. Three million years is a *very* long time. And in another three million years, the Big Island will be sitting where O'ahu is now. It's on its way there right now, charging across the ocean floor at the rate of about three inches a year.

A Hawaiian Way-Wayback Machine

The Big Island rose out of the ocean less than half a million years ago, Kaua'i about 5.1 million years ago, and Kure Atoll—the first of the Hawaiian Islands—about 30 million years ago. The first seamount in the Emperor Seamount Chain, which were formed by the same volcanic vent as the Hawaiian Islands, is 81 million years old. That is *old!* But Hawai'i's Hawksbill sea turtles have been around for *300* million years. They probably watched the creation of all the islands and spread to each new island as it formed.

Hanalei Valley Then and Now

Hanalei Valley as it looked in 1912. BAKER-VAN DYKE COLLECTION

Hanalei Valley as it looks today. JOHN RICHARD STEPHENS

Living with Celebrities

Hawai'i is the vacation spot of choice for many of the rich and famous. In fact, you'd be hard pressed to find celebrities who have *not* been to the Paradise of the Pacific. Not surprisingly, many love it so much that they get vacation homes here or decide to live here. In fact, a lot of them do—particularly on Maui.

Living in Hawai'i is interesting in that you can be surrounded by celebrities and never really know it. Everything is low key here and on the rare occasions they are spotted, they're usually left in peace. Of course, there are occasionally paparazzi who follow them to the beach, hoping to get some bathing suit shots. But more often than not, they aren't even recognized. They're able to pass for one of the crowd, and they seem to like that. Other times they are noticed and word gets around. Alice Cooper is regularly spotted on the golf courses. A friend will tell you Cher was seen grocery shopping at Safeway or that someone saw Steven Tyler in Longs Drugs. Perhaps you will wander down to the beach for the evening and discover Sting is playing a private corporate-sponsored concert outside at one of the resorts. All of these things have happened. Where else can you sit on the beach in the moonlight listening to a live Sting concert for free?

Did you know...

Duke Kahanamoku competed in four Olympics from 1912 to 1932, winning three gold medals and two silver.

The Attack on Pearl Harbor Predicted

It was Obvious to Him

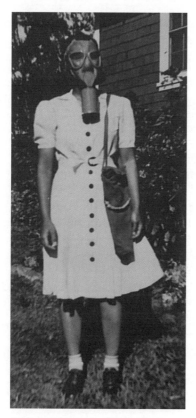

A Maui girl shows off a popular fashion accessory during the war. Gas masks for babies in case of an invasion were called Bunny Masks.

General Billy Mitchell—the father of the U.S. Air Force—predicted the attack on Pearl Harbor in 1924 after on a nine-month trip around the Pacific Ocean that included visiting Hawai'i. He wrote in his official report that Japan's imperialism would eventually bring it into war with the United States. He said it would begin with a carrier-based surprise attack by Japan on Pearl Harbor and followed by an assault on the Philippines, writing, "Attack will be launched as follows: bombardment, attack to be made on Ford Island [in Pearl Harbor] at 7:30 a.m. Group to move in column of flights in V [formation]. Each ship will drop...projectiles on the targets...Attack to be made on Clark Field [in the Philippines] at 10:40 a.m."

He later added that this would happen on a Sunday.

What Happened

His predictions were amazingly accurate. While the actual attack on Pearl Harbor didn't start until 7:55 a.m., Japanese planes were circling overhead at 7:30 a.m., but they were ordered not to begin until the slower planes with torpedoes arrived. The attack on Clark Field in the Philippines began at 12:35 p.m. that same day, which was a Sunday.

Mitchell made his prediction 17 years before the attack.

"*It might seem dramatically wrong to refer to the morning of December 7th, 1941 as "peaceful." Yet, until a few minutes before 8:00 a.m., that is exactly what it was. When explosions rattled windows and smoke billowed in the distance, most of those who could see what was going on just did not accept the possibility that they were watching an earthshaking historical event.*"

"*At the outset, we, and probably a great many other people, thought the military were carrying on a maneuver. Many people gathered out in the streets and craned their necks to watch the 'show.'*"

—DeSoto Brown

Predicting the Pearl Harbor Attack—Déjà Vu

The Story

Actually, General Billy Mitchell wasn't the only person to predict the attack. In 1928 a short story was published which contains a line describing an attack on Pearl Harbor that is eerily prophetic of what actually happened in 1941. The story "The Black Tsar" was written by French diplomat, novelist, playwright and poet Paul Morand for his book, *Magie noire*. The book was translated from French and published in America as *Black Magic* in 1929.

You can Skip This if You Want

The story itself—which is marred by racism—is not important, but for those who will no doubt be curious, here's a brief synopsis. It begins in 1927 during the U.S. occupation of Haiti from 1915 to 1934. The main character is a Haitian lawyer named Occide, who idolizes everything African and despises the United States. After setting off a bomb in a U.S. club, he hides out in the hills, living primitively and studying under a man called Clairvoyant, who believes that people can use dreams to see the future. Clairvoyant tells Occide not to fight the occupation, as it will end in its own time. Eight years later it does end and Occide takes over as President of Haiti. Modeling himself on Soviet dictator Vladimir Lenin, he launches a world-wide black communist movement, but he is soon overthrown and the Haitians welcome the return of the U.S. forces.

Okay, that's the story in a nutshell. Now you can forget it.

The Prediction

The interesting thing is *why* the U.S. ends its occupation. Paul Morand's fictional reason for this was, "The Yankees withdrew during the month that followed the opening of hostilities between the United States and Japan, after the indecisive battle of Pearl Harbour in the Hawaiian Islands." He wrote this in 1927 setting it about ten years in the future. It was actually fourteen years later in 1941 that the Japanese bombed Pearl Harbor.

Things are Always Changing
Waikīkī and the War

Private Angelo Reina, of Utica, New York, guards a Kahuku beach on O'ahu in 1945. U.S. Army

World War II had a huge impact on the world, and Hawai'i in particular. Ronn Ronck wrote in *Hawaiian Yesterdays*, "Waikīkī, of course, was forever changed by the war. Many of the men who had seen the islands during their tours of duty took their military discharges here and the population of Hawai'i rose dramatically. Waikīkī Beach was no longer a place where friends stopped and chatted. It was now a place full of strangers..."

Nostalgia

Kuʻu Home

In its glory days, Old Plantation hosted many exclusive social gatherings. The sisters were musical; they played and sang the popular Hawaiian and English-language songs of the day. One song, written for them, is still popular: "Kuʻu Home."

Pua wale mai nōke aloha
Ka paia puīa i ke ʻala
I ka wai huʻihuʻi aniani
Ko ʻiawe ka huila wai
Aia i laila ka ʻiʻini
Ka ʻanoʻi a koʻu puʻuwai

Love and affection ever rise
For the fragrance of flowers I adore
Bubbling water, sparkling and refreshing
Come from yonder water wheel
The charms and pleasures I hold dear
A spot that is dear to my heart.

Hui:
Old Plantation nani ʻoe
Home pumehana i ke aloha
I ka ʻolu o ka niu
I ka poli o ke onaona.

Chorus:
Old Plantation, how beautiful you are
Home ever warm with love
In the shade of the waving palms
In the bosom of fragrance
Softly-scented are the flowers
Moistened by the touch of dew

Nahenahe ke ʻala o na pua
I ka peʻia e ke kehau
Hoʻolaʻi na manu i laila
Hoʻoipo i ke oho o ka niu
Luhe ʻehu ka palai i ka nuʻa
I ka ʻolu o ka Old Plantation

It is there that birds find solace
And romance among the coconut fronds
Palai ferns lean and bend in abundance
In the pleasant surroundings of Old Plantation.

The lyrics were written by Mary Jane Montano, the music by David Nape. The song was copyrighted in 1938.

It is still a local favorite and has inspired other musicians to compose their own tributes to their beloved homes: "Kuʻu Home ʻo Kahaluʻu," "Kuʻu Home ʻo Maui," and so on.

—KAREN LOFSTROM

The Sad History of Old Plantation

Honolulu's Neil Blaisdell Center (concert hall, exhibition center, and arena) was built on the site of Old Plantation, a Honolulu mansion with a long, eventful, and sometimes sad past.

The Mansion

The mansion was built in the early 1880s for Curtis Ward, his part-Hawaiian wife Victoria, and their seven daughters. It stood on what were then the outskirts of Honolulu; its extensive grounds stretched from Thomas Square all the way to the sea. The two-story house was encircled by wide lanais and screened from the road by hundreds of trees. Extensive vegetable gardens and a fish pond supplied the house with food, with enough left over to sell.

Curtis Ward died unexpectedly in 1882, leaving his widow to deal with a large business and a sprawling property. She proved an astute businesswoman and left a substantial estate when she died in 1935.

Sinking into Decay

Four of her seven daughters married, to prominent Honolulu businessmen. Three of the daughters, Hattie, Kathleen, and Lucy, never married. They remained at Old Plantation. Once active in the community, they grew more reclusive as they aged. The house and grounds sank into decay.

Dementia and Death

In 1951, two of the married daughters brought suit to declare Hattie, the oldest of the three spinsters, incompetent to manage her own affairs. They claimed that she suffered from dementia and wanted her share of the estate to be managed by a local trust company. A long, sad, legal wrangle followed, pitting the married sisters and their children against the three unmarried sisters. Hattie was declared incompetent, as was another sister, Kathleen, a few years later. Lucy died in 1954.

The way was clear for the sale of Old Plantation. In 1957, the city of Honolulu bought it for $2.5 million. The house was razed and Blaisell Center rose in its place. Only a few of the original coconut trees are left of the once-thriving farm.

Hattie and Kathleen, declared incompetent and removed from their childhood home, died soon afterwards: Kathleen in 1958, Hattie in 1959.

—KAREN LOFSTROM

What Were They Thinking?
Preserving Mana

Ancient Hawaiian chiefs and royalty believed they were imbued with divine power, or mana, causing them to resort to incest in order to keep it in the family and from being weakened. This was similar to what the bluebloods and royalty of Europe were doing, believing they were superior than everyone else and had to keep their blood "pure." The science of genetics has shown us the opposite is true.

Did you know...

The Hawaiian Blue Ginger plant is not a ginger and it's not blue—it's purple. It's also from Brazil.

More Spirits of Aloha

The Blue Hawai'i

The Blue Hawai'i cocktail was invented in 1957 by Harry Yee, a bartender at the Hilton Hawaiian Village Resort and Spa on Waikīkī Beach. This predates the 1961 Elvis Presley movie of the same name and both probably get their names from the popular Bing Crosby song "Blue Hawaii" which was featured in the 1937 film *Waikiki Wedding*. The Blue Hawai'i—not to be confused with the Blue Hawaiian—came about because Bols had just come out with its Blue Curaçao liqueur and one of their representatives asked Harry Yee to create a new cocktail featuring that as its main ingredient. The result was this very popular tropical Hawaiian drink.

Pour these ingredients in this order into a 12 oz. glass with ice:

> 3 oz. pineapple juice
> 1 oz. sweet and sour mix
> 1/2 oz. blue Curaçao
> 3/4 oz. vodka
> 3/4 oz. light rum

Gently stir and garnish with a pineapple slice and vanda orchid. In Hawai'i, cocktails are often ornamented with orchids—usually a delicate purple and white variety.

That's Yee's original recipe. Over the years some bartenders have slightly modified the ingredients, often adding a dash of cream or Creme de Coconut to give the drink an attractive opalescent hue.

Sammy's Maui Rocker

Maui-resident and rocker Sammy Hagar is well known for his many solo albums, along with being the front man for the bands Montrose, Van Halen, and Chickenfoot. He also distills Sammy's Beach Bar Rum, which is made on Maui using the island's pure cane sugar. So, what's the best thing to do with authentic Hawaiian rum? Why, make tropical drinks, of course. And here's Sammy's own recipe for a hard-rockin' Hawaiian drink.

Crank up "I Can't Drive 55" on the stereo and then pour the following ingredients into a mixing glass:

> 1.5 oz. Sammy's Beach Bar Rum
> 1.5 oz. pineapple juice
> 1 oz. fresh sour
> 0.5 oz. orange Curaçao
> 0.25 oz. grenadine
> Several ice cubes.

Shake, rattle, and roll it into a punch glass, while straining out the cubes. Garnish with an orange wedge and a pineapple slice. Do not chug.

What's in a Name?
(Kahoʻolawe)

- **Kahoʻolawe** (island): carrying away by the currents. Others say it means "gatherer of driftwood," because trees trunks and debris from the Pacific Northwest are found on the island's Kanapoʻu Beach.
- **Makawao** (district): edge of the forest.
- **Kanapoʻu** (bay, beach): this is probably a contraction of Keanapou, which means "the canoe cave" or "the vaulted cave."
- **Lua Makoa** (volcano): crater of Makoa, which is the name of a large rock in the area.

The World's Tallest Sea Cliff

According to guidebooks and the *Guinness Books of World Records,* Kalaupapa on Moloka'i—next to Father Damien's old leper colony—is the tallest sea cliff in the world. Well, that depends on your definition of a sound, because there are four taller ones on sounds. Dictionary.com says a sound is "an inlet, arm, or recessed portion of the sea." So, if you really want Kalaupapa to be the highest sea cliff in the world, then you need to consider these arms of the sea as not being part of the sea. Otherwise, you have to contend with Mitre Peak, which rises 5,522 feet from Milford Sound in New Zealand, and South Greenland's 5,118-foot Maujit Qaqarssuasia, which has the easier to pronounce nickname, the Thumbnail. Milford Sound also has the 4,272-foot-tall Lion and the roughly 3,871-foot Elephant. Kalaupapa is a still highly respectable 3,314 feet. On the other hand, Mitre Peak is more than a mile high.

Moloka'i is actually only half a mountain. Around 1.5 million years ago, the northern half of the mountain collapsed and slid into the ocean, which must have caused quite a tsunami.

Did you know...

Bananas ripen at the same time by giving off ethylene gas, which will ripen all other fruit nearby.

Mark Twain Tries Surfing

In 1866, Mark Twain was canoeing down the coast of the Big Island near Hōnaunau on his way to the City of Refuge, when he saw some surfers. He wrote:

> In one place we came upon a large company of naked natives, of both sexes and all ages, amusing themselves with the national pastime of surf-bathing. Each heathen would paddle three or four hundred yards out to sea, (taking a short board with him), then face the shore and wait for a particularly prodigious billow to come along; at the right moment he would fling his board upon its foamy crest and himself upon the board, and here he would come whizzing by like a bombshell! It did not seem that a lightning express train could shoot along at a more hair-lifting speed.
>
> I tried surf-bathing once, subsequently, but made a failure of it. I got the board placed right, and at the right moment, too; but missed the connection myself.—The board struck the shore in three quarters of a second, without any cargo, and I struck the bottom about the same time, with a couple of barrels of water in me. None but natives ever master the art of surf-bathing thoroughly.
>
> —MARK TWAIN

Traditional Saying

Mahala ka pua, ua wehe kaiao.

("The blossoms are opening, for dawn is breaking." In other words, we are looking forward to a happy event.)

An Island Treasure

ʻĪao Needle

JOHN RICHARD STEPHENS

What is It?

The ʻĪao Needle is one of the most famous natural features on Maui, along with Haleakalā and the road to Hāna. It is a beautiful and amazing rock formation that is the highlight of ʻĪao Valley. This narrow valley was created when the caldera of the volcano that created the West Maui Mountains eroded from the heavy rains on the mountain's peak. The ʻĪao Needle is a volcanic monolith that was once inside the volcano, but has since been exposed by thousands of years of erosion. It now rises 1,200 feet above the valley floor, which astonishingly is just fifty feet short of the height the Empire State Building's roof, not counting its antenna spire.

The Valley of the Kings

'Īao Valley was once exclusively reserved for Maui's royalty most of the year, all except for the winter months of the Makahiki festival when the kapus were lifted. It was where the remains of many of Maui's royalty were placed. This was also the site of the conclusion of the great battle where Kamehameha attacked Maui's chiefs in 1790 to gain control over the island.

What They Don't Tell You

You will hear that the ancient Hawaiians considered the Needle to be the phallic stone of Kanaloa, the ocean god, but what you won't find in any tour books, or at the state park, is that the Hawaiian name for the 'Īao Needle—Kūkaemoku or Kuka'emoku—literally means "broken excrement."

Now, you have to wonder how exactly scholars came by this information. Presumably they had more than one source, and their sources were reliable, but you can almost picture an ethnologist walking up to a group of teenagers hanging out in 'Īao Valley, and pointing up at the Needle, asking them in Hawaiian, "What do you call that?"

They glance up and one of them responds, "What? You mean that piece of..."

Did you know...

In Hawai'i there are two days a year—early in summer and mid or late in summer—when certain objects fail to cast a shadow because the sun is directly overhead. It's called Lahaina Noon. This doesn't happen in any of the other states.

Who Would Have Guessed

The State Fowl

Hawai'i's official state bird is *not* the chicken, although it probably should be. It's the Nēnē (pronounced *nay-nay*), which is a type of goose that is only found on the islands. They're cool, too, but chickens taste better and can be used in a wider variety of dishes. Also, Nēnē are an endangered species, so it's better not to eat them.

Nēnē crossing on Haleakalā, Maui.
JOHN RICHARD STEPHENS

Uncommon Knowledge

Ask a Stupid Question...

When Cambridge professor and English classical scholar, Richard Porson, was asked in the late 1800s, "Was Captain Cook killed on his first voyage?" he promptly replied, "I believe he was, but he did not mind it much, but immediately entered on a second."

What Does It All Mean?
(O'ahu)

- **O'ahu (island):** the name of the child of the goddess Papa from her affair with the god Lua.
- **Diamond Head (crater):** formerly called Lae'ahi (brow or crest of the 'ahi fish) and sometimes Kaimana Hila (Diamond Hill) in the 1800s.
- **Waikīkī (beach):** spouting water.
- **Mānoa (valley):** vast.
- **Ko'olau (mountain range):** windward.
- **Honolulu (district, city):** protected bay.
- **Māmala (bay):** named for a mythical shark woman said to protect the entrance to the bay.
- **Hālawa (town):** curve.
- **'Aiea (town):** Nothocestrum tree.
- **Waimalu (town):** sheltered water.
- **Waipi'o (town):** curved water.
- **Mililani (town):** beloved place of chiefs.
- **Waipahu (town):** bursting water from underground.
- **'Ewa (district, town, beach):** crooked.
- **Makakilo City (town):** watching eyes.
- **Wai'anae (mountains, district, town):** mullet water.
- **Nānākuli (town):** look at knee, or look deaf. The former refers to the tattooed knee of a kahuna named Ka-'ōpulupulu, whose chief was deaf to his advice. The latter refers to an incident when the people who lived there pretended to be deaf because they didn't have enough food to offer passersby.
- **Mā'ili (town):** pebbly.
- **Mākaha (valley, town):** fierce.
- **Wahiawā (district, town):** milkfish place.
- **Leilehua (plain):** this is an ancient name that doesn't appear to have a translation.
- **Waialua (bay, district, town):** this might mean "two waters."
- **Hale'iwa (town):** house of a frigate bird.
- **Waimea (valley, falls, beach):** reddish water.
- **Pūpūkea (town):** white shell.

- **Koʻolau (mountain range):** windward.
- **Koʻolauloa (district):** a fishline for a specific type of fish that is 90 feet long.
- **Kahuku (town):** the projection.
- **Lāʻie (town):** an ʻie leaf.
- **Koʻolaupoko (district):** this is an ancient name that doesn't appear to have a translation.
- **Kāneʻohe (bay, town):** a variety of sweet potato.
- **Kailua (town):** two seas, or two ocean currents.
- **Waimānalo (beach, town):** drinking water.

Looking down on Diamond Head and its surroundings. JOHN RICHARD STEPHENS

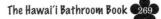

Did you know...

The Pacific Ocean covers one-third of the earth, contains half of the world's water, and probably has more than 7,500 islands.

Go for Broke!

Sending Americans to the Camps

We don't normally hear the internment camps for Japanese-Americans called concentration camps, but that's what they were. The *Collins English Dictionary* defines the term as, "a guarded prison camp in which nonmilitary prisoners are held," while the *Random House Dictionary* says it's "a guarded compound for the detention or imprisonment of aliens, members of ethnic minorities, political opponents, etc." That's exactly what they were. Of course, they were nothing like the Nazi's concentration and death camps with their horrendous horrors.

Shortly after the war the U.S. Secretary of the Interior Harold Ickes said, "As a member of President Roosevelt's administration, I saw the United States Army give way to mass hysteria over the Japanese...Crowded into cars like cattle, these hapless people were hurried away to hastily constructed and thoroughly inadequate concentration camps, with soldiers with nervous muskets on guard, in the great American desert. We gave the fancy name of 'relocation centers' to these dust bowls, but they were concentration camps nonetheless."

The U.S. Government Apologizes

We use the term to refer to camps in other countries, but not our own. We don't like the idea that our country would do such a thing, but eventually the U.S. government admitted what it had done was racist and apologized for it. The official apology was signed in 1988 by President Ronald Reagan, who said, "It was based solely on race, for these 120,000 were Americans of Japanese descent."

Hawai'i Resists

Most of those interned were from the West Coast states of California and Oregon, most of whom had been born and raised in the United States. Hawai'i had a larger population of Japanese-Americans than both of those states put together.

Here they made up a third of the population, numbering more than 150 thousand, yet only 2,200 to 2,800 of these were interned. There was a lot of pressure from the U.S. government to intern Hawai'i's entire Japanese-American population, but Hawai'i was a territory, not a state, so the territorial governor was able to resist. It was also under martial law, which made potential spying and sabotage more difficult. Removing one third of Hawai'i's population would have devastated the economy and been far more damaging than anything spies or saboteurs could have done. Those that were interned were sent to the five concentration camps on the islands, or to one of the many camps on the mainland.

Most of those interned felt there was nothing they could do about it, so they just went along with it, partly out of a sense of duty to the U.S. government. They had a saying— *"shikata ga nai,"* which loosely translated means "it is what it is."

Oddly, no one thought of doing this to German-Americans. They didn't question the loyalty of General Eisenhower, General Spaatz, or Admiral Nimitz.

The beginning of the attack on Pearl Harbor photographed from one of the Japanese planes.

Japan's Spy Network

They did all of this as a precaution against spying and sabotage. They needn't have bothered. Long after the war it was revealed that Imperial Japan had only one spy in the U.S. and he left Honolulu right after the attack. His name was Takeo Yoshikawa. He was sent to Honolulu about eight months before the attack to gather all the information he could on the fleet and Pearl Harbor. This he did, and it was the intelligence he provided that made the attack so devastating.

No one would have suspected he was a spy. He was very cautious not to raise suspicion. With his photographic memory, he didn't have to take any notes. He gathered all his information legally, but he couldn't reveal what he was doing to anyone. As he later said, all the Japanese-Americans "were loyal to the United States."

After the war he was ostracized in Japan. The Japanese had paid a terrible price and many people blamed it on him—even the two atomic bombs. The government refused him a pension and he died penniless.

Emblem of the 100th Infantry Battalion.

Volunteering to Fight and Die

In spite of the internments, many Japanese-Americans volunteered to fight in the war. They were placed together in the 442nd Regimental Combat Team, which, for its size and length of service, became the most decorated unit in U.S. military history. Around 14,000 Nisei served in the unit, receiving 18,143 awards, which included 21 Medals of Honor, a Congressional Gold Medal, 8 Presidential Unit Citations, and 9,486 Purple Hearts. They had a very high casualty rate of 93%. They fought in Europe, primarily against the Germans. They're best known for rescuing the "Lost Battalion" that was surrounded by Germans.

Initially 3,000 primarily Nisei from the Hawaiian National Guard were formed into the 100th Infantry Battalion—the One-Puka-Puka, whose motto was "Remember Pearl Harbor." They were later joined by and placed under the command of the 442nd. The motto of the 442nd was "Go for Broke!" This is an excerpt from their unit song:

> We're the boys of Hawai'i nei—
> We'll fight for you
> And the Red, White and Blue,
> And go to the front...
> And back to Honolulu-lulu.
> Fighting for dear old Uncle Sam
> Go for broke! *Hooh!* We don't give a damn!

Hawai'i's 442nd off to war in a ceremony at Iolani Palace on March 28, 1943. HAWAI'I STATE ARCHIVES

Did you know...

To prove their courage, Hawaiian chiefs dove off the eighty-foot Wailua Falls.

 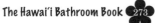

Revenge?

A Little Present from the Whalers

Rev. William Richards, c.1843.
HAWAI'I STATE ARCHIVES

Mosquitos first hitched a ride over to Hawai'i in 1826 on the British whaling ship *Wellington* in water casks that were filled in San Blás, Mexico, and then dumped at the port in Lahaina on Maui before the casks were refilled with fresh water. However, there is a story that the sailors dumped a cask of wriggler-infested water near the houses of missionaries Rev. William Richards and that of Rev. Ephraim Spaulding—whose house is now known as the Baldwin House and Museum—because of their ongoing feud with the missionaries, who, in an attempt to prevent prostitution, were keeping Hawaiian women from sailing out to greet the incoming ships. From the common Hawaiian women's point-of-view, consorting with sailors was a fun way of obtaining Western goods, which otherwise were only available to the chiefs, so they weren't happy about the restrictions. The missionaries were hard at work with the ali'i writing the Ten Commandments into the laws of the Kingdom of Hawai'i.

Fighting Back

The sailors, of course, were furious. They wanted to enjoy themselves when they came ashore and they felt the missionaries were overstepping their bounds by outlawing everything they liked. The previous year, in October 1825, the crew of the whaler *Daniel IV* marched on Rev. Richards' house threatening to kill him, but Richards was saved by the Native Hawaiians.

Then in 1826, sailors attacked Lahaina, but Rev. Richards and his family escaped. The following year the British whaler *John Palmer* tried to bombard the Richards' house while Rev. Richards and his family hid out in the cellar, but all five cannonballs missed their target.

That was the same year the *Wellington*'s crew is thought to have dumped the mosquito larvae outside the missionaries' houses, introducing the pest to Hawai'i.

The Weird and the Wild
Attack of the Biting Mosquitoes

Whether the infestation of Hawai'i with mosquitoes was on accident or on purpose, within ten years they had spread to O'ahu and Kaua'i. There are now two night-biting species on Hawai'i. The Southern House Mosquito is the most common and was the one that arrived in 1826. The other is the Inland Floodwater Mosquito. It came to Hawai'i in 1962 and is now on all the main islands, except Maui. The Asian Tiger Mosquito, which arrived in 1896, was the first of four day-biting species. In 1981 the Bromeliad or Pineapple Lily Mosquito became established on Kaua'i, O'ahu and the Big Island. The following year the Yellow Fever Mosquito established itself in small pockets on the Big Island and Moloka'i, although some of the latter were found on O'ahu in 2012. Hawai'i's sixth biting mosquito—the Japanese or Rockpool Mosquito—settled in on the east coast of the Big Island in 2004. State quarantine officers have prevented the arrival of more than forty other mosquito species, and they have to be constantly vigilant.

Tiny Vampires

Vegetarians and Bloodsuckers

It's only the female mosquitoes that are bloodsuckers. The males are all vegetarians, drinking flower nectars or fruit juices. They never bite. The females need to drink blood in order to produce their eggs. After biting you, they lay around for a few days while their eggs develop. Once they lay them, they're off searching for someone else to bite so they can lay more eggs.

Bad News for Birds

Mosquitoes can spread human diseases, but this is rare in Hawai'i and generally not of much concern. What is alarming is that they are contributing to the extinction of some very beautiful birds are found only in Hawai'i. The avian pox virus and avian malaria, which are harmless to humans, has decimated some bird populations, particularly the Hawaiian honeycreeper species. A third of these species went extinct before the Southern House Mosquito arrived in 1826 and another third after. It's thought that as the avian pox wiped out bird populations, cage birds were brought over and released to replace those that were dying, but that this introduced the avian malaria, which was even worse than the pox.

Vanishing Honeycreepers

The Hawaiian honeycreepers evolved from some cardueline finches that came here three to four million years ago when only Ni'ihau, Kaua'i, and Oahu were the main Hawaiian Islands. They slowly evolved over the many, many centuries into at least 56 species and subspecies of honeycreepers by the time the first Polynesians arrived. Now most of these are gone. Of the 17 that remain, six are critically endangered, four are endangered, five are vulnerable, and only two of these widely varying species are doing okay. Some have retreated to high elevations where it's too cold for the bloodsuckers. With the disappearance of the honeycreepers, seven species of mountain hibiscus—which are only found in Hawai'i—have pretty much been wiped out largely because they need honeycreepers for pollination.

Eradicating the Little Buggers

Of course, there have been some attempts to wipe out the mosquitoes. According to the *Hawaiian Almanac and Annual for 1903*, "The introduction of toads a few years ago to rid these islands of the mosquito pest had a like effort much earlier through Dr. Wm. Hillebrand, as mention is made in the papers of the day of his receiving five frogs and a lizard from San Francisco in September 1857, which he turned loose in his gardens to propagate and remedy this very evil. Another lot of toads, frogs, etc., as a set-off to mosquitos were also imported in November of the same year, with a number of deer, by M. M. Russell, in the bark *Yankee* from San Francisco. The new toads are said to be thriving,—and so are the mosquitoes."

The introduction of minnows from Texas to streams and ponds in 1905 has helped reduce the mosquito population.

Did you know...

Hawai'i is the only state with tropical rainforests.

Did you know...

Female coqui frogs don't sing, so what you hear are males serenading the females.

Black Sand, White Sand, Red Sand, Green Sand

Hawai'i's white sand beaches are primarily made of the hard parts of marine organisms—coral, shell fragments, bits of marine skeletons—with a small amount of volcanic material mixed in. Black sand beaches are primarily erosion from volcanic rocks. Most of the black sand beaches are found on the Big Island, with a few on Maui. There are also some red sand beaches which come from cinder cones, and some really beautiful tan sand beaches. There is even a green sand beach. The green sand beach is near the Big Island's South Point and contains the volcanic mineral, olivine. On Kaua'i, there's Glass Beach and Swiss Cheese Shoreline that are largely made up of small, water-worn bits of discarded man-made glass from an old dump site, but it is rapidly disappearing as glass enthusiasts and beachcombers haul it away and no new glass is dumped to replace it. These glass pebbles come in a wide variety of colors, from brown to blue to green to clear.

Tan sand at Big Beach in south Maui. JOHN RICHARD STEPHENS

Forget About Columbus

Hawai'i is one of three states that do not recognize Columbus Day; the other two being South Dakota and Alaska. South Dakota, along with several cities and counties around the country, have replaced Columbus Day with Native American Day or Indigenous People's Day. Hawai'i unofficially celebrates Discoverers' Day, which honors the first Polynesians who discovered the islands sometime around 100 to 300 AD, settling at the southern tip of the Big Island. Only federal government offices are closed on this day.

The U.S. Government is Sorry

In 1993 the U.S. government officially said it was sorry for the overthrow of the Kingdom of Hawai'i, stating that "the United States Minister assigned to the sovereign and independent Kingdom of Hawaii conspired with a small group of non-Hawaiian residents of the Kingdom of Hawaii, including citizens of the United States, to overthrow the indigenous and lawful Government of Hawaii" and that "without the active support and intervention by the United States diplomatic and military representatives, the insurrection against the Government of Queen Lili'uokalani would have failed." It acknowledged that the "illegal acts of the conspirators" and the subsequent U.S. invasion were an "act of war" on "the government of a peaceful and friendly people."

The U.S. government hoped the apology would facilitate a reconciliation with the Native Hawaiians without doing anything further.

Adam Sandler on Location

Adam Sandler has made several romantic comedies in Hawai'i. Referring to filming here, he told Jay Leno on *The Tonight Show* how much he loved it, adding, "You try to learn something when you're shooting a movie. You try to learn something new every time. The first movie—I shot *Punch-Drunk Love* there—I said, 'Let me learn how to surf.' I shot the second movie—*50 First Dates*—I said, 'Let me learn how to scuba dive.' This past movie I said, 'Let me learn how to fall in love with a Samoan man.' So I did that. If he's watching, his name is Kamana Kup'abala."

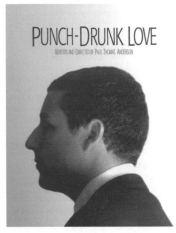

Punch-Drunk in Honolulu

Punch-Drunk Love (2002): Sandler's character is the beleaguered owner of a novelties company, selling items like themed toilet plungers. He meets and falls in love Emily Watson's character and pursues her to O'ahu using some of the million frequent flyer miles he obtained from buying pudding (that last part is based on a true story). There are problems, but he ends up with the gal in the end.

Most of this movie was filmed in Los Angeles, but the O'ahu scenes were shot in the Honolulu area and include Waikīkī Beach and the Kāhala Mandarin Oriental Hotel at 5000 Kāhala Avenue.

50 First Dates on O'ahu

50 First Dates (2004): Set in Hawai'i, a womanizing marine-life veterinarian (Sandler) falls in love with the woman of his dreams (Drew Barrymore), but she suffers from amnesia.

Each day when she wakes up, she can't remember anything that's happened to her since her car accident a year before, including meeting Sandler's character, so he has to introduce himself to her every day.

Much of this movie was filmed on the windward side and North Shore of O'ahu; more specifically, in Makapu'u, Waimānalo, Kāne'ohe, Kāne'ohe Bay, Waikāne Pier, Ka'a'awa, Wahiawā, and Waimea Valley. Some scenes were also shot in Honolulu and at Honolulu's Hawai'i Film Studio on 18th Avenue and Diamond Head Road. The boat *Sea Serpent* is berthed in Ko 'Olina and is actually named *Viking Spirit*. Some shots, such as the golf course and interior scenes, were filmed in and around Los Angeles. Others were filmed in Alaska and San Francisco, while the walrus tank is in Vallejo, California. They also filmed at the Dillingham Estate at 68434 Farrington Highway in Mokulē'ia; Kualoa Ranch at 49560 Kamehameha Highway in Ka'a'awa; and at Sea Life Park in Waimānalo.

Just Go With It on Maui

Just Go With It (2011): This film is loosely based on the 1969 romantic comedy *Cactus Flower* starring Walter Matthau, Ingrid Bergman, and Goldie Hawn, which in turn was based on a French play.

Adam Sandler's character—a plastic surgeon—pretends to be unhappily married to avoid commitment in relationships. When he meets a much-younger woman who won't have anything to do with him because she thinks he's married, he assures her he's getting a divorce. She, then, insists on meeting the estranged wife he doesn't have, so he talks his assistant (Jennifer Aniston) into posing as his wife, but her two kids blackmail him into taking everyone to Maui. Aniston's character then does everything she can to throw monkey wrenches at him while more lies ensue.

The primary scenes were filmed in Wailea on Maui at the Waldorf Astoria's Grand Wailea Beach Resort, which is one of Hawai'i's most gorgeous resorts. There are scenes at the nearby Gannon's Restaurant and the wedding was at the Maui Prince Resort's Maluaka Beach in Mākena. The tiki bar was constructed for the film at the Grand Wailea. The luau was also at the Grand Wailea. Over on Kaua'i, scenes were filmed at the magnificent St. Regis Princeville Resort and the beautiful Kīlauea Falls, also known as Rainbow Falls. The rickety rope bridge leading to the falls was made for the film.

Did you know...

On arriving in Hawai'i, Adam Sandler's character in *Punch-Drunk Love,* says, "It really looks like Hawaii here."

The Nightmarchers Walk Among Us

Collector of Hawaiian ghost stories, Glen Grant, received the following firsthand account of an eerie encounter with the nightmarchers from a Polynesian man who was 22 years old at the time Grant recorded his experience in 1993.

This account is a bit unusual for Hawai'i in that these were interracial nightmarchers.

One of the best sources for ghost stories are night watchmen who have to spend the night in haunted places while the rest of us are safely at home. While they have more to fear from the living than the dead, once in a while a security guard will encounter the unknown.

One guard who claimed to have experienced nightmarchers in 1989 was parked one morning at 3 a.m. in front of a church in Kahuku. He had just checked to make sure that the gate to the church was locked when he took a break in his front seat. As he was taking a drink of freshwater from this thermos, *Whack!*—a force struck him right in the forehead, throwing him back into the seat and then hurling him down. Struggling against something he could not see, he felt a force grab his hands and then pull them across his chest. With his arms crossed like a dead man in a coffin, this invisible force began to press him into the seat. He was unable to move or breathe.

Then he felt the tips of two ice-cold fingers suddenly press on his eyelids, tightly closing his eyes. As he was lying in the front seat of his car, pressed to the front seat, his hands crossed and eyes shut, the gate to the church grounds which he had locked, slowing began to open with a long, creaking sound from its rusty hinges. The gate slowly creaked open, then he heard the sounds of dozens of people walking by his car. All the people were talking with one another. He recognized the language—it was a Chinese dialect. The voices passed right by his car.

Unable to breathe or move, the guard struggled against the force, his fists tightly closed as he pushed up unsuccessfully. Then he realized that if he relaxed and opened his fists, he could actually pry his eyelids open with his fingers. When he pushed open his eyelids so that he could see what it was that was holding him down, he saw two tall Hawaiian men standing at each of his front windows, each man with his head in the open windows staring at the immobilized guard. He knew the gaze of the two men looking at him, one at his feet and one at his head, was the force which kept him pressed.

When the procession of talking Chinese finally passed by his car, the gate suddenly slammed shut. And the two Hawaiian men at both sides of his automobile dematerialized. He drove to the nearest phone booth and called in to the security office for an emergency substitute. He told me that he refused to spend the rest of the night in Kahuku.

The next day he was certain that if he hiked mauka of the church into the woods of the valley he might find the cause of his strange encounter. Sure enough, there it was—an old Chinese graveyard for the early immigrants of the last century who once worked on the Kahuku sugar plantation. Their graves were in a direct line down through the church, past his car and to the sea. He was convinced that the night-marchers had passed his automobile.

In modern Hawaii, I have collected stories from people of all backgrounds who believe the nightmarchers they have encountered was comprised of people of all races, not just Hawaiians. While a multicultural procession of huakai o ha po would not be in accordance with traditional Hawaiian belief, who is to know what may occur today in the spirit realm?

—GLEN GRANT (*OBAKE FILES*)

Spirits on the March

Accounts of marching spirits, similar to the nightmarchers, can be found in other cultures. In Ireland they are armies of sidhe (spirit) warriors. In the U.K. it's usually marching Roman soldiers that are seen—sometimes marching on old roads now buried so that only the upper half of their bodies are above ground or they are seen marching through stone walls which weren't there in Roman times. In the Eastern U.S., people see marching soldiers from the Revolutionary War or the Civil War. In most of these cases they seem oblivious to the living. That is, except for the sidhe. They can be very dangerous. It's said if they spot you, chances are you'll be stuck in their world and will never make it back to the world of the living.

Fun and Games

Hawaiian Sledding

David Malo was a leading Native Hawaiian historian who lived through King Kamehameha I's reign. Originally written in the 1830s in the Hawaiian language, Malo here describes one type of ancient Hawaiian recreation.

Sledding as a Sport
Sliding down hill on the holua-sled was a sport greatly in vogue among chiefs and people, and one on the issue of which they were very fond of making bets, when the fit took them.

The holua was a long course laid out down the steep incline of a hill and extending onto the level plain. Rocks were first laid down, then earth was put on and beaten hard, lastly the whole was layered with grass, and this was the track for the holua-sled to run on.

The Sleds

The runners of the holua-sled were made of ma-mane, or of uhiuhi wood, chamfered to a narrow edge below, with the forward end turned up, so as not to dig into the ground, and connected with each other by means of cross-pieces in a manner similar to the joining of a double-canoe.

On top of the cross-pieces boards were then laid, as in flooring the pola of a canoe. This done and the runners lubricated with oil of the kukui-nut, the sled was ready for use.

The bets having been arranged, the racers took their stations at the head of the track; the man who was ranged in front gave his sled a push to start it and mounted it, whereupon his competitor who was to his rear likewise started his sled and followed after. He who made the longest run was the victor. In case both contestants travelled the length of the course, it was a dead heat and did not decide who was victory.

The victory was declared for the player who made the best run.

David Malo's book also contained the following notes written by his book's translator, Dr. N. B. Emerson. He refers to the sled tracks as they were in 1898.

Old Courses

The course of an old-time holua slide is at the present writing clearly to be made out sloping down the foot-hills back of the Kamehameha School. The track is of such a width—about 18 feet—as to preclude the possibility of two sleds travelling abreast. It is substantially paved with flat stones, which must have held their position for many generations. The earth that once covered them has been mostly washed away. The remains of an ancient kahua holua are also to be made out at Keauhou, or were a few years ago.

Daredevil Feats

From the sample of the holua sled to be seen at the Bishop museum, it seems a wonder that any one was able to ride the sled down such a descent as either one of the two just mentioned, or to keep on the thing at all. The two runners are—in the specimen at the museum—twelve and a half feet long, are set about two and a half inches apart at the narrow, sliding edge, and about six inches apart on top, where the body of the man rests.

A more difficult feat by far it must have been to ride on this tipsy affair at speed than to keep one's balance on the back of a horse, a la circus-rider; yet it is asserted that there were those who would ride down hill on the holua-sled at break-neck speed maintaining at the same time an erect position. It hardly seems credible. The swift rush of the toboggan is as nothing to this.

—DAVID MALO (*HAWAIIAN ANTIQUITIES*)

Uncommon Knowledge

Kaua'i Saves Sinatra, Twice

The rescue of Frank Sinatra in rough waves off Wailua is well-known on Kaua'i. What's little known is the spark the island people gave to Sinatra when he was in the doldrums in 1952.

Sinatra at the Kaua'i County Fair

Longtime Kaua'i resident and Sinatra fan Lillian Daily of 'Anini traveled from her hometown in Roselle, New Jersey to the Paramount Theater in Manhattan in the bobbysocks era of the 1940s to hear Sinatra during his early ascent to fame. But her most memorable Sinatra concert took place in April 1952 under a leaky County Fair tent at a spot near the Wailua golf course.

"It was unforgettable," said Daily, who came to Kaua'i in the late 1940s when her husband launched Love's bread operation here. "Sinatra was at a low ebb in his life. He was offered a job as a soloist at the Kaua'i County Fair...can you believe that!"

"It was where the second nine holes of the golf course is today," she remembered. "It was a rainy Sunday afternoon and he did his regularly scheduled show, avoiding all these leaks. When that was pau, he walked to the edge of the stage and sat down and looked out at the audience and said 'What do you want to hear?' and what ever anybody called out he sang...he sang his heart out."

Sinatra's daughter Nancy Sinatra, writing in her book *Frank Sinatra: An American Legend* calls the Kaua'i County Fair appearance her dad's big "Comeback Concert."

A Warm Reception
The singer's buddy in Hawai'i, the late Buck Buchwach, then a reporter with the *Honolulu Advertiser*, recalled how Sinatra reacted to the concert. Frank told him, "I wondered if the show really did have to go on. Then I peeked out at the audience. There were a few hundred, tops. They weren't wearing fancy clothes or expensive jewelry. They wore aloha shirts, jeans, mu'umu'u and such. Homey. And their warmth and friendliness smacked me in the face. And when two brown-skinned young girls gave me a couple of handmade lei and little kisses, I almost broke down."

Buchwach said after singing for the county fair audience—accompanied only by a pianist—Sinatra had tears in his eyes and said that the night marked the first night on his way back to the top.

"From that moment, everything seemed to go right for him," Buchwach wrote.

Sinatra and Ava Gardner
Well, maybe not everything, according to Mike Ash-

man of Princeville who was then a KTOH radio announcer who interviewed the singer on the air and got to know Sinatra during his first visit.

"Sinatra had agreed to come to Po'ipū and play volleyball on Sunday morning and he never showed up," Ashman said. "He was staying at the Kaua'i Inn, at the end of Rice Street, and Ava Gardner had flown in."

Sinatra and Gardner married in Pennsylvania previous November, but her career soon eclipsed his after the singer's record sales cooled off. Their stormy marriage lasted only a few years.

"I drove to Lihue and he was in the dining room with Ava Gardner having a very serious conversation," Ashman said. "He saw me and gave me a negative wave and I left. Shortly after that they broke up, and the break up was apparently in discussion then. She left Kaua'i and went back to Honolulu."

That November Gardner, along with the singer's friendship with movie mogul Harry Cohn, helped Sinatra get the role of Maggio, his Oscar-winning role in the O'ahu-made film *From Here to Eternity*, a role that for good turned his career around and led to his major stardom.

Caught in the Undertow
On a return visit in 1964, Sinatra came within minutes of drowning in the surf off Wailua Beach. He was here to direct and star in the film *None But the Brave* and chose an isolated beach north of Moloa'a as the principle location.

Toward the end of the filming Sinatra spent a Sunday afternoon relaxing at a beach front home once located near where the Lae Nani condominiums are today. The home became known as "The Frank Sinatra House" and was later trailered up to Wailua Homesteads. Joining him were long-time pal July Rizzo, producer Howard W. Koch and his wife Ruth Koch, and some of the cast.

In an interview for *The Kaua'i Movie Book* Koch described the day to me. He said despite his warning not to go in the ocean, his wife decided to take a swim and Sinatra, noticing that the surf was up, said he would go in her to protect her from the undertow. They were wading just offshore when the inside wash from a big set of waves swept them away. The next wave drew Koch toward shore, but dragged Sinatra about 200 yards out.

Sinatra Turning Blue

While a young actor tried to get Sinatra in, the others ran for help. Eventually assistance came from county supervisor Louis Gonsalves and Harold Jim, then an assistant manager at the Coco Palms, and from the Kaua'i Fire Department.

"Sinatra was in the water for about twenty minutes, in another five minutes he would have been gone," Fire Lieutenant George Keawe told *The Garden Island*. "His face was starting to turn blue."

Sinatra finally made it to the beach and he was carried into the beach house on a stretcher. After a checkup a doctor found he was okay, but exhausted. His daughter remembers that she made him eggs and peppers and the two watched TV until he fell asleep. But producer Koch recalls that he and others who watched helplessly on the beach started drinking and didn't stop "until we didn't know where we were."

Koch took over the director's chair the next day, but Sinatra was soon back in action to complete the American-Japanese production.

—Chris Cook (*A Kaua'i Reader*)

The Wiggling Black Tail

An Unknown Creature

In the fall of 2010, my girlfriend and I were staying in a vacation rental in the Mormon town of Laie on O'ahu, where they lock up the beaches on Sundays, or at least the parking lots to the beaches. It was late at night—about 2 a.m.—and I had just finished brushing my teeth when I saw a thin black tail wiggling along under the bathroom door. My girlfriend, Elaine, was asleep in bed right on the other side of the door and I know very well how she feels about rats, mice and anything else with thin hairless tails. While I think opossums are kind of cute, she's convinced they're the devil's spawn and should be blasted from the face of the planet, preferably with massive amounts of napalm. No matter how often I tell her they're marsupials, not rodents, she's still convinced they're just giant rats, or the result of interbreeding between rats and raccoons. I tell her that's impossible, but she doesn't believe me.

Anyway, I knew I had to protect her from this unknown creature, so I grabbed my flashlight, opened the door, and on my hands and knees I chased the wriggling tail into the bedroom closet. I quickly realized that there was no body attached to the tail and that it resembled an earthworm, but was much darker. It looked like a wiggly pencil lead about four inches long. It was moving along very quickly, but I wasn't prepared for what it did when I touched it. Suddenly it went into a frenzy of spasms, very rapidly flopping around, obviously trying to scare away whatever had assaulted it.

As Fast as Greased Lightning

I'm always amazed at how fast some of Hawai'i's scarier creatures move. Centipedes move like lightning. These guys can grow to about a foot in length and they're built like little armored vehicles. I slammed a shoe down on a six-inch centipede a couple of times and it just ran away. I had to corner it again and hit it harder a couple more times before it started to look a little dizzy. While I don't like to harm critters and will generally catch them and release them outside, I don't want creatures that bite or sting around the house where they can reproduce and come back in, so I do send these to an early grave.

Scorpions are just about as fast, but four- or five-inch cane spiders are even faster. I've tried hitting a couple of them before and both times they got away. They are also very tough. When I tried to smash them near the ceiling with the bristles of a broom, they just dropped to the floor and ran away. I never found them again, so I was left hoping I annoyed them enough that they found their outside way on their own. I've since learned that the best way of dispatching cane spiders is to hose them with bug spray, but they still get away. I've only caught two, but they were distracted and slowing down after I doused them a couple of times.

A four-inch Hawaiian Blind Snake in my backyard. Its head is at the top. There were two or three others with it. JOHN RICHARD STEPHENS

The Pencil-Lead Critter

Well, the pencil-lead creature was about as fast as a centipede. While I have no problem exterminating scorpions and centipedes, I don't like killing things that are harmless, and the wiggling pencil lead looked like some sort of shiny but dry worm, so I picked it up and took it outside to let it go. It was scaly, but I couldn't see any eyes or a mouth. After it shot away to safety, I looked it up and discovered that contrary to popular opinion, there *are* snakes in Hawai'i. There are actually two kinds of snakes here: the Hawaiian Blind Snake and the Yellow-Bellied Sea Snake, which are rather rare.

This one was a blind snake, which is also known as the

Brahminy Blind Snake and the Island Blind Snake. They were introduced to Hawai'i from the Philippines sometime around 1930. I suspect the blind snakes are quite common because a few months later I was digging some dirt in a gully next to my house near Wailea on Maui, when one of these snakes shot out from under some leaves and up into my sandal. While I'm not nearly as fast as they are, I quickly shook it off my foot—or I should say "I shook *her* off my foot" since all blind snakes are female. They reproduce through parthenogenesis, which means they don't need males to get pregnant—they all have virgin births. I think people must come across these snakes all the time and just think they're worms—especially since these are burrowing snakes. I would have been convinced the second snake was an earthworm if I hadn't had my close encounter with the first one.

I have since come across about a dozen of these snakes in my backyard. They are safe to pick up. While holding them, I've seen them trying to bite me, but their mouths are so small that I couldn't feel anything.

Traditional Saying

Ahu ka ʻala ʻala palu.

("A heap of relish made of octopus liver." Mashed octopus liver was used as bait, not food. The phrase is used to refer to something that is not worth worrying about.)

The World's Tallest Mountain

Climbing Mt. Everest

Ever dream of climbing Mt. Everest? It's fun to consider, but most people have absolutely no desire to hike for six to nine weeks over hideous terrain to a place that's freezing, windy, and has an oxygen-depleted atmosphere which will give you frostbite, hypothermia, snow blindness, severe headaches, nausea, vomiting, and/or death. All so you can brag that you are one of about 3,500 people who made it to the top of world's tallest mountain. Or join the nearly 200 people who died trying. And it will cost you between $25,000 and $100,000. Forget that! Besides, whether Mt. Everest is actually the world's tallest mountain or not, all depends on how you measure it.

The Challenger

The summit of Mt. Everest reaches 29,035 feet above sea level. Now, Hawai'i's tallest mountain, Mauna Kea, rises 13,792 feet above sea level, but that's just the tip of the iceberg. Just as Everest is part of the Himalayas, Mauna Kea is part of the Hawaiian-Emperor Seamount Chain, most of which is underwater. From its base on the sea floor to its summit is 33,476 feet. Since Mt. Everest sits on the Tibetan Plateau, its height from the lowest point of its base is only 15,260 feet. Measuring it this way, Mauna Kea is the world's tallest mountain, beating out Everest by 18,216 feet.

Relative sizes of Mauna Kea and Mt. Everest. JOHN RICHARD STEPHENS THIS IS A MODIFIED VERSION OF A DIAGRAM BY THE U.S. GEOLOGIC SURVEY.

It's Not Just a Mountain

Not only that, Mauna Kea is also the world's largest volcano. It last erupted about 4,600 years ago and is one of five hot-spot volcanoes on the Big Island. Being a volcano, Mauna Kea is a huge pile of lava that doesn't sit flat on the ocean floor. It actually presses down into the ocean floor in an inverted cone shape—sort of a mirror image of the volcano above. If you include this as being part of the volcano, then Mauna Kea is about 59,500 feet tall.

Skiing on Mauna Kea with Mauna Loa way off in the distance. DOUGLAS PEEBLES

Forget Climbing

But, get this: the greatest thing Mauna Kea has over Everest is that you can drive there! Not only that. *You can drive up to the top of the world's tallest mountain—you can even snowboard and ski—and then head back down to hang out on the beach drinking Mai Tais or banana-mango smoothies, all in the same day!!!* How cool is that?

Another One

There's more. Right next to Mauna Kea is Mauna Loa. This one is an active volcano that last erupted in 1984 and has erupted thirty-three times since 1843. Its peak is 13,674 feet above sea level, or 33,358 feet from its base on the sea floor, which makes it 18,098 feet taller than Everest. It's the world's second tallest mountain and the largest active volcano. Measuring it this way, even Alaska's Mt. McKinley is taller than Everest.

Everest Shmeverest

One other thing: Mt. Everest's summit is not even the highest point on Earth. Because of the Earth's irregular potato shape, if you measure from the center of the Earth, the highest spot on the planet is actually the summit of Chimborazo in Ecuador, which rises 20,565 feet above sea level, though its peak is 3,967 miles above the center of the Earth.

All of this means Mt. Everest is just another mountain.

 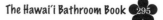

A Pacific Hero

Herb Kawainui Kāne's statue more closely resembles the king. JOHN RICHARD STEPHENS

Kamehameha or Not Kamehameha

The most famous statues of King Kamehameha I are not really of him. How this happened is an interesting story.

Kamehameha, of course, is best remembered for uniting seven of the eight main Hawaiian islands, forming the Kingdom of Hawai'i in 1810. The first statue was proposed to the Hawaiian legislature in 1878 by Walter Gibson. He chose a Boston sculptor named Thomas Gould to design it. Gould had never been to Hawai'i, but he was sent reference photographs. King David Kalākaua decided to use his friends, John Timoteo Baker and Robert Hoapili Baker, as models for the statue. He chose the Bakers, who were part Caucasian and part Hawaiian, because he felt that foreigners would find their features more pleasing. But Gould did use an old engraving of Kamehameha.

Kamehameha Caesar

Gould was living in Florence, Italy, when he designed the statue, drawing inspiration from those of Roman emperors and generals. He apparently took the pose from a statue of Augustus Caesar. The Kamehameha statue has Grecian sandals, a longer, draping Roman-influenced robe and sash-like malo, but more importantly, Kamehameha has a Roman-looking nose. The spear was later modified from the original design to more closely match Hawaiian spears and Gibson requested that the face be altered to more closely match Kamehameha's. While they intended the statue to be accurate, they also wanted ed to create what they called a "Pacific hero."

Lost and Found

The eight-and-a-half-foot statue was cast in Paris and was to be shipped from Germany to Hawai'i around Cape Horn, but the ship carrying it caught fire and sank at the Falkland Islands. The legislature used the insurance money to cast a replacement from the same mold. This one was installed in Honolulu, across from the 'Iolani Palace. It was unveiled in 1883 by King Kalakaua during his coronation, which had been delayed for nine years.

The original slightly damaged statue was recovered and eventually installed in Kapa'au on the Big Island, close to where Kamehameha was born. For the unveiling, the concrete in the base wasn't dry, so they had to suspend the statue above the base with straps passing under the statues arms. When Princess Kekaulike pulled off the covering, the audience was horrified. It looked like Kamehameha had been hanged, dangling above the stand. But they soon recovered and began clapping.

While portions of the other statues are decorated with gold leaf, this one is entirely painted to make it more lifelike. Many people today who grew up seeing the unadorned statues of ancient Greece and Rome, view these as classic works of art and look askance at painted statues, not realizing that all of the ancient statues were originally painted.

More Kamehamehas

Since then four more large bronze statues have been cast. The third used molds made from Gould's Honolulu statue. This was installed in National Statuary Hall in Washington, D.C., in 1969, and was moved to Emancipation Hall in 2012. This one weights of more than six tons.

A fourteen-foot bronze statue—eighteen, if you count the

spear—was cast in Vicenza, Italy, for the Princeville Resort, but following protests by Kaua'i's residents, it was placed in storage in 1963. The resort tried to donate it to the county, but they didn't want it. Not everyone likes Kamehameha, particularly in the places he captured by force. Kaua'i was never conquered. Its king negotiated a treaty whereby he remained in charge of the island, but was nominally under Kamehameha. Eventually the statue was donated to Hilo, where it was placed on display in Wailoa State Park in 1997. Hilo was his first capital after he gained control over the Big Island. While the sandals on this statue are more Hawaiian, his features are more European.

The most accurate of all the statues was created in 1990 by Hawaiian artist Herb Kawainui Kāne. This nine-and-a-half-foot statue stands facing the Grand Wailea Resort on Maui. Oddly, there is also a large bronze statue in Las Vegas, of all places, beckoning people to enter the Hawaiian Marketplace, although about the only thing Hawaiian there is the statue.

Shown on the right, is perhaps the most famous statue of Augustus Caesar at the Vatican museum in Rome. Augustus is pointing, while Kamehameha is making a beckoning gesture, and he carries a staff instead of a spear; otherwise, the pose is about the same. Authentic Hawaiian feather cloaks were less robe-like than what adorns the Kapa'au statue on the right. It should be similar to a short cape—shaped like a crescent with the points cut off— while the malo would not be thrown over the cloak. In Gibson's instructions to Gould, Kamehameha's beckoning gesture shows "the successful warrior inviting the people to accept the peace and order he had secured."
JOHN RICHARD STEPHENS

The Hawaiian Essence

Whether the statues resemble the king or not is insignificant to the local populations. The statues have great cultural significance to the populace and they are heavily adorned with long, flowing leis twice a year, on Lei Day and on King Kamehameha Day. Some feel the statues represent their ancestors, not just the king. There are those who talk to the statues and there are those who say they hear the statues speak to them. As Kohala community organizer, Sharon Hayden, put it, "We feel the statue [at Kapaʻau] is the embodiment of Kamehameha and the Hawaiian essence. It's not an icon or symbol, it's the real essence. We're honored and protected by it." Ultimately, the blending of Hawaiian and European features in the statues are representative of the modern mix of Hawaiʻi's society as a whole.

Blast from the Past

Qualifications

Colonel Alexander K. McClure's *"Abe" Lincoln's Yarns and Stories* contains the following:

> "A Commissioner to the Hawaiian Islands was to be appointed by President Abraham Lincoln, and eight applicants had filed their papers, when a delegation from the South appeared at the White House on behalf of a ninth. Not only was their man fit—so the delegation urged—but was also in bad health, and a residence in that balmy climate would be of great benefit to him.

> "The President was rather impatient that day, and before the members of the delegation had fairly started in, suddenly closed the interview with this remark: 'Gentlemen, I am sorry to say that there are eight other applicants for that place, and they are all sicker'n' your man.'"

—Colonel Alexander K. McClure

The Statue Worshipper

Every day for 35 years, Jose de Medeiros spent the daylight hours standing in front of King Kamehameha's statue in Honolulu. The barefoot Portuguese-Hawaiian would shuffle back and forth staring up at the statue. He became known as the "Statue Worshipper" and the "Mystery Man of Honolulu."

Beginning in 1896 at the age of 16, he continued every day until he died in 1932 at age 52. As for why, he explained simply, "Someday he step down—then we talk." Others who knew him said he did it because when he was young, a calf kicked him in the head.

Did you know...

King Kamehameha the Great married his favorite wife—Queen Kaʻahumanu—when she was thirteen years old and he was about twenty-three.

Uncommon Knowledge
Hordes of Mongeeses

A mongoose relaxing in a Kailua-Kona mall parking lot on the Big Island. Even mongooses take it easy in Hawai'i. ELAINE MOLINA

The plural of mongoose is mongooses, although the Merriam-Webster Dictionary is one of the few dictionaries which accepts that it can be mongeese because of common usage (or misusage), even though that is etymologically incorrect. It is never mongeeses, polygoose or mongi.

Now, whether they come in herds, troops, gaggles, swarms, companies, gangs, tribes, mobs, fesnyings, or whatever, it's difficult to say. A few sources say that collectively they're called bands or packs. The ones around Hawai'i seem pretty solitary. Still, the sound of *parties* of mongooses has a ring to it. It makes one want to join them for piña coladas.

Even Workers Have Fun

On the mainland you often come upon signs that say "Work Crew Ahead" or "Cleanup Crew Working." Not in Hawai'i. Here you see signs like, "Survey Party Ahead." It hardly even sounds like work.

Did you know...

Mauna Kea's longest ski run is five miles.

Obama on Hawai'i

Barack Obama's wife, Michelle, has said, "You can't really understand Barack until you understand Hawai'i." Here are a few things he has said about his home. This first one was written in 1999 while he was an Illinois state senator:

> "Wherever I go in Chicago, people ask me two questions. First, they ask me how a nice guy like me ever got involved in politics. Second, once they've found out that I grew up in Hawaii, they ask me what the heck I'm doing in a cold place like Chicago.

> "I admit that there are times when I ask myself the same questions. Every year, my family and I take a Christmas trip to Hawaii to visit my grandmother, and usually at some point during those trips—maybe while I'm sitting on the beach watching our one-year-old daughter, Malia, dig her perfect brown toes into the sand, or maybe while I'm taking an early morning jog through Kapi'olani Park, with a soft ocean breeze brushing against my cheeks—I will think about the snow and sleet and darkness that awaits me back in Chicago, and the pressures and tensions of the next campaign [for U.S. Congress], and wonder if I'm certifiably crazy to have left Hawaii.

> "The irony is that my decision to work in politics, and to pursue such a career in a big mainland city, in some sense grows out of my Hawaiian upbringing, and the ideal that Hawaii still represents in my mind....

> "And yet, when I look back on my years in Hawaii, I realize how truly lucky I was to have been raised there. Hawaii's spirit of tolerance might not have been perfect or complete, but it was—and is—real. The opportunity that Hawaii offered—to experience a variety of cultures in a climate of mutual respect—became an integral part of my world view, and a basis for the values that I hold most dear.

"All of which explains both my choice of professions and my life in Chicago. For it was only when I went away to college, first in Los Angeles and later in New York, that I was able to appreciate how unique Hawaii truly was."

(Barack Obama, "A Life's Calling to Public Service," Punahou Bulletin, Fall 1999.)

"No place else could have provided me with the environment, the climate, in which I could not only grow but also get a sense of being loved. There is no doubt that the residue of Hawai'i will always stay with me, and that it is a part of my core, and that what's best in me, and what's best in my message, is consistent with the tradition of Hawai'i."

(Speech at the Hilton Hawaiian Village in Honolulu, Dec. 16, 2004.)

"People ask me, 'What do you still bring from Hawai'i? How does it affect your character, how does it affect your politics?' I try to explain to them something about the Aloha Spirit. I try to explain to them this basic idea that we all have obligations to each other, that we're not alone, that if we see somebody who's in need we should help...that we look out for one another, that we deal with each other with courtesy and respect, and most importantly, that when you come from Hawai'i, you start understanding that what's on the surface, what people look like—that doesn't determine who they are.

"And that the power and strength of diversity, the ability of people from everywhere...whether they're black or white, whether they're Japanese-Americans or Korean-Americans or Filipino-Americans or whatever they are, they are just Americans, that all of us can work together and all of us can join together to create a better country.

"And it's that spirit, that I'm absolutely convinced, is what America is looking for right now."

(Speech in Ke'ehi Lagoon Beach Park, O'ahu, Aug. 8, 2008.)

"I'm going to get a plate lunch. I might go to Zippy's."

(Also at Ke'ehi Lagoon Beach Park)

—President Barack Obama

What's in a Name?

(Kaua'i)

- **Kaua'i** (island): this is an ancient name that doesn't appear to have a translation.
- **Līhu'e** (district, town): cold chill.
- **Nāwiliwili** (harbor): the wiliwili trees.
- **Kōloa** (district, town): a Hawaiian duck, or tall sugarcane.
- **Po'ipū** (town): completely overcast or crashing (as waves).
- **Lāwai** (valley, town): (wa'i) day to end [fishing taboo].
- **Hanapēpē** (town): crushed bay (due to land-slides).
- **Waimea** (canyon, bay, district, town): reddish water.
- **Na'pali** (coast): this is an ancient name that doesn't appear to have a translation.
- **Hanalei** (bay, district, town): crescent bay.
- **Nāmolokama** (mountains): interweaving, bound fast together.
- **Kalihiwai** (town): kalihi (with a) stream.
- **Kīlauea** (town): spewing eruption.
- **Kawaihau** (district): ice water.
- **Anahola** (mountains, bay, beach, town): this is an ancient name that doesn't appear to have a translation.
- **Kapa'a** (beach, town): the solid or the closing.
- **Wailua** (river, town): two waters.
- **Hanamā'ulu** (beach, town): tired (as from walking) bay.

Traditional Saying

Aia ke ola i ka ihu o ka lio. ("Life is where the horse's nose points." Follow the scent of food for nourishment.)

Lucy Thurston's Endurance

Missionaries Asa and Lucy Thurston were celebrating their fortieth wedding anniversary in Honolulu when this photograph was taken in 1859. Looks like it was a lively celebration.
HAWAI'I STATE ARCHIVES

Lucy Thurston was among the first group of missionaries who came to Hawai'i in 1920. Her husband, Asa Thurston, had graduated from Yale College and Andover Theological Seminary. As a newly ordained minister, he and Lucy came to proselytize among the Hawaiians. They found a receptive audience, particularly among the ali'i.

Then in 1855, at the age of sixty, she discovered she had breast cancer and had to undergo a mastectomy without anesthesia, except for some alcohol. They had chloroform, but were afraid to give it to her because of a previous bout with paralysis. She must have been a very strong woman, since she held up amazingly well. A month later she wrote about the operation in a letter to her daughter, Mary, saying:

> [The doctor said,] "I am going to begin now." Then came a gash long and deep, first on one side of my breast, then on the other. Deep sickness seized me, and deprived me of my breakfast. This was followed by extreme faintness. My sufferings were no longer local. There was a general feeling of agony throughout the whole system. I felt, every inch of me, as though flesh was failing. During the whole operation, I was enabled to have entire self control over my person, and over my voice. Persis and Asa [her daughter and son] were devotedly employed in sustaining me with the use of cordials, ammonia, bathing my temples, etc. I myself fully intended to have seen the thing done. But on recollection, every glimpse I happened to have, was the doctor's right hand completely covered with blood, up to the very

wrist. He afterwards told me, that at one time the blood from an artery flew into his eyes, so that he could not see. It was nearly an hour and a half that I was beneath his hand, in cutting out the entire breast, in cutting out the glands beneath the arm, in tying the arteries, in absorbing the blood, in sewing up the wound, in putting on the adhesive plasters, and in applying the bandage....

The doctor, after removing the entire breast, said to me, "I want to cut yet more, round under your arm." I replied, "Do just what you want to do, only tell me when, so that I can bear it." One said the wound had the appearance of being more than a foot long. Eleven arteries were taken up....

Up to this time, everything is fresh to my recollection. Of that afternoon and night, I only remember that the pain in the wound was intense and unremitting, and that I felt willing to be just in the circumstances in which I was placed....I have since told Persis, that "I thought they kept me well drugged with paregoric [a camphorated tincture of opium]." He [her doctor] replied, "We did not give you a drop." "Why then do I not remember what took place?" "Because you had so little life about you."

By morning light the pain had ceased.

—Lucy Thurston

The operation was successful and she lived another twenty-one years.

Getting to the Point

Not Quite Southernmost

Ka Lae, also known as South Point or "the point," is the southern tip of the island of Hawai'i. Road signs and guidebooks will tell you it's the southernmost point of the United States, but that's wrong. The United States consists of the fifty states, the District of Columbia, Native American reservations, U.S. territories, American embassies and consulates, and U.S. military bases. There are the unincorporated territories of Guam, the Northern Mariana Islands, American Samoa, Puerto Rico, and the U.S. Virgin Islands. Then there are the three sovereign nations which are in free association with the United States: the Republic of the Marshall Islands, the Federated States of Micronesia, and the Republic of Palau. While the U.S. reserves the right to lay claim to a portion of Antarctica, it has yet to do so and so far doesn't recognize any country's claims.

Setting aside embassies, consulates and military bases, Rose Atoll of American Samoa is the southernmost point of U.S. controlled territory. Guam, Puerto Rico, the U.S. Virgin Islands, and half a dozen other islands are all further south than Ka Lae.

While Ka Lae is not the southernmost point of the United States, it is the southernmost point of the fifty states.

Home Sweet Home

It is thought that Ka Lae was the first inhabited area of the Hawaiian Islands and it appears to have Hawai'i's oldest ruins. It's believed the Polynesians first arrived here between 100 and 300 AD, and it's odd they settled there since it's a pretty desolate spot. You'd think they would have immediately moved on to someplace nicer, like the Hilo or Captain Cook areas, but there are many ruins at Ka Lae. Life must have been difficult. There are lava fields and not much vegetation. It's very windy. In fact, the wind constantly blows 27 knots per hour from east to west, 24 hours a day, every day. The currents are treacherous and they had to dive underwater in the ocean to get their drinking water from freshwater vents along the coast. But the ancient Polynesians were a strong and hardy people, so perhaps they thought nothing of it.

A few did move on to greener pastures. Hanalei, Kaua'i, is the location of another of the oldest settlements.

Did you know...

The ancient Hawaiians had more than sixty recreational pastimes—everything from wrestling matches to flying kites to sledding on mats of ti leaves.

What Were They Thinking?

Snake Smugglers

While the Hawaiian Islands are essentially free of snakes, unfortunately some ignorant boneheads smuggle them in and then when they escape or are released, they have the potential to cause all sorts of problems. Fortunately it doesn't happen very often and when it does, it usually becomes a featured news story.

Now, as fun as it would be to bring in a few bonobos, loads of monkeys, a couple dozen koalas, a mob of meerkats and a three-toed sloth, this is an extremely bad idea for the wonderful critters that are already here.

Did you know...

In 1974, someone submitted to the State Agriculture Board a proposal to raise 10,000 monkeys on Moloka'i to sell for scientific research because of a worldwide shortage of disease-free monkeys.

Hula Hoops

Origins

Hula hoops are not Hawaiian and don't have anything to do with hula. It's said they date back at least to the fourteenth-century England where they were popular for entertainment and exercise, but some doctors blamed them for causing back ailments and heart attacks. About the same time, Native Americans independently began using smaller versions in hoop dances. For British sailors returning from Hawai'i in the early 1800s, the movement of the hips in hooping reminded them of the hula dancing they'd seen, so they began calling them hula hoops. The British took the idea with them to Australia where they were used in exercise classes.

There's Always Someone to Spoil the Fun

It was from an Australian that the two California toy inventors behind Wham-O® heard of them. They began selling their Hula Hoops® in 1958, which instantly became a tremendous fad. Japan quickly banned them in public because they deemed the hip movements to be indecent. Indonesia banned them out of fear they "might stimulate passion." The Soviet Union said they were a "symbol of the emptiness of American Culture," while the People's Republic of China proclaimed them to be "a nauseating craze." As in much of the rest of the world, after more than half a century they remain popular in Hawai'i.

Surfing with Sharks

S.S. Hill's account of surfing and how the Hawaiians dealt with sharks was published in 1856:

> About mid-day we reached the village of Keauhua [just south of Kailua-Kona on the Big Island], where I had the satisfaction of witnessing, for the first time, the famous ancient sport of the country played in the water, upon what is termed by Europeans the surf-board.
>
> This is truly a famous and animating diversion, but, for what reason I know not, now discouraged by the missionaries, and no longer played with the same spirit among the islanders wherever the Europeans are mingled among them....

A Very Different Kind of Surfing

> The great difficulty, and therein the chief merit of the performance, consists in keeping upon the steepest part of the rolling sea, which brings the swimmer so near its foam, that he is sometimes lying in almost a perpendicular position, with his head downwards, upon the advanced side of the white-topped swell, as it sweeps on towards its goal. By this he is exposed to the effects of the crash of the broken water before he has time to dive, and, after making a summerset [i.e. somersault], with the temporary loss of his board, to the laughter of the rest of the swimmers as well as the spectators on shore.
>
> While we sat watching them, the parties were distributed between the two lines of breakers, and within the inner line, in the act of rolling onward, or returning to the bars, or lying between the breaking seas, diving and reappearing, till the time seemed favourable for their long roll towards the shore.

Combatting Sharks

> The women, whom we could distinguish by their long hair, and also the girls and boys, appeared to

us to perform their part amidst the turmoil of the minor line of breakers as dexterously as the men along the outer line. That they do not generally trust themselves farther from the shore, is rather on account of the sharks, which the men are prepared for, and seek to contend with, than from any distrust of their capabilities in the water. The sole weapon used by the men in combating the shark is a dagger or knife, which on other occasions, when fishing, they stick in their maro [a loincloth that wrapped around the waist and up between the legs], to be used merely when, as it frequently happens, their canoe is upset, and they are attacked by the voracious fish before they can put their little craft again upon her bottom and resume their seats.

But when they are engaged in this sport, the weapon is attached to the surf-board. If now attacked, the shark has no chance with them. At the approach of their enemy, they feign fear and swim away from him, at the same time exhibiting all sorts of awkwardness, until they give the equally cautious as voracious animal, sufficient confidence to approach them. Then they dive under him, for he is not an active fish in the water, and thrust their dagger into the under part of his body; upon which, even the stoutest of the species will turn and retreat, sometimes to escape, but often in such a condition as to be easily pursued and vanquished, and after the action triumphantly towed on shore....

Surfer Girls
We frequently expressed our admiration at what we saw, to the great delight of all the party; but upon asking the little girls near us, whose ages were probably between seven and nine, whether they intended, when a little older, to join in the sport, they declared it to be their daily amusement; and, without waiting to be asked to display their dexterity, they ran and picked up two small surf-boards that were lying near us, and set off in great haste to join one of the parties in the water.

Arrived at the beach, the girls slipped off their sole robe, and after leaping into the sea, soon reached and mingled with the rest in the exciting sport; and I confess, when I saw these little creatures sliding down the side of the swell which runs with such rapidity before the rolling surf, and diving to avoid its crash, when the curling wave was about to break over them, there seemed to me to be something absolutely superhuman in the feats they accomplished, so far were they above anything I had deemed it possible for any creatures whatsoever to perform in an element not their own....

Surfing King
The healthful diversion is still the favourite of the few remaining national exercises of the natives throughout the group. I was informed by the missionaries and by others, in proof of its popularity, and of the constancy with which it must have been practiced for ages, that many of the natives spend whole days in enjoying themselves in this manner in the water. I was informed also, that Kamehameha III., then the reigning king, was known thus to divert himself even from sunrise to sunset, taking his meals of poi during the day without ever coming on shore.

—S.S Hill (*Travels in the Sandwich and Society Islands*)

Did you know...

Only the ali'i were allowed to use the longest, thickest surfboards. These were kapu to everyone else.

Did you know...

Poi is sometime referred to as Hawaiian Super Glue, perhaps because of its consistency or because it can stop you up.

Woody Harrelson

A pedestrian crossing sign in the surfer/hippie community of Pa'ia on Maui near where hemp-advocates Woody Harrelson and Willy Nelson live. JOHN RICHARD STEPHENS

Woody Harrelson has played a wide range of rolls from the champion bowler who lost his hand in the Farrelly brothers' slapstick comedy, *Kingpin,* to a serial killer in Oliver Stone's *Natural Born Killers* and the alcoholic mentor in *The Hunger Games.* He was awarded an Emmy for his work, along with five Emmy nominations and two Academy Award nominations.

Woody lives in a sustainable community on Maui's North Shore, amidst organic gardens and fruit trees. He says he has a difficult time accepting movie roles, because he doesn't want to leave. While filming in New Orleans, he told *Men's Journal* magazine, "I've never had a harder time leaving home, where it just felt like ripping my heart out. I cried the day I left. Maui is heaven. My family is there, and my buddies...the good times never stop. A year could pass and you wouldn't even notice. Kitesurfing, soccer, living off the grid, eating fruit from your trees. That's my heaven. That's how life is meant to be lived."

Amazing Gecko Facts

A Gold-Dust Day Gecko in Keal-akekua on the Big Island. JOHN RICHARD STEPHENS

Gecko toes. JOHN RICHARD STEPHENS

The Sound of One Gecko Laughing

Geckos sometimes make noises. They usually chirp, but they also make clickings and whirrings. They appear to chirp to call out to one another and it's usually five to nine times in rapid succession, although they do make single chirps. They're quite loud and can probably be heard a hundred yards away. It almost sounds like they're laughing. It's rare that they make clicking sounds. Like chirpings, their clicks are given in sequence, but spaced out more, with perhaps a couple of seconds between each click. They sound like a swiveling fan when it gets stuck. They make the whirring or trilling sound during territorial disputes, sometimes right before they start fighting.

Eyes Wide Shut

And here's something interesting: geckos have eyelids, but they're transparent. Their eyelids are permanently closed, but they can see through them. This makes them look like they're eyes are always open. Since they can't blink, they have to lick their eyelids clean with their long tongues.

Sticky Toes

People often confuse geckos with other kinds of lizards and

you occasionally see pictures of other lizards—particularly anoles, which are also common in Hawaii—wrongly labeled as being geckos. They do look similar, until you become familiar with them. One way to recognize geckos is by their characteristic waddle when they walk or run. They are also pudgier than other lizards. A quick way to recognize them is by looking at their toes. Gecko toes are bulbous. It's their toes that enable them to cling to glass windows and crawl upside-down on ceilings.

Some people wrongly believe geckos have tiny suction cups on their toes. Actually they have microscopic hairs that are split at the end which use molecular attraction to cling to surfaces, but only when the surfaces are tilted greater than a certain angle, thus their feet grip vertical surfaces, but not horizontal ones. The molecular attraction, known as the van der Waals force, is so strong that a gecko can hang on to pane of glass by one toe. This is also how insects walk on ceilings and glass.

The Weird and the Wild
Know Your Geckos

There are at least nine species of wild geckos residing in Hawai'i. It's likely all were introduced by humans, either as stowaways or brought as pets. Four species were probably brought over by the Polynesians, although it is possible their eggs floated here on their own or a few geckos arrived on a raft of debris. Since most geckos reproduce without males, all it would take is for just one to make it. The remaining species came more recently.

Most of these grow up to five inches from snout to tail tip. Their eggs are white and about the size of a pea. The mother can stick them to things and it's common to see two eggs stuck to each other. Sometimes you'll see the mother transporting them in her mouth. It takes one to three months for them to hatch, and then one to three years before the gecko is full grown. If all goes well, they live from five to seven years, although the larger varieties can reach twenty years of age.

Extreme Hawai'i

Weed Wacking the Lawn

In Hawai'i, many people mow their lawns with weed whackers. Even professional gardeners do it, as you can see here. This is not a golf course, but it is a huge lawn that had two gardeners weed whacking it. Apparently it has something to do with the type of grass. JOHN RICHARD STEPHENS

O Whyhee?

In the 1700s, Europeans referred to Hawai'i as the Sandwich Islands. Their maps, charts and illustrations give the following names and spellings for the individual islands:

- **O-Why-ee** or **o Whyhee** (the Island of Hawai'i)
- **Mawhee** or **Mowee** (Maui)
- **Tahoorowa** (Kaho'olawe)
- **Ranai** (Lāna'i)
- **Morotoi** (Moloka'i)
- **Woahoo** (O'ahu)
- **Honoruru** (Honolulu)
- **Atooi** or **Tauai** (Kaua'i)
- **Oneeheow** (Ni'ihau)

The Sailor's Honolulu

"Honolulu grew up a seagoing city, smelling of bilge-water, sandalwood, sperm oil, manila cordage, oakum, molasses, and split rum. After dark the loudest sounds were ships' bells by the score telling the watches of the night and the oaths of liberty men pitching out of taverns on their heads in Fid Street. [Note: "Fid" was a sailor's term for "booze." Fid Street was lower Nu'uanu Avenue.] The first seamen's chaplain of the town used to scull about the moorings in a little boat handing up temperance tracts to larboard, for the sailors to throw promptly over the side to starboard. It was the whalerman's joy to drink his earnings, put as much extra grog as he could on the credit slate, and steal away with the tide, paying his debts at the foremast, as the saying went."

—WILLIAM BROWN (*A Hawaii Anthology*)

 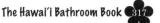

Sleepy Days of 30s Hawai'i

With great nostalgia I remember those days in the 1930s when Honolulu was a sprawling small city. It reached up into valleys and moved out toward Kuapa Pond, now filled in and called Hawaii Kai. Its streets were hidden in the rich foliage of coconut palms, monkeypod trees, shower trees mangos, poincianas. I remember spending summers in Kailua, Kona, on the Big Island. Those beautiful volcanic slopes of Hualalai and Mauna Loa were dotted with just a few villages then—some along the mountain road for coffee growers and other farmers, and other Hawaiian places along the shore that had been there at least from the historic past. There were only two or three hotels in Kona then, notably the Managa Hotel on the mauka road and Kona Inn in Kailua. There were few—very few—tourists in all Hawaii. There was little traffic in the streets of Honolulu or on the Kona roads. The days moved quietly. The islands still had remnants of the feelings and attitudes of the nineteenth century. Jet planes had not yet interrupted the serene skies. Statehood was yet to come.

I remember the people of those days fifty years ago. Their lives were closer to the natural round of day and night, to tidal ebb and flow, to the growth, blooming, and fruiting of trees and plants, to the constant awareness of human progress through the generations of families. There were, of course, the discords and struggles which occur when people of many different races come together in a small archipelago. But these had not, as yet, been complicated, intensified, dramatized by the rapid growth of big business and tourism and an exploding population.

—Marjorie Sinclair (*Kona: A Novel of Two Generations in Hawai'i*)

Big Yellow Hawaiian Taxi

On Joni Mitchell's first trip to Hawai'i, she arrived at night and took a taxi to a Honolulu hotel. When she awoke the next morning, she threw back the curtains and saw the lush mountains off in the distance. Then she looked down and saw a huge parking lot. Struck by the stark contrast which she said "broke her heart," she sat down and wrote:

> They paved paradise and put up a parking lot,
> With a pink hotel, a boutique and a swinging hot spot.

The pink hotel is the Royal Hawaiian on Waikīkī. Then she wrote:

> They took all the trees and put 'em in a tree museum
> And they charged all the people a dollar and a half just to see 'em.

This refers to Honolulu's Foster Botanical Gardens, which features 24 "exceptional trees" because of their "age, rarity, location, size, aesthetic quality, endemic status or historical and cultural significance."

Mitchell's hit song from 1970, "Big Yellow Taxi," emphasizes how we rarely appreciate the wonderful things in life until it's too late.

> Don't it always seem to go
> That you don't know what you've got 'til it's gone.

But we're still paving over Hawai'i to put in more parking lots.

Honolulu in the 1830s

Honolulu, "A Hard Old Camp"

Honolulu was a hard-looking old camp in those days [the 1830s]. A drawing of it in the early thirties, afterwards engraved at Lahainaluna, is to be seen in the Honolulu Reading Room. It gives some notion of the facts. Most of the dwellings were native thatched cottages, chiefly pili-grass. They were irregularly scattered in enclosures of rotten adobe walls.

Few Streets

One main street, now King street, of good width, extended from the present corners of South and Bethel streets. Quite a lane followed the course of Merchant street. Fort and Nuʻuanu streets had no existence. There was a lane up Punchbowl to Beretania, and along Beretania to Union. A number of other narrow lanes ran here and there. There were irregular fragments of street near the waterfront from Fort to Nuʻuanu, where were three or four stores of traders, mostly stone or adobe structures of one story.

Dreary, Uncomfortable and Unsanitary

There were scarcely any trees in the town. A few hau trees were in some premises. About 1836, Pride of India [trees] appeared. Occasionally cocoanuts and pandanus were seen. The only drinking water was drawn from the shallow wells dug through the coral to tide level. Being slightly brackish, it was distasteful to us, who were used to mountain water. Probably it was rather insanitary.

Barren

The mission dooryards were nearly devoid of vegetation, the mānienie, or Bermuda grass, not having become common. Nothing could be less attractive than the general aspect of the town, of which its present inhabitants can form little idea.

Few Houses

Of foreign-built houses there were few in 1832, when my definite memory begins. The King lived chiefly at Lahaina, but had a house on the Fort-wall here, and perhaps near the present Capitol. Near the south corner of that enclosure was a fairly good stone house occupied by Auhea, or Kekāuluohi, the mother of the late King Lunalilo. A dwelling-house of some importance was that of the British Consul, Richard Charlton, later occupied by his successor, General Miller, which stood there for seventy years, adjacent to the ex-queen's premises.

Pearl Oysters and Clams

The lochs or lagoons of Pearl River were not then as shoal as now [in 1901]. The subsequent occupation of the uplands by cattle denuded the country of herbage and caused vast quantities of earth to be washed down by storms into the lagoons, shoaling the water for a long distance seaward. No doubt the area of deep water and anchorage has been greatly diminished. In the thirties the small pearl oyster was quite abundant, and common on our table. Small pearls were frequently found in them. No doubt the copious inflow of fresh water favored their presence. I think they have become almost entirely extinct, drowned out by the mud. There was also at Pearl River a handsome speckled clam, of delicate flavor, which contained milk white pearls of exquisite luster, and perfectly spherical. I think that clam is still found in the Ewa lochs.

—REVEREND SERENO EDWARDS BISHOP (*REMINISCENCES OF OLD HAWAII*)

Uncommon Knowledge

History of Honolulu Street Names

For Windward Oʻahu residents driving to Honolulu from the Windward side, there can be a lesson in Oʻahu's history.

The Honolulu-bound Pali Highway becomes Nuuanu Pali Road upon exiting the tunnel under the lookout. Wood Street, four miles past the tunnel, is named after Massachussettsborn John H. Wood (1816-1892), who first came to O'ahu in 1846 on the brig *Henry*, accompanied by other illustrious immigrants including Charles Reed Bishop (1822-1915), later husband of Princess Bernice Pauahi Bishop (1831-1884). Wood arrived with considerable financial strength and he constructed Honolulu's very first brick building on Fort Street, where he opened a shoe store.

In 1849, he departed for California with his brother and others to add to his fortune by gold mining during the great gold rush. Very successful, Wood returned to his native Massachusetts to marry Sarah Hardy and accumulate a large stock of merchandise. He then returned to O'ahu in 1850 to stay, adding to his fortune by selling the goods.

Wood sent to Boston for a prefabricated house and erected it on a large tract of land near the present Wood Street. It was the family home for over thirty years. Here Wood raised sugarcane for a time until 1870 when he converted the property to a livestock ranch. The sugarcane plantation was the first on the Honolulu side of the Koolau Mountain Range.

One of Wood's daughters, Florence Jones, became a longtime friend of Queen Emma, not surprising as they were practically neighbors during the time that Queen Emma spent at her Nuuanu Summer Palace. It was a close-knit society among the wealthy and alii (high chiefs) during the times of the Hawaiian monarchy and much of it centered in the spacious homes located in Nuuanu Valley.

Next after Wood Street is Dowsett Street, named after James Isaac Dowsett (1829-1898) believed to be the first Caucasian child born in Hawai'i not of missionary parentage. Childhood friend of Kings Kamehameha IV, V, and Lunalilo, Dowsett became a tycoon in island shipping and, later, in ranching and sugarcane farming on Maui and O'ahu. He accumulated vast landholdings and later in life served in the House of Nobles during the reigns of King Kalakaua and Queen Liliuokalani.

Dowsett and his wife, the former Annie Green Ragsdale, had thirteen children who were left with wide business and ranching interests, many surviving to this day. The Nuuanu Valley location known as Dowsett Highlands is named for this kamaaina family.

The next place of historical significance is a street sign for Puiwa Street, where over two-hundred years ago in 1795, a historic battle took place. It is here that Kalanikupule, ruler of Oʻahu, and his army made their stand against the invading forces of Kamehameha I behind a stone wall located here.

Next is the location of Queen Emma's Summer Palace. Born Emma Kalanikaumakeamano, she was queen consort of Kamehameha IV, whom she outlived by 19 years. Queen Emma was instrumental in founding the hospital that bears her name as well as St. Andrews Episcopal Church and St. Andrews Priory School. Emma had several other summer residences—Allerton Gardens on Kauai in Lawai and a summer house located near the shore on the airport side of the entrance to Pearl Harbor, the location later of Fort Kamehameha which is now integrated into the Hickam Air Force Base reservation.

The last thing that catches the eye is the large sign attached to a substantial overpass denoting Wyllie Street. Robert Crichton Wyllie (1798-1865) was a Scotsman and bachelor businessman who arrived in Hawaiʻi in 1844. His acumen attracted the notice of Kamehameha III and, until his death in 1865, he served as minister of foreign affairs for Kamehameha III and IV. He was an indefatigable letter writer, using that method to promote treaties to protect Hawaiʻi from the encroachment of foreign powers. His handwriting was almost indecipherable and one is puzzled as to how the recipients of his letters made perfect sense of them. Nevertheless, his efforts were successful as Hawaiʻi was able to stave off aggression by European powers during his stewardship.

Wyllie founded Princeville Plantation on Kauai and was a staunch supporter of Queen Emma in her efforts to establish the Episcopal Church in Hawaiʻi.

So, any time you are stuck in a slow-moving line of motorists moving towards downtown Honolulu, relive Honolulu's history via the street signs.

—WILLIAM DORRANCE (*OʻAHU'S HIDDEN HISTORY*)

Old Honolulu
The Road Less Taken

Nuuanu Pali Drive winds through a bower of trees for almost three miles before rejoining the Nuuanu Pali Road. This winding and colorful road became obsolete when today's modern highway opened in 1957. At that time a question arose about what to do about the old road. "Close it," said the practical-minded. "No, no," said the sentimental, "it's a beautiful stretch of tree-shaded road of which we have too few on O'ahu."

The sentimental-minded won out and this stretch of road remains as a bucolic bypass to the new road, rejoining it north of Wood Street. A driver loses little time if he takes this bypass to recapture some of the mystique of old-time O'ahu.

During this drive a pond and reservoir can be seen which played a key role in Honolulu's first street-light system, established in the last quarter of the nineteenth century. Water from the reservoir drove a hydroelectric generator that provided electricity for the system until it shut down in the early 1930s.

—WILLIAM DORRANCE (*O'AHU'S HIDDEN HISTORY*)

Did you know...

In 1918, Duke Kahanamoku insured his feet for $50,000.

Did you know...

Sea turtles tagged at Moloka'i have been found as far away as the Marshall Islands and the Philippines.

 The Hawai'i Bathroom Book

Traditional Sayings Regarding Life

"Everything's beautiful from one end of Puna [on Kaua'i] to the other." This means there's nothing to complain about.

"He (or she) has sunk in the bog of Alaka'i [on Kaua'i]." Refering to someone who is overwhelmed by troubles.

"He (or she) was pounded flat by the 'Āpa'apa'a wind [of Kohala on the Big Island]." This is said of someone who has suffered an overwhelming trauma or disaster.

"Only the mists know the storm that made the rivers swell." This means that only the people who are close to someone will understand his or her suffering.

"The sea is deep and rough, but the coral rock is still standing." This refers to someone who remains calm through difficult times.

"The rustling sound of falling leaves is like whispering to the living." Meaning that it's those who are alive who can appreciate these things.

Streetcar

If you are seeking views and thrills,
Take the car for College Hills,
Where residents, as you'd supposed,
Pungle high for bungalows. [Pungle is "to pay"]

To behold the city and all its sights
Or count its myriad lights o' nights,
Take Wai'alae car for Kaimuki Heights,
Palolo Valley lies close by,
Its inmost reaches rising high,
Taking for in extinct crater
Splendid for the sweet potato!

(*PARADISE NEWS*, FEBRUARY 1919)

That's Bowangus, Dude!

Duke Writes of Old-School Surfing

The following is from an article on surfing Duke Kahanamoku wrote in 1911 when he was twenty-one years old:

To Stand Like a God

I have never seen snow and do not know what winter means. I have never coasted down a hill of frozen rain, but every day of the year, where the water is 76, day and night, and the waves roll high, I take my sled, without runners, and coast down the face of the big waves that roll in at Waikiki. How would you like to stand like a god before the crest of a monster billow, always rushing to the bottom of a hill and never reaching its base, and to come rushing in for half a mile at express speed, in graceful attitude, of course, until you reach the beach and step easily from the wave to the strand?...

Perhaps the ideal surfing stretch in all the world is at Waikiki beach, near Honolulu, Hawaii. Here centuries ago was born the sport of running foot races upon the crests of the billows, and here bronze skinned men and women vie today with the white man for honors in aquatic sports once exclusively Hawaiian, but in which the white man now rivals the native.

A Born Surfer

I mastered the art of riding the surf-board in the warm Hawaiian waters when I was a very small child, and I never gaze out upon the ocean in any part of the island that I do not figure out how far each wave, as it comes rolling in, would carry me standing on its crest. There are great, long, regular, sweeping billows, after a storm at Waikiki that have carried me from more than a mile out at sea right up to the beach; there are rollers after a big kona storm that sweep across Hilo Bay, on the Big Island of Hawaii, and carry native surfboard riders five miles at a run, and on the island of Ni'ihau there are even more wonderful surfboard feats performed...

Riding a Log
In the old days the natives were wont to use cocoanut logs in the big surf off Diamond Head, and sometimes six of them would come in standing on one log, for, of course, the bigger and bulkier the surfboard the farther it will go on the dying rollers; but it is harder to start the big board, and, of course, on the big logs one man, the rear one, always had to keep lying down to steer the log straight with his legs.

The Surfing Queen and Amazing Feats
At Waikiki beach, Queen Emma, as a child, had a summer home, and always went out surfing with a retainer, who stood on the board with her. Today it is seldom that more than one person comes in before the wave on a single board, although during the past year some seemingly wonderful feats have been attempted.

I have tried riding in standing on a seven-foot board, with a boy seated on my shoulders, and now I find it not impossible to have one of my grown companions leap from his board, while it is going full speed, to mine, and then clamber up and twine his legs about my neck. Lately I have found a small boy, part Hawaiian, who will come in with me on my board, and when I stand, he stands on my shoulders, and even turns round. But this is as nothing when we read... of the feats of the old Hawaiians...

The Important Thing in Life
Native legends abound with the exploits of those who attained distinction among their fellows by their skill and daring in this sport; indulged in alike by both sexes. Necessary work for the maintenance of the family, such as farming, fishing, mat and kapa making and such other house-hold duties re-

quired and needing attention, by either head of the family were often neglected for the prosecution of the sport.

Taking It a Bit Too Far

Betting was made an accompaniment thereof, both by the chiefs and the common people. Canoes, nets, fishing lines, kapas, swine, poultry and all other property were staked, and in some instances life itself was put up as wagers, the property changing hands, and personal liberty, or even life itself sacrificed, according to the outcome of the match in the waves.

—Duke Kahanamoku

"*Duke was to swimming what Babe Ruth and Joe Dimaggio combined were to baseball.*"

—*The New Yorker*, March 12, 1990,
on the centennial of his birth

Did you know...

Duke Kahanamoku's father was a policeman and Duke served as a military police officer during World War II. He was Honolulu sheriff from 1933 to 1961, but this position was ceremonial.

Academic Zombies

The Hawaiians have a saying: Ua aʻo a ua ʻailolo. This means, "He trained until he ate brains." In the old days, when someone completed a course of study, they would offer an animal—such as a fish or hog—to the deity of whatever it was that they had studied and the student would eat a portion of the brains of his or her offering. So instead of getting a diploma, they ate some brains and were then considered to be an expert.

Blast from the Past

A Hawaiian Doctor's Certificate

This doctor's certificate from 1865 was originally written in the Hawaiian language:

Certificate of a Doctor for Hawaii Nei.
It is decided to be proper that ....
.... should act as a medical doctor, for under me, he having exhibited to my satisfaction his qualifications as such doctor. Therefore, I hereby give my sanction to his practicing medicine from Hawaii to Kauai, so long as he obeys my directions and observes the laws of the King of this government and conducts himself properly and honestly.

The following is the scale of fees to which I consent, if a cure is affected:

1. Very great sickness ....$50.
2. Less than that ....$40.
3. A good deal less ....$30.
4. Small sickness...$20.
5. Very small ....$10.
6. Attending a friend.......................................$5.
7. Incantation to find out disease.....................$3.

8. Taking a case from another doctor ....$10.
9. Certificate of a doctor ....$3.
10. Refusal by the patient to pay ....$10.

Given under my hand this .... day of .... 18........

S.W. Kapu
W.E.P. Daniels
Head of Hawaiian Doctors

Now that's affordable health care. It would be nice to return to this fee schedule, but then, the old adage that you get what you pay for, would probably be true in this case.

All this is not reflective on the traditional Hawaiian medical kāhuna, who promoted healing with the use of medicinal herbs and plants, massage, steam baths, diet, enemas, and rest, which were probably more effective than the bleeding, blistering, and snake oil remedies that were common in Western medicine at that time.

Aloha

What's aloha? It's the Hawaiian word for love and compassion. According to an anonymous acrostic, it is:

Akahai (gentleness)
Lokahi (harmony)
ʻOluʻolu (politeness)
Haʻahaʻa (humility)
Ahonui (patience)

Did you know...

Macadamia nuts can be fatal to dogs, sometimes causing seizures and kidney failure.

Bigfoot

Screaming Big Foot

Rob Carlson was a "military brat" who grew up at Schofield Barracks, graduated from Leilehua High School and attended the University of Hawai'i. In a personal story that he recorded in 1973, he described his own encounters with a Hawaiian "bigfoot."

One night he had gone to the river in Whitmore Village, by the Wahiawa Mountains, with his friends to catch catfish. They laid traps in the river for about an hour, intending to come back in the morning to gather up the fish. As they were busy putting in their traps, they heard a bloodcurdling scream.

"It sounded at first like a wild man screaming in the bushes right next to us. I thought at first it was a joke by one of my friends, but we were all standing there, and the screaming was in the bushes. We looked at each other and we ran like hell up the side of the embankment. We just ran, totally panicked."

He was Coming Right for Us!

As they got to the top of the hill, running down a little trail, they came to a curve in the path. As they entered the curve, they all stopped dead in their tracks. An 8-foot-tall man was walking down the trail, heading right for them. He was naked except for a cloth around his waist.

"I tell you, he was coming right for us! So we turned and ran back to the river. As he stumbled down the side of the embankment, a giant woman stepped out from behind a tree. She must have been at least seven feet tall!"

Turning downriver, they ran and ran until finally they came out of the ravine safely.

Big Footprints

"It was one helluva night," Rob continued. "I didn't sleep at all. But in the morning, we figured it was safe to go back and get our traps. We couldn't believe our eyes when we arrived at the river. There were huge footprints in the ground near the place where we had been laying the traps. Giant footprints at least two to three feet long! We never will go back fishing at that river near Whitmore Village at night. Never."

—GLEN GRANT (*OBAKE FILES*)

Supernatural Hawai'i

The Man-Eater

Glen Grant's books contain a number of accounts and tales of giants in the Wahiawa-Whitmore Village part of Central O'ahu. They are called Aikanaka, which means "man-eater." It's probably a good thing to stay away from anything called a "man-eater."

Contemporary Poetry

Handicap

No need fell sorry
   for the crippled man
      down on the sidewalk
         in Waikiki—

There are a lot more crippled
   minds
      limping araound,
feel sorry for them!

—WAYNE KAUMUALI'I WESTLAKE (*MALAMA: HAWAIIAN LAND AND WATER*)

Did you know...

Gilligan's Island, as shown in the opening credits of the TV show, is actually Mokuolo'e Island, also known as Coconut Island, in Oahu's Kāne'ohe Bay.

Uncommon Knowledge

What Does It Mean?

(Ni'ihau)

- **Ni'ihau** (island): this is an ancient name that doesn't appear to have a translation.
- **Waimea** (district): reddish water.
- **Pu'uwai** (town): heart.
- **Ki'eki'e** (town): lofty.
- **Lehua** (island): lehua flower.

That's Just Rude

What *Were* Her Parents Thinking?

In 2008 a New Zealand court gave a nine-year-old girl the right to change her name from "Talula Does The Hula From Hawaii." The poor girl was so embarrassed by her name that she told even her closest friends that her name was "K," or so all the news reports insisted, although it's possible the court used the abbreviation to hide her identity. Her parents must not have wanted her to change her name since the court had to take custody of her until after the change became legal. For Talula's protection, her new name was kept secret. New Zealand registration officials did block someone from naming their sprout "Twisty Poi," but oddly they allowed "Number 16 Bus Shelter." Perhaps that's where that sprocket was conceived.

"*It's not the kids who are different today. It's the parents!*"
—Charles Onaka
(*THE LESSONS OF ALOHA, ED. BROTHER NOLAND*)

The Hawai'i Bathroom Book 333

Firsthand Encounters with Lava

Obviously getting close and personal with lava is very dangerous. It has killed several sightseers, who are usually asphyxiated by gases. George Ulrich, Norman Banks, and Jeffery Judd were geologists working for the Hawaiian Volcano Observatory collecting samples when they broke through the crust they were standing on and their legs went into the molten lava. They were extremely fortunate in that it could have gone a lot worse for them. As Norman Banks pointed out, the lava he took a dip in was fourteen times hotter than boiling water.

"Flames Blasted from the Hole Around My Burning Leg"

Jeffrey described his experience saying, "One day, I was assigned to drive out as far as I could and then hike about a mile out to collect fresh lava samples with two visiting geologists. I sat our guests down in a safe place while I edged out on new crust that was forming on the side of an active lava channel. I was leaning out to scoop up a sample with my pick, when all of a sudden my boot poked through the crust and my right leg followed to about my knee. I fell backwards as flames blasted from the hole around my burning leg. I immediately yanked it free and pounded out the flames, but my other clothes were also catching on fire from the hot crust I was rolling around on. Burned, cut up, and bleeding badly, I hiked out, made a call on my two-way radio and was evacuated to the Hilo hospital. I was treated for second- and third-degree burns and released from the hospital after three weeks with only minor permanent damage."[142]

"#%@&, That's Hot!"

When Norman fell in, he was out about fifteen feet onto the flow. The nearest members of his team were about fifty feet away. He wrote:

"I remember clearly the conversation going on in my mind—'#%@&, that's hot! #%@&! I've just lost my leg. #%@&! Maybe

I'm going to die. Jump back out! Damn! My foot is going deeper and the other is breaking through. Jeff said he rolled on his back to extract his legs. What if the crust won't hold and my back goes in? I'm going to die anyway.'

"All this took less than one to two seconds. I dropped to my back and was then able to lift my legs with my stomach and thigh muscles, then rolled over and over to shore.

"When I got to the shore, I jerked off the remains of my left boot and socks to see if my foot was still there. The only damage was burns under each rivet and eyelet in the boot. My left boot almost vaporized, and my jeans and Nomex flight suit did vaporize up to my crotch, and the upper suit and work shirt had holes burned in them. I had second degree burns up to both knees, but my third degree burns were spotty and small except for a soft-ball-sized one on my left calf, which curiously looked like a map of the Big Island. Hot gases from my vaporized boot and clothing probably contributed to the burns, and continued upward as far as mid chest as my body was black from soot from boot top to mid chest."

Even though the crust was only about three-quarters of an inch thick, it held when he fell back onto it. He was treated by the Navy's top burn specialist at Kīlauea Military Camp and, amazingly, was back at work the next day. The specialist allowed him to keep the burn kit so he could treat his wounds himself. He continued, "It took about a month for the largest third degree area to close over from skin growth from the edges and from a few skin buds scattered through the exposed meat. I had to scrub the burns with a sterile sponge until they bled and then apply Silvadene and a fresh bandage three times a day."

Even When Cautious, Accidents Happen

Norman always carried that kit with him after that and it came in handy when he sank into a pyroclastic flow at Mount St. Helens, receiving another small third degree burn. He also used it to save a colleague's life in the Philippines who was burned over 85% of his body when a dike path through some mud pots collapsed. Clearly volcanology can take a life-threatening turn very quickly. In another accident at Kīlauea, Ed

Wolfe fell into an empty lava tube and was burned by hot gasses.

"The Molten Lava Engulfed My Legs"

George's accident was worse than Norman's and Jeffery's. He said, "I walked quickly across the crusted surface, assuming I would easily recognize the newly cooled lava flow....I reached what I thought was the place where we had extracted the thermocouple moments before. I averted my face toward the right, intending to scoop up the molten lava sample on the pick in my left hand. I bent over to pierce the new crust. As I looked down, I saw the crust open up and felt it give way beneath me. The molten lava engulfed my legs..."

He was only in the liquid rock for about five seconds, but that was five seconds too long. When Italian volcanologist Dario Tedesco, from the observatory at Mount Vesuvius, pulled him out, George's fire retardant suit was on fire. He suffered third-degree burns on his left kneecap and upper thigh, with possible third-degree burns on his right kneecap, in addition to second-degree burns over much of the rest of his legs, and first-degree burns to parts of his arms, hands, and face; all of which landed him in the hospital for two months. He was able to recover after several months of physical therapy, although this terrible calamity probably still haunts his nightmares.

"Leaving Hawai'i is like going from color to black and white."
—John Richard Stephens, author/editor

Small, Maybe, but We Make Up for It in Length... *and* We've Got You Outnumbered

The Hawaiian Islands are an archipelago of 132 scattered points of land, consisting of eight main islands and a plethora of tiny islands, atolls and shoals that extend in a row from northeast to southwest, covering 1,523 miles. While Hawai'i is the fourth tiniest state (or the eighth if you include water), it is the nation's widest state, beating out Alaska by about a hundred miles. It's almost *twice* the length of Texas's longest dimension. In addition, the Hawaiian Islands are the longest chain of islands in the world.

Midway Atoll is controlled by the U.S. Navy and is not part of the State of Hawai'i.

The Hawaiian Island Chain is superimposed on the United States. JOHN RICHARD STEPHENS

Going Somewhere?

Fahget About It

How many miles is it from Honolulu to:

Los Angeles, California	2,563
Samoa	2,611
Seattle, Washington	2,682
Vancouver, B.C., Canada	2,711
Tahiti	2,755
Las Vegas, Nevada	2,758
Anchorage, Alaska	2,787
Fiji	3,154
Mexico City, Mexico	3,788
Guam	3,805
Tokyo, Japan	3,860
Chicago, Illinois	4,254
Auckland, New Zealand	4,402
Seoul, South Korea	4,548
Washington, D.C.	4,834
Miami, Florida	4,860
New York City, New York	4,965
Beijing, China	5,075
Sydney, Australia	5,080
Taiwan	5,113
Manila, Philippines	5,305
Hong Kong	5,556
London, England	7,236
Berlin, Germany	7,317
Delhi, India	7,408
Paris, France	7,446
Rome, Italy	8,036
Rio de Janeiro, Brazil	8,297
Athens, Greece	8,349
Cape Town, South Africa	11,549

Note that these are the shortest distances by air. Many airline routes are longer, particularly if they have to refuel. For example, it's unlikely you'll be able to fly nonstop from Hawai'i over Antarctica to Cape Town as measured here.

A Snowbird that Vacations in Hawai'i

Home Life in Alaska

Kōlea, or Pacific Golden Plovers, are amazing birds who spend their winter vacations in Hawai'i and throughout the South Pacific, flying in from Alaska and Siberia. Who can blame them? Alaska and Siberia are pretty inhospitable places, but that's where they nest and raise their families.

The Hawaiian kōlea begin returning to Alaska in the end of April. The males return first so they can claim the best territories, while females tend to go to a different spot each year to pair up with new males. The females are only there for about three months and the males for four, so they get right to work. The males go through a variety of dances and displays trying to get a female's attention. Eventually they pair up and a few weeks later the female lays up to four eggs, which collectively can weigh almost as much as she does when she's not pregnant. Imagine, losing half your weight by laying four giant eggs.

Domestic Difficulties

The parents take turns incubating the eggs for 22 to 30 days. This is a difficult period, since Arctic Foxes and birds called Long-Tailed Jaegers want to eat their babies. Even caribou will eat their eggs and chicks. The parents will fight predators or pretend to have a broken wing in order to draw the predators away from the nest. Their nests are just simple depressions in the ground, so there's also the danger a caribou herd will accidentally stomp all over the eggs.

On the Run

Because of all this, once the last chick hatches, they don't waste time hanging about. Within hours they set off across the tundra on foot, with the chicks immediately being able to feed themselves by eating bugs, seeds, and berries. About 25 days later the chicks become fledglings and the parents take off, leaving them behind to fend for themselves. The female takes off first so she can bulk back up before making her long migratory flight, leaving the male to tend the chicks on his own.

Hightailing It Out of the Frozen North

Non-breeding adults depart around mid-July, parents leave in August, and the juveniles skedaddle in September and October. Those from Siberia head off throughout Asia, with some ending up in Japan, India, Africa, and Australia. Those from Alaska fan out to winter in the South Pacific, New Zealand, and South America. A few lazily make their way down the Pacific coast of Canada and the United States until they reach San Francisco or Los Angeles. Some vagrants have been seen wintering in Europe and the Mediterranean. Amazingly they make one of the longest migrations of any animal in the world.

A Nonstop Flight

Now get this: Since they're not sea birds, their feathers aren't waterproof, which means they can't pause to rest on the ocean. They have to keep flying. They also can't glide or soar, so they have to keep flapping their wings twice per second. Yet they can fly at up to 70 miles per hour, reaching altitudes more than three and a half miles high, and they can do this for at least 70 hours straight, enabling them to travel 6,360 miles nonstop. It takes them just two days to fly the 2,500 miles from Alaska to Hawai'i.

Time to Parrr-tay!

Once here, they are transformed from frantic parents to relaxed and carefree vacationers. Even their plumage changes. Instead of trying to blend into the background hiding from predators, they stand around in the open. Here, they like to hang out on beaches, parks, athletic fields, and golf courses while chowing down on cockroaches, crickets, grasshoppers, grubs, moths, earwigs, spiders, mollusks, and crustaceans. They've even been known to eat lizards, bird's eggs, small fish, rice, and French fries. Some hang out in small groups, while others maintain feeding territories—smaller than their breeding grounds—that they protect from intruders by patrolling its borders. At night they get together as a group so they won't be snatched in their sleep by an owl or cat.

All Good Things Must Come to an End

At the end of April, after fattening up, they begin to get antsy and over several days up to 200 of them will gather together in a flock. Then, just before dusk they'll begin their flight back to Alaska. The Hawaiian's have songs about the kōlea where they sing about how these birds get fat before they set off to some mysterious faraway place to lay their eggs. These songs were written long before they ever heard of Alaska, and before Alaska Airlines began flying to the islands several times a day. The Hawaiians even have a hula of the kōlea where kneeling dancers imitate the kōlea's movements.

Some believe that the Polynesians discovered the Hawaiian Islands by following the kōlea.

This Has Been Going On for an Extremely Long Time

Interestingly, fossils on Oʻahu indicate the kōlea have been coming here for at least 120,000 years—about ten times longer than the existence of human civilization and about twenty times as long as Stonehenge and the Great Pyramid of Giza have been around.

Did you know...

The Hawaiian Owl, or Pueo, is one of the few daytime owls. They nest on the ground, which makes their eggs vulnerable to mongooses and rats.

So sorry. Gotta go! Gotta go! JOHN RICHARD STEPHENS

Pau

Sources

The author wrote or compiled all uncredited entries, along with the background introductions to credited selections. Mutual Publishing added some entries from its books and manuscripts after deciding to lengthen the book.

For ease of reading and because this bathroom reader is not a scholarly book, there are no footnotes and reference endnotes. Instead, this source list should provide references to most of the selections. Generally for short quotations by well-known personages, the original source is not cited unless the source is often misattributed.

If you are unable to locate a source for a passage using this source list, please email Mutual Publishing at info@mutual-publishing.com or snail mail to 1215 Center Street, Suite 210, Honolulu, HI 96816. If you have additional information on a topic, send that as well. It might be included in volume two of *The Hawai'i Bathroom Book.*

A

Ahlbrandt, Thomas S. "What are 'booming sands' and what causes the sounds they make?" *Scientific American,* Oct. 20, 1997, http://www.scientificamerican.com/article.cfm?id=what-are-quotbooming-sand.

Ahrens, C. Donald. *Essentials of Meteorology.* Independence: Cengage Learning, 2008.

American Chemical Society. "Cone of poison: The secret behind the cone snail's venom pump." *ScienceDaily,* Oct. 27, 2010, http://www.sciencedaily.com /releases/2010/10/101027124732.htm

Armstrong, William. *Around the World with a King.* Honolulu: Mutual Publishing, 1995.

Ashley, Randy and Jay Robinson. *Mauna Ulu Eruption Guide.* Hawai'i Volcanoes National Park, Interpretive Planning and Media Development Branch, 2010, http://www.nps.gov/havo/planyourvisit/upload/mauna_ulu_trail_guide-1.pdf.

B

Baldwin, H. P. *The Sugar Industry in Hawaii.* Overland Monthly 25, 1894.

Banks, Leo. "Petrified With Fear!" Tucson Weekly, Dec. 15, 1997, http://weeklywire.com/ww/12-15-97/tw_curr3.html.

Bartholomew, Gail and Bren Bailey. *Maui Remembers: A Local History*. Honolulu: Mutual Publishing, 1994.

Bingham, Hiram. *A Residence of Twenty-One Years in the Sandwich Islands*. Hartford: Hezekiah Huntington, 1848.

Bingham, Jon-Paul, Joycelyn Chun, Do Kim, and Jeffrey Milisen. "Local 'killer' slugs provide novel leads for medical science and pesticide development." *CTAHR Research News*, Jan. 2010, http://www.ctahr.hawaii.edu/site/downloads/crn/CTAHR_Research_News_Jan_10.pdf.

Bird, Isabella L. *The Hawaiian Archipelago: Six Months in the Sandwich Islands*. Honolulu: Mutual Publishing, 2007.

Bishop, Sereno Edwards. *Reminiscences of Old Hawaii*. Edited Lauren Andrews Thurston. Honolulu: Hawaiian Gazette Company, 1916.

Bitner, Arnold and Phoebe Beach. *Hawaii's Tropical Rum Drinks and Cuisine by Don the Beachcomber*. Honolulu: Mutual Publishing, 2001.

Boyd, Robynne. "Genetically Modified Hawaii." *Scientific American*, Dec. 8, 2008, http://www.scientificamerican.com/article.cfm?id=genetically-modified-hawaii.

Budnick, Rich. *Hawaii's Forgotten History*. Honolulu: Aloha Press, 2005.

Burns, Stephanie. "Name Change Ruling for Tula Does the Hula." *The Daily Express* (UK), Jul. 25, 2008, http://www.express.co.uk/posts/view/53968/Name-change-ruling-for-Tula-Does-The-Hula.

Bushnell, O. A. *Ka'a'awa*. Honolulu: University of Hawai'i Press, 1972.

Bushnell, O. A. *The Gifts of Civilization: Germs and Genocide in Hawaii*. Honolulu: University of Hawaii Press, 1993.

Bushnell, O. A. *The Stone of Kannon*. Honolulu: University of Hawaii Press, 1979.

C

Ching, Carrie. *Things Hawai'i*. Honolulu: Mutual Publishing, 2010.

Choy, Sam, Lynn Cook, and Arnold Hiura. *With Sam Choy: Cooking from the Heart*. Honolulu: Mutual Publishing, 1995.

Choy, Sam with Lynn Cook. *A Hawaiian Luau with Sam Choy and the Mākaha Sons*. Honolulu: Mutual Publishing, 2003.

Christie, Agatha. *An Autobiography*. London: HarperCollins, 1997.

Clifford, Edward. *Father Damien*. London: MacMillan & Co., 1889.

Coke, Henry J. *A Ride Over the Rocky Mountains to Oregon and California: With a Glance at Some of the Tropical Islands, Including the West Indies and the Sandwich Isles*. Gale, Sabin Americana, 2012.

Cook, Captain James and Rev. James King. *A Voyage to the Pacific Ocean vol. 3.* London: G. Nicol and T. Cadell, 1785.

Cook, Chris. *A Kauai Reader.* Honolulu: Booklines Hawaii, 2007.

Cooper, George and Gavan Daws. *Land and Power in Hawaii.* Honolulu: University of Hawaii Press, 1990.

Corbett, Bob. "The Black Tsar in *Black Magic.*" 1996, http://www.webster.edu/~corbetre/haiti/bookreviews/morand.htm.

D

Dampier, Robert and David W. Forbes. *Encounters with Paradise: Views of Hawaii and its People, 1778-1941.* Honolulu: University of Hawaii Press, 1992.

Day, A. Grove. *Books about Hawaii: Fifty Basic Authors.* Honolulu: University of Hawaii Press, 1977.

Day, A. Grove. *Mad About Hawaii.* Honolulu: Mutual Publishing, 1987.

DeLima, Frank. *Frank DeLima's Joke Book.* Honolulu: Bess Press, 1991.

Division of Forestry & Wildlife and Division of Aquatic Resources. *Hawaii's Comprehensive Wildlife Conservation Strategy.* 2005, www.state.hi.us/dlnr/dofaw/cwcs/Conservation_need.htm and www.state.hi.us/dlnr/dofaw/cwcs/files/NAAT%20final%20 CWCS/Appendices/Appx%20A%20Animal%20SGCN%20 NAAT%20final%20!.pdf.

Dooley, Jim. "Suspect charged in Four Hawaii bank robberies." Honolulu Advertiser, Jan. 5, 2008, http://the.honoluluadvertiser.com/article/2008/Jan/05/ln/hawaii801050333.html.

Dorrance, William. *Oahu's Hidden History.* Honolulu: Mutual Publishing, 1998.

Duffield, Wendell A. *Chasing Lava: A Geologist's Adventures at the Hawaiian Volcano Observatory.* Missoula: Mountain Press Publishing Co., 2003, pp. 102-03.

E

Emerson, Nathaniel B. *Unwritten Literature of Hawaii.* Washington, DC: Government Printing Office, 1909.

F

Fairfax, Geoffre W. *The Architecture of Hawaii.* Honolulu: Island Heritage, circa 1970.

Frierson, Pamela. *The Burning Island: A Journey Through Myth and History in Volcano Country, Hawaii.* Random House, 1991.

G

Giambelluca, T. W., Q. Chen, A. G. Frazier, J. P. Price, Y-L. Chen, P-S. Chu, J. Eischeid, and D. Delparte. *The Rainfall Atlas of Hawaiʻi.* 2011, http://rainfall.geography.hawaii.edu.

Gibson, Walter Murray. *The Diaries of Walter Murray Gibson, 1886, 1887.* Edited Jacob Adler and Gwynn Barrett. Honolulu: University of Hawaiʻi Press, 1973.

Grant, Glen. *Chicken Skin Tales.* Honolulu: Mutual Publishing, 1998.

Grant, Glen. *From the Skies of Paradise: The Big Island of Hawaii.* Honolulu: Mutual Publishing, 1992.

Grant, Glen. "Introduction" to *Rape in Paradise* by Theon Wright. Honolulu: Mutual Publishing, 2005.

Grant, Glen. *Obake Files.* Honolulu: Mutual Publishing, 1996.

Grant, Glen and Bennett Hymer. *Hawaii Looking Back: An Illustrated History of the Islands.* Honolulu: Mutual Publishing, 1999.

Greene, Linda Wedel. A Cultural History of Three Traditional Hawaiian Sites on the West Coast of Hawaiʻi Island. United States Department of the Interior, National Park Service, Denver Service Center, 1993, http://www.nps.gov/history/history/online_books/kona/history5a.htm.

Gregg, David Lawrence. *The Diaries of David Lawrence Gregg.* Edited Pauline King. Honolulu: Hawaiian Historical Society, 1982.

Guy, Jenny. "Pearl of the Pacific." *The Sunday Tribune* (UK). Feb. 18, 2007, http://tribune.maithu.com/article/2007/feb/18/pearl-of-the-pacific/.

H

Hagar, Sammy. "Sammy's recipes." http://www.sammysbeachbarrum.com/recipes.php.

Hall, A. D. *Hawaii.* Forgotten Books, 2012.

Harden, M. J. *Voices of Wisdom.* Aka Press, 1999.

Harney, Jodi N. "Sand in Hawaii." University of Hawaiʻi, http://hawaii.gov/dlnr/occl/manuals-reports/sand-in-hawaii.

Hawaii Conservation Alliance. "Mosquitoes in Hawaiʻi." Position Paper 2005-02, 2005, http://hawaiiconservation.org/files/content/resources/publications/position_papers/mosquitos.pdf.

Hawaii State Data Book. Honolulu: Mutual Publishing, 2012.

"Hawaiian Place Names", Ulukau: The Hawaiian Electronic Library, www.ulukau.org/gsdl2.5/cgi-bin/hpn?.

"Hawaiian Punch: Our History", http://www.drpeppersnapplegroup.com/brands/hawaiian-punch/.

Hedegaard, Erik. "Woody Harrelson's (Mostly) Happy Ending." *Men's Journal*, Apr. 2012, http://www.mensjournal.com/woody-harrelson.

Heenan, Bobby. *Monday Night Raw*. Jul. 11, 1993, http://en.wikiquote.org/wiki/Bobby_Heenan.

Henke, L. A. "A Survey of Livestock in Hawaii." Honolulu: University of Hawai'i, Aug. 1929, http://www.ctahr.hawaii.edu/oc/freepubs/pdf/RP-5.pdf

Hill, S. S. *Travels in the Sandwich and Society Islands*. London: Chapman & Hall, 1856.

Holmes, Gillian S. "Hula Hoop." How Products are Made, vol. 6, http://www.madehow.com/Volume-6/Hula-Hoop.html. Anonymous, "History of Hula Hooping", http://www.hulahooping.com/history.html. Anonymous, "Wham-O's History", http://www.wham-o.com/history.html.

Holt, John Dominis. *Monarchy in Hawaii*. Honolulu: Ku Paa Publishing, 1995.

Holt, Kermit. "Hawaii: The Pacific's Fairest Fleet." *The Rotarian*, Apr. 1962, http://books.google.com/books?id=UDcEAAAAMBAJ&pg=PA64.

Homeland Defense Public Affairs Office. "Navy Emergency Preparedness Liaison Officers and Defense Coordinating Element Visit Kauai" Press Release. http://www.usarpac.army.mil/docs/jtf-hd/news/dcodcepmrf.asp.

Hopkins, Jerry. *The Hula*. Apa Productions, 1982.

Hula: Hawaiian Proverbs and Inspirational Quotes Celebrating Hula in Hawaii. Honolulu: Mutual Publishing, 2003.

I

Imada, Lee. "'Big Bog' ranks among wettest spots in Hawaii, possibly world." *The Maui News*, March 21, 2012, http://www.mauinews.com/page/content.detail/id/559332.html.

Imada, Lee. "OHA funds will help endangered seabird." The Maui News, Feb. 14, 2010, http://www.mauinews.com/page/content.detail/id/528637.html

International Astronomical Union, The. "IAU names fifth dwarf planet Haumea." Sept. 17, 2008, http://www.iau.org/public_press/news/detail/iau0807/.

J

James, Van. *Ancient Sites of Hawai'i*. Honolulu: Mutual Publishing, 1995.

Jardine, Detective John. *Crimes in Honolulu*. Honolulu: University of Hawaii Press, 1984.

Jones, James. *From Here to Eternity*. New York: Dell Publishers, 1951.

K

Kalākaua, King David. *The Legends and Myths of Hawaii*. Honolulu: Mutual Publishing, 1987.

Kahanamoku, Duke Paoa. "Riding the Surfboard." *The Mid-Pacific Magazine*, vol. 1, no. 1, Jan. 1911.

Kakesako, Gregg K. "Lethal sarin tested on Big Island." Honolulu Star-Bulletin, Oct. 31, 2002, http://archives.starbulletin.com/2002/10/31/news/index4.html.

Kapu, S. W. and W. E. P. Daniels. *P.C. Advertiser*, Jul. 15, 1865.

Knowles, Lori. "Paradise found." Welland Tribune (Canada), August 8, 2009, http://www.wellandtribune.ca/ArticleDisplay.aspx?e=1692086&auth=LORI%20KNOWLES,%20SUN%20ME-DIA.

"Kōlea or Pacific Golden-Plover." *Hawaii's Comprehensive Wildlife Conservation Strategy*, State of Hawaii, Division of Forestry and Wildlife, Oct. 1, 2005, http://www.state.hi.us/dlnr/dofaw/cwcs/files/NAAT%20final%20CWCS/Chapters/Terrestrial%20Fact%20Sheets/Migratory%20Birds/Pacific_Golden_Plover%20NAAT%20final%20!.pdf.

L

Lazell, James D. Jr., Timothy W. Sutterfield, and William D. Giezentanner. "The population of rock wallabies (genus *Petrogale*) on Oahu, Hawaii." *Biological Conservation*, vol. 30, no. 2, 1984.

Leskiw, Tom. "The Discovery of the Hawaiian Islands: A Case of Human-Bird Mutualism." Vartan P. Messier and Nandita Batra, eds., *This Watery World: Humans and the Sea*, Newcastle upon Tyne: Cambridge Scholars Publishing, 2008, http://www.sterlingbirds.com/Leskiw/Discovery%20of%20Hawaiian%20Islands.html.

Lili'uokalani, Queen. *Hawaii's Story*. Honolulu: Mutual Publishing, 1990.

Livett, Dr. Bruce. "Revenge of the Killer Snails." University of Melbourne, Australia, http://grimwade.biochem.unimelb.edu.au/cone/deathby.html.

London, Jack. "My Hawaiian Aloha." *Cosmopolitan Magazine*, Oct. 1916.

London, Jack. *Stories of Hawaii*, Honolulu: Mutual Publishing.

Loomis, Ilima. *Rough Riders*. Waipahu: Island Heritage, 2006.

Lubove, Seth. "Republic of Hawaii: Hawaii is a nice place to visit but you wouldn't want to do business there." *Forbes*, June 16, 1997.

Lum, Curtis. "Police arrested man suspected of 2 bank robberies." *Honolulu Advertiser*, Jun. 4, 2009, http://the.honoluluadvertiser.com/article/2009/Jun/04/br/hawaii90604100.html.

Lush Pops. http://www.lush-pops.com.

Lydgate, J. M. "Some Plantation Memories." Edited Thos. G. Thrum. *Hawaiian Almanac and Annual for 1918*, Honolulu, 1918.

M

MacMillan, Ian. *The Red Wind*. Honolulu: Mutual Publishing, 1998.

Malama: Hawaiian Land and Water. Edited Dana Naone Hall. Honolulu: Bamboo Ridge Press, 1985.

Maugham, W. Somerset. "Honolulu." *The Trembling of a Leaf*. Honolulu: Mutual Publishing, 1985.

Maui Ocean Center Marine Life Profile, "Parrotfish", http://www.mauioceancenter.com/marinepdf/parrotfish.pdf.

McClure, Colonel Alexander K. *"Abe" Lincoln's Yarns and Stories*. Chicago: The Educational Co., 1901.

McDermott, John F., Wên-Shing Tsêng, Thomas Maretzki. *People and Cultures of Hawaii: A Psychocultural Profile*. Honolulu: University of Hawaii Press, 1980.

McMahon, Barbara. "Parents lose custody of girl for naming her Talula Does the Hula From Hawaii." *The Guardian* (UK), Jul. 24, 2008, http://www.guardian.co.uk/lifeandstyle/2008/jul/24/familyandrelationships.newzealand.

Mehta, Julie. *Mele Kalikimaka: Christmas in Hawaii*. Honolulu: Mutual Publishing, 1991.

Mykkānen, Juri, *Inventing Politics: A New Political Anthropology of the Hawaiian Kingdom*. Honolulu: University of Hawai'i Press, 2003.

N

National Museum of the U.S. Air Force. "Brig. Gen. William 'Billy' Mitchell." 2010, http://www.nationalmuseum.af.mil/factsheets/factsheet.asp?id=739.

NOAA National Weather Service Honolulu Forecast Office. http://www.prh.noaa.gov/hnl/climate/phto_clim.php.

NOAA Satellite and Information Service. "Global Measured Extremes of Temperature and Precipitation." U.S. Dept. of Commerce, National Climactic Data Center, www.ncdc.noaa.gov/oa/climate/globalextremes.html.

NOAA Western Regional Climate Center. http://www.wrcc.dri.edu/.

Northwestern University. "Synthetic Adhesive Mimics Sticking Powers of Gecko and Mussel." *ScienceDaily*, Jul. 18, 2007, http://www.sciencedaily.com/releases/2007/07/070718140750.htm.

O

Obama, Barack. *Dreams From My Father*. New York: Crown Publishers, 2005.

Obama, Barack. "A Life's Calling to Public Service." Punahou Bulle-

tin, Honolulu: Punahou School, Fall 1999, http://www.punahou.
edu/uploaded/News_Content/Media/Pun_Bull_Obama_article.
pdf.

Obama, Barack. Speech in Keehi Lagoon Beach Park. Oʻahu, Aug.
8, 2008.

Obama, Barack. Speech quoted in "Obama: At Home in the Islands." *New York Times*, The Caucus blog, August 10, 2008.

OnoPops Honolulu. http://www.onopops.com.

P

"Pair charged in robberies to appear in court today." *Honolulu
Star-Bulletin*. Jun. 8, 2009, http://archives.starbulletin.com/
content/20090608_police_and_fire.

Peluso, Beth. "The Original 'Snowbirds': Pacific Golden-Plovers."
Juneau Empire (Alaska). Feb. 3, 2012, http://juneauempire.com/
outdoors/2012-02-03/original-snowbirds-pacific-golden-plovers.

La Perouse, Jean-Francois de Galup. *Carte des iles Sandwich*.
Paris, 1786.

Petras, Ross and Kathryn. *The 776 Stupidest Things Ever Said*. New
York: Doubleday, 1993.

Piercy, LaRue W. *Hawaii This and That*. Honolulu: Mutual Publishing, 2003.

Polancy, Tony. *Hawaiʻi in Love*. Kīhei: Barefoot Publishing, 2001.

Polancy, Tony. *The Hawaiʻi Pet Book*. Kīhei: Barefoot Publishing,
2003.

Pukui, Mary Kawena. *ʻŌlelo Noʻeau: Hawaiian Proverbs & Poetical
Sayings*. Honolulu: Bishop Museum Press, 1983.

Pukui, Mary Kawena, Samuel H. Elbert, and Esther T. Mookini.
Place Names of Hawaii. Honolulu: University of Hawaiʻi Press,
1966.

Q

Quayle, Dan. Speech in Hawaii, Apr. 25, 1989 quoted in *Esquire*,
Aug. 1992.

R

Reddall, Henry Frederic. *From the Golden Gate to the Golden Horn*.
New York: Phillips & Hunt, 1885.

Robinson, Pete. "Agatha Christie's surfing secret revealed." The
Guardian (UK), Jul. 29, 2011, http://www.guardian.co.uk/
books/2011/jul/29/agatha-christie-hercule-poirot-surfing-se-
cret.

Roe, Stephen. "A climate for every occasion." *The Independent* (Ireland), March 28, 1999, http://www.independent.co.uk/travel/a-
climate-for-every-occasion-1083548.html.

Ronck, Ronn. *Hawaiian Yesterdays.* Honolulu: Mutual Publishing, 1982.

Rubinoff, Daniel and William P. Haines. "A New Species of Snail-Feeding Caterpillar (*Lepidoptera: Cosmopterigidae: Hyposmocoma*) from Maui, Hawaii." *Science,* Mar. 10, 2006, vol. 311, no. 5766.

S

Sack, Kevin. "The 1992 Campaign: Political Memo; Quayle's Working Hard To Give a Better Speech." *New York Times,* October 7, 1992.

Schmitt, Robert C. and Ronn Ronck. *Firsts and Almost Firsts in Hawai'i.* Honolulu: University of Hawai'i Press, 1995.

Schweitzer, Sophia V. *Tiki of Hawai'i: A History of Gods and Dreams.* Honolulu: Mutual Publishing, 2005.

Shaka Pops Maui, http://www.shakapopsmaui.com.

Simonson, Douglas, Ken Sakamata, and Pat Sasaki. *Hawaii To Da Max.* Honolulu: Bess Press, 1992.

Simpson, MacKinnon. *A Century of Aloha.* Honolulu: Mutual Publishing, 2005.

Sinclair, Marjorie. *Kona: A Novel of Two Generations in Hawaii.* Honolulu: Mutual Publishing, 1986.

Singletary, Milly. *Hilo Hattie: A Legend in our Time.* Honolulu: Mutual Publishing, 2006.

Smithsonian Institution. "A More Perfect Union." http://american-history.si.edu/perfectunion/non-flash/internment_permanent.html.

Smyser, A. A. Bud. *John A. Burns the Man and his Times.* Honolulu: University of Hawaii Press, 2000.

Song, Jaymes. "Cookie king seeks to be muffin mogul." Associated Press, *Los Angeles Times,* Jul. 13, 2007, http://articles.latimes.com/2007/jul/13/business/fi-amos13.

Squires, Nick. "Tourists return stones to 'cursed' Ayers Rock." The Telegraph (UK), May 12, 2008, http://www.telegraph.co.uk/news/newstopics/howaboutthat/1948843/Uluru-Tourists-return-stones-to-cursed-Ayers-Rock.html.

Stanton, Joseph. *A Hawaiian Anthology.* Honolulu: University of Hawaii Press, 1997.

State of Hawai'i Dept. of Health. "Mosquitoes." n.d., http://hawaii.gov/health/environmental/vector/mosquitoflyer.pdf. U.S. Geological Survey, "Feral Pigs, Introduced Mosquitoes, and the Decline of Hawai'i's Native Birds", USGS FS 2006-3029, February 2006, http://biology.usgs.gov/pierc/Fact_Sheets/Pigs_and_mosquitoes.pdf.

Stevenson, Robert Louis. *Father Damien.* London: Chatto & Windus, 1890.

Subiono, Keoni. "The battle of the littler big man." *Honolulu Star-Bulletin*, April 28, 2007.

T

Tan, Ria. "Pacific Golden Plover." Singapore, 2001, http://www.naturia.per.sg/buloh/birds/Pluvialis_fulva.htm.

Taylor, Clarice B. *Hawaiian Almanac.* Honolulu: Mutual Publishing, 1995.

Theroux, Paul. "Happily a State, Forever an Island." *New York Times*, August 21, 2009.

Theroux, Paul. "The City: Honolulu." Newsweek, Jun. 26, 2011, http://www.thedailybeast.com/newsweek/2011/06/26/paul-theroux-reflects-on-honolulu-hawaii.html.

Thomas, Craig, M.D., and Susan Scott. *All Stings Considered: First Aid and Medical Treatment of Hawaiʻi's Marine Injuries.* Honolulu: University of Hawaiʻi Press, 1997, http://www.aloha.com/~lifeguards/alsting1.html.

Thrum, Thos. G. *Hawaiian Almanac and Annual for 1903.* Honolulu, 1903.

Thurston, Lucy. *Life and Times of Mrs. Lucy G. Thurston.* Ann Arbor: S. C. Andrews, 1882.

Tonouchi, Lee. *Hybolics, Issue One.* Honolulu: Hybolics, Inc., 1999.

Twain, Mark. *Following the Equator: A Journey Around the World.* Hartford: American Publishing Company, 1897, pp. 52-53.

Twain, Mark. *Roughing It.* 1872.

Twain, Mark. *Sacramento Daily Union*, May 21, 1866.

U

U.S. Geological Survey. "70 percent of beaches eroding on Hawaiian islands Kauai, Oahu, and Maui." *ScienceDaily*, May 7, 2012, http://www.sciencedaily.com//releases/2012/05/120507165601.htm.

U.S. Geological Survey. "The Hawaiian Archipelago—An Ecosystem in Crisis." The Biocomplexity Project, 2003-2012, http://www.uhh.hawaii.edu/~biocomp/hawaii.php.

University of Calgary. "Geckos' Amazing Grip is Triggered by Gravity. *ScienceDaily*, Aug. 4, 2009, http://www.sciencedaily.com/releases/2009/08/090804210625.htm.

University of Calgary. "Sticky Questions Tackled in Gecko Research." *ScienceDaily*, Dec. 20, 2007, http://www.sciencedaily.com/releases/2007/12/071220133448.htm.

V

Voosen, Paul. "King Corn Takes Root in Hawaii." *New York Times*, Aug. 22, 2011, http://www.nytimes.com/

gwire/2011/08/22/22greenwire-king-corn-takes-root-in-ha-
waii-28466.html.

Vorisno, Mary. "Obama pushes message of diversity." *Honolulu Star-Bulletin,* Dec. 17, 2004, http://archives.starbulletin.
com/2004/12/17/news/index2.html.

W

Watts, Robert M. "On location in Hawai'i: Two Perspectives." *Honolulu Magazine,* Nov. 1995, http://www.hawaii-nation.org/watts.
html.

Westervelt, W.D. *Legends of Old Honolulu.* Honolulu: Mutual Publishing, 2003.

Wordsworth, R. D. *"Abe" Lincoln's Anecdotes and Stories.* Boston:
The Mutual Book Co., 1908.

Further Reading

To learn more about the Mutual Publishing titles
that were the sources of some of the selections in this book,
visit www.mutualpublishing.com.

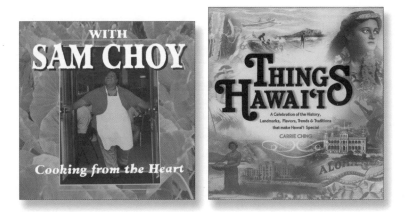

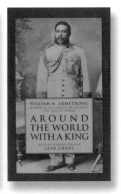

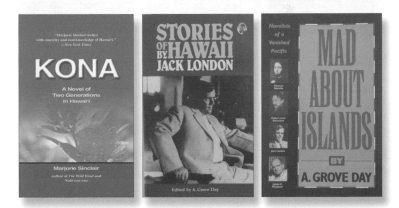

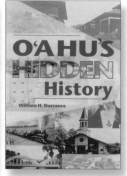

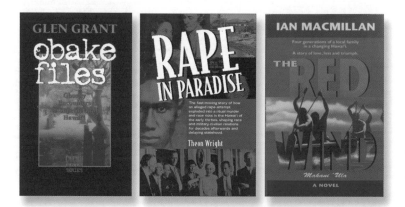

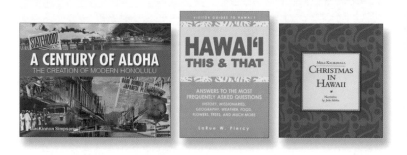

About the Author

John Richard Stephens is the author/editor of sixteen books, including *Wyatt Earp Speaks!*, *Adventure*, and *Voodoo*. His books have been selections of the Preferred Choice Book Club, the Quality Paperback Book Club and the Book of the Month Club. His work has been published as far away as India and Singapore and has been translated into Japanese and Finnish.

WANTED

Funny stories, unusual experiences, interesting newspaper magazine clippings, internet sightings, believe-it-or-not tales.

Suggestion Box for Volume 2

- Did we miss anything that belongs?
- Do you want us to cover a particular subject?
- Do you want to submit your own entry (500 words or less)? If we use your piece, you will receive a free copy plus $25.
- What topics would you like to see covered more?

Please email or write us at:
info@mutualpublishing.com

Or snail mail us at: Hawaiian Bathroom Book, Mutual Publishing, 1215 Center St., Ste. 210, Honolulu, HI 96816.

Remember, it has to be about Hawai'i!